M000170108

PRAYERPOINTS™

*Prayer*POINTS™

PRAYING GOD'S PROMISES
at Your Point of Need

—————————— ⇒⇒ ——————————

KEN PETERSEN, GENERAL EDITOR

Tyndale House Publishers, Inc. Carol Stream, Illinois

Visit Tyndale online at www.tyndale.com.

TYNDALE, Tyndale's quill logo, and *LeatherLike* are registered trademarks of Tyndale House Publishers, Inc. *PrayerPoints* is a trademark of Tyndale House Publishers, Inc.

PrayerPoints: Praying God's Promises at Your Point of Need

Designed by Jennifer Ghionzoli

Unless otherwise indicated, all Scripture quotations are taken from the *Holy Bible*, New Living Translation, copyright © 1996, 2004, 2007, 2013 by Tyndale House Foundation. Used by permission of Tyndale House Publishers, Inc., Carol Stream, Illinois 60188. All rights reserved.

Scripture quotations marked ESV are taken from *The Holy Bible*, English Standard Version® (ESV®), copyright © 2001 by Crossway, a publishing ministry of Good News Publishers. Used by permission. All rights reserved.

Scripture quotations marked MSG are taken from *THE MESSAGE* by Eugene H. Peterson, copyright © 1993, 1994, 1995, 1996, 2000, 2001, 2002. Used by permission of NavPress Publishing Group. All rights reserved.

Scripture quotations marked NIV are taken from the Holy Bible, *New International Version,® NIV.®* Copyright © 1973, 1978, 1984, 2011 by Biblica, Inc.® (Some quotations may be from the earlier NIV edition, copyright © 1984.) Used by permission. All rights reserved worldwide.

Scripture quotations marked NKJV are taken from the New King James Version,® copyright © 1982 by Thomas Nelson, Inc. Used by permission. All rights reserved.

ISBN 978-1-4964-0950-8

Printed in China

21	20	19	18	17	16	15
7	6	5	4	3	2	1

INTRODUCTION

*PrayerPoints: Praying God's Promises
at Your Point of Need*

WELCOME TO *PrayerPoints*! This book is designed to help with any specific need you may have, no matter what season of life you're in. Each entry provides Bible verses, a promise from God, and a prayer to help you along. As you pray, you can claim the promise for whatever concern you may have in the moment. *PrayerPoints* features nearly 250 entries and addresses more than 170 topics, so most any need or problem you wish to address will have at least one entry. Entries are listed alphabetically, and multiple entries for the same topic are differentiated by the sub-heading. Additionally, a Guide to Prayer Topics is located in the back; it can help you find specific entries related to emotional, physical, relational, and spiritual needs. A Scripture index directly follows and allows you to quickly find a Bible verse for the problem you're facing.

Each entry in this book is an invitation into a private encounter with God. After all, prayer is, quite simply, a conversation with God. Yet too often we make the conversation one sided, using the time to talk at God rather than listen to him. This book encourages you to give God time to speak to you—to listen for his voice. How so? Located at various points within each prayer is a special mark that looks like this: ⸎. It indicates a pause and provides you with a chance to add what is personal to you and specific to the need you have. It's also a moment for you to stop and listen for God speaking to you. When you do, something special happens.

There are many different ways that we may address God when we pray. Some of these prayers address him as "Lord," others as "Jesus," others as "Father," and some simply as "God." God is revealed to us as three distinct persons—the Trinity of Father, Son (Jesus), and Holy Spirit. The Bible gives examples of addressing God using all these terms, as well as others, but it is clear we are always praying to the one sovereign God. In your prayers, feel free to either use the words provided or to address God however you feel most comfortable.

As you pray these prayers, note that within each entry, the Bible promise is highlighted in **bold**. Within the written prayer, the part that echoes the Bible promise is likewise presented in **bold**. Each entry is short and can be read in a matter of a few minutes. But it also gives you the opportunity to enjoy time spent sitting in God's presence and listening for his voice.

We hope that this book becomes a handy go-to prayer guide in your daily life. Start to experience God in a whole new way as he speaks into your every need.

Ken Petersen,
GENERAL EDITOR

ABANDONMENT · EMBRACING THE PRESENCE OF GOD

At a time when you're feeling rejected, know that God is present. Quiet your heart. Enter into his presence right now . . .

GOD'S PROMISE

PSALM 142:4-6 • *I look for someone to come and help me, but no one gives me a passing thought! No one will help me; no one cares a bit what happens to me. Then I pray to you, O LORD. I say, "You are my place of refuge. You are all I really want in life. Hear my cry, for I am very low."*

PSALM 27:10 • *Even if my father and mother abandon me, the LORD will hold me close.*

ROMANS 8:38-39, ESV • *I am sure that neither death nor life, nor angels nor rulers, nor things present nor things to come, nor powers, nor height nor depth, nor anything else in all creation, will be able to separate us from the love of God in Christ Jesus our Lord.*

PRAY GOD'S PROMISE

Lord Jesus, in these moments I feel a sense of worthlessness. I pretty much feel abandoned right now. It makes me angry toward the person who has left me, but most of all it just deeply hurts inside. ✤ I hear your words that even if my mother and father abandon me, you will hold me close. Jesus, I believe you love me, but I need to feel your presence in a special way. So I come to you and ask that you will be with me right now. ✤ *I claim your promise that nothing can separate me from the love of God in you, Christ Jesus.* I embrace your promise, just as you embrace me.

Let yourself, in silence, experience his arms around you. Let Jesus whisper to you in these moments.

———————————— ⋅◇⋅ ————————————

ABUSE · GOD RESCUES THOSE IN NEED

Come to God with your hurt and heartbreak. Listen for his counsel . . .

GOD'S PROMISE

ZEPHANIAH 1:9, ESV · *That day I will punish everyone who leaps over the threshold, and those who fill their master's house with violence and fraud.*

2 THESSALONIANS 3:6, NKJV · *We command you, brethren, in the name of our Lord Jesus Christ, that you withdraw from every brother who walks disorderly and not according to the tradition which he received from us.*

2 PETER 2:9, ESV · **The Lord knows how to rescue the godly from trials, and to keep the unrighteous under punishment until the day of judgment.**

PRAY GOD'S PROMISE

Lord God, I have been suffering physical harm at the hands of someone I have loved. My heart is broken and my bruised body aches. I have no energy to confront this situation, Lord. I cannot bear it anymore. ⚜ I pray for your healing hand and soothing presence in the midst of this suffering. ⚜ *Help me to remember this promise that you know full well how to rescue me from this trial and that your justice will prevail in the life of my perpetrator.* Grant me hope and patience, Lord, as I await your deliverance.

The Bible authorizes those who have been hurt by someone's disorderly, abusive behavior to withdraw from that person. God allows you to find protection. Listen to him speak to you about what you need to do.

ABUSE · GOD'S SAFE HOUSE FOR YOU

In this difficult time of feeling neglected and abused, come to God for strength. Listen to his words . . .

GOD'S PROMISE

JOEL 3:16-17, MSG • *GOD roars from Zion, shouts from Jerusalem. Earth and sky quake in terror. But GOD is a safe hiding place, a granite safe house for the children of Israel. Then you'll know for sure that I'm your GOD . . .*

PROVERBS 30:5 • *Every word of God proves true. He is a shield to all who come to him for protection.*

JOHN 14:26-27, MSG • **The Friend, the Holy Spirit whom the Father will send at my request, will make everything** *plain to you. He will remind you of all the things I have told you. I'm leaving you well and whole. That's my parting gift to you. Peace. I don't leave you the way you're used to being left—feeling abandoned, bereft. So don't be upset. Don't be distraught.*

PRAY GOD'S PROMISE

Lord Jesus, I pray to you right now for comfort and provision. I have been left in a difficult place, hurt by someone close. I have physical needs, healing needs, heart needs. Touch me, Lord Jesus. ❧ I trust you to be my hiding place, a safe house for my body and my life. I look to you in these next days for those gifts. ❧ *And I claim your promise that the Holy Spirit, my best Friend, will provide for my healing, safety, and provision.* Thank you, Jesus.

In these next moments, list the primary needs you have right now. Share them with God and listen for his counsel about finding provision for each one.

———————————— ❖ ————————————

ABUSE • STRENGTH IN OVERCOMING UNTHINKABLE HURT

You're feeling the pain of many deep, difficult emotions right now. Come to God with all of them. Receive his comfort. Listen for his counsel . . .

GOD'S PROMISE

PSALM 9:9, MSG • *GOD's a safe-house for the battered, a sanctuary during bad times.*

PSALM 62:5-8, ESV • *For God alone, O my soul, wait in silence, for my hope is from him. He only is my rock and my salvation, my fortress; I shall not be shaken. On God rests my salvation and my glory; my mighty rock, my refuge is God. Trust in him at all times, O people; pour out your heart before him; God is a refuge for us.*

PHILIPPIANS 4:19, MSG • ***You can be sure that God will take care of everything you need.***

PRAY GOD'S PROMISE

Lord God, it's hard to believe I'm in a situation in which someone with whom I share a close relationship is actually abusing me. I am helpless in this, and I cannot protect myself. I feel betrayed, fearful, and heartbroken. I'm desperate for your help. ❧ You are my rock, my fortress, and my salvation, Lord. I pray for something in this situation to change soon, but if it doesn't, then show me what to do, Lord. ❧ *I embrace this promise that you will indeed take care of the painful difficulties I'm experiencing in this situation.* I look to you for the resources I need. Help me find protection, Lord.

God can rescue you out of this situation. Pray to him for his words of counsel. What is he whispering to you? Who is he telling you to go to for help in dealing with this abuse?

———————— ❖ ————————

ADDICTION · OVERCOMING A LIFE OF DECEPTION

You already know that a life of addiction is a life of lies. As you come to God right now, drop the pose. Be honest with him. After all, he already knows the truth about your situation. Be real with him about the struggles you face . . .

GOD'S PROMISE

EPHESIANS 4:25 • *Stop telling lies. Let us tell our neighbors the truth, for we are all parts of the same body.*

ROMANS 7:15, MSG • *What I don't understand about myself is that I decide one way, but then I act another, doing things I absolutely despise.*

ISAIAH 41:10 • *Don't be discouraged, for I am your God.* **I will strengthen you and help you.** *I will hold you up with my victorious right hand.*

PRAY GOD'S PROMISE

Oh Father God, I come to you experiencing a great struggle. I've tried over and over to stop. But I can't. I always go back to it. As a result I'm living a lie in front of others—acquaintances, my friends, even my family. ॐ I want to end this behavior, yet I still find myself repeating it—even though it's something I absolutely despise. I know I cannot overcome this through my own power. ॐ *So right now I claim your promise, God, to strengthen me and help me.* Come to my rescue, Father. I need you, only you, to deliver me from this.

In these moments, take this God time a step further. Tell him, literally, the things you have done. Confess them to him, one by one. Let the urges, the compulsions, the addiction be brought into the light of God your Father.

———————————— ⟨·⟩ ————————————

ADVERSITY · DEFEATING DAY-TO-DAY OBSTACLES

You're going through a lot right now, and it's leaving you feeling tired and bone-weary. In these quiet moments, rest in God. Let go of your frustrations while God speaks into your life . . .

GOD'S PROMISE

JOB 7:3-4 · *I, too, have been assigned months of futility, long and weary nights of misery. Lying in bed, I think, 'When will it be morning?' But the night drags on, and I toss till dawn.*

1 CORINTHIANS 15:43 · *Our bodies are buried in brokenness, but they will be raised in glory. They are buried in weakness, but they will be raised in strength.*

1 PETER 5:10, ESV · **After you have suffered a little while, the God of all grace, who has called you to his eternal glory in Christ, will himself restore, confirm, strengthen, and establish you.**

PRAY GOD'S PROMISE

Dear God, oh my. I'm so frustrated by all the obstacles that have popped up in the road I'm on. And I'm tired—truly exhausted from having to deal with one thing after another. I identify with Job's expressions of futility and sleeplessness. ⚜ I believe this journey is what you want for me—but God, why does it have to be so hard and tiring?

I need your restoring touch. ❧ In all of this, I thank you for these words of Scripture. I like the sound of "suffered a little while," for I hope and pray it will not be much longer for me. But even if it does last a while more, *I embrace this promise: that you, the God of all grace, will restore, confirm, strengthen, and establish me.* Thank you, God, for encouraging me today.

Ask God what he wants you to do. It isn't wrong to ask him for a break, for some downtime. Pay attention to his voice guiding you forward.

———————————— ❖ ————————————

ADVERSITY · TURNING DARKNESS INTO LIGHT

Sometimes adversity serves to make us more aware of what others are going through. Sometimes *our need* gives us an understanding of *someone else's need*. In this time of difficulty, quiet your heart, come to God, and listen to him speak to you . . .

GOD'S PROMISE

2 CORINTHIANS 1:4 · *He comforts us in all our troubles so that we can comfort others. When they are troubled, we will be able to give them the same comfort God has given us.*

ISAIAH 58:11, ESV · *And the LORD will guide you continually and satisfy your desire in scorched places and make your bones strong; and you shall be like a watered garden, like a spring of water, whose waters do not fail.*

ISAIAH 58:10, ESV · *If you pour yourself out for the hungry and satisfy the desire of the afflicted, **then shall your light rise in the darkness and your gloom be as the noonday**.*

PRAY GOD'S PROMISE

Oh God, I come to you right now with so many burdens. I have so much to do, and many things keep getting in my way. I find myself discouraged—sometimes too discouraged to go on. ⚜ But these words help me see something I haven't seen before—that my own difficulties serve to refine and equip me for doing your work in the world. Help me to accept whatever this might mean in this season of my life. ⚜ And God, I thank you for the encouragement in these verses. *I embrace your promise that as I reach out to help others, my light will rise in the darkness.* Help me recognize opportunities to do just that—to help others and be less focused on myself.

Spend some more time with God, and think about the needs others around you have. Consider a way in which you can help one of them. Listen for God's direction, and see how your own troubles start to melt away as you reach out to someone else.

———————— ⟨◇⟩ ————————

AGING · THE PROMISE OF ETERNAL LIFE

Growing older often leads us to worry about the future and life after death. The good news is that through Christ we have clarity and assurance about the life to come. Spend some time listening to God about what he has in store for you . . .

GOD'S PROMISE

1 CORINTHIANS 13:12, NIV • *Now we see only a reflection as in a mirror; then we shall see face to face. Now I know in part; then I shall know fully, even as I am fully known.*

HEBREWS 13:14, ESV • *Here we have no lasting city, but we seek the city that is to come.*

REVELATION 21:1, 3-4 • *I saw a new heaven and a new earth, for the old heaven and the old earth had disappeared. . . . I heard a loud shout from the throne, saying, "Look, God's home is now among his people!* **He will live with them, and they will be his people. God himself will be with them.** *He will wipe every tear from their eyes, and there will be no more death or sorrow or crying or pain. All these things are gone forever."*

PRAY GOD'S PROMISE

Father in heaven, hallowed be thy name. You know I have prayed this many times before, and yet now I am thinking more and more about heaven and the afterlife I am heading into. It's not so much that I fear it, but I have some doubts about what is going to happen. ❧ I pray to you, Father, and ask you to reassure me. Please give me clarity about your plans for me. Help me to have confidence about what is to come. I do seek the city that is to come, the Kingdom of Heaven that is your promise. ❧ *And so I cherish and embrace the promise that you will live with us, that you will be with us.* You will be with me. That's all I really need to know.

In this time of quiet, talk with God about what it means to you that "he will wipe every tear" from our eyes. What difficult situations will your tears represent? Imagine God tenderly wiping them away.

———————————— ❖ ————————————

ALCOHOLISM · GRABBING HOLD OF GOD

What you're struggling with is something you can overcome only with God's help. Coming to him in prayer is a powerful first step. Enter into his presence. Share with him the truth of your life. Let him speak to your soul . . .

GOD'S PROMISE

PROVERBS 23:29-33, ESV · *Who has woe? Who has sorrow? Who has strife? Who has complaining? Who has wounds without cause? Who has redness of eyes? Those who tarry long over wine; those who go to try mixed wine. Do not look at wine when it is red, when it sparkles in the cup and goes down smoothly. In the end it bites like a serpent and stings like an adder. Your eyes will see strange things, and your heart utter perverse things.*

ROMANS 7:15-20, ESV · *I do not understand my own actions. For I do not do what I want, but I do the very thing I hate. . . . For I have the desire to do what is right, but not the ability to carry it out. For I do not do the good I want, but the evil I do not want is what I keep on doing. Now if I do what I do not want, it is no longer I who do it, but sin that dwells within me.*

PSALM 103:2-4, ESV · *Bless the LORD, O my soul, and forget not all his benefits, **who forgives all your iniquity, who heals all your diseases, who redeems your life from the pit.***

PRAY GOD'S PROMISE

God, you know who I am and what I struggle with. And you know how difficult that struggle has been for me. I have tried to stay sober but have repeatedly failed. I understand too well the meaning of the verses that speak of alcohol biting like a serpent. I know this is the enemy's way of taking over my life. ⚜ God, I want to be done with this. Yet though I say I want this to be over, I know a part of me still wants it. Just as your Word says, I don't do the thing I want but wind up doing the thing I hate. God, help me. ⚜ I ask for your deliverance. I need your power to overcome this. *I claim your blessing right now that you can forgive my sin and heal me and redeem my life from the pit.* That's the only way I can conquer this, God.

Establish with God an agreement that every day you will spend time pouring out your heart to him, just like this.

———————— ◇ ————————

ALIENATION FROM FAMILY

• FINDING THE HEART OF RECONCILIATION

When a family member becomes distant from you, you suffer a unique emotional pain. Bring your ache to God in these next moments as you talk with him . . .

GOD'S PROMISE

JOB 19:13, NIV • *He has alienated my family from me; my acquaintances are completely estranged from me. My relatives have gone away; my closest friends have forgotten me.*

MATTHEW 18:21-22, NIV • *Peter came to Jesus and asked, "Lord, how many times shall I forgive my brother or sister who sins against me? Up to seven times?" Jesus answered, "I tell you, not seven times, but seventy-seven times."*

2 CORINTHIANS 5:18-19 • *God has given us this task of reconciling people to him.* **For God was in Christ, reconciling the world to himself, no longer counting people's sins against them.** *And he gave us this wonderful message of reconciliation.*

PRAY GOD'S PROMISE

Father God, I am feeling hurt by someone in my family. I feel shut out and left in the dust. It seems as if this person is upset with me, and I wonder if it might have something to do with a recent conversation we had, but I don't know for sure. ⚜ I understand these words about forgiving many times more than I think I need to. I don't know whether I am to forgive or to ask forgiveness. So, Father, I ask you to show me what to do. ⚜ *I see your example of reconciliation, of no longer counting people's sins against them.* I pray for your help in making peace with my family member.

What do you hear God whispering to you right now? Is it possible your family member, who has been so distant, might be feeling alienated by you? Or perhaps there's no clear reason behind this painful situation. Whatever the case, know that God is for you. Claim his peace . . . trust his guidance.

———————— ❖ ————————

ANGER · OVERCOMING PERSONAL ANIMOSITY

Take a deep breath. Feel yourself calming down. Anger in itself is not wrong, but left unchecked, it can lead to wrong actions. So unburden yourself in these moments of prayer as you bring your frustrations to God . . .

GOD'S PROMISE

PROVERBS 14:29 • *People with understanding control their anger; a hot temper shows great foolishness.*

EPHESIANS 4:26-27 • *Don't sin by letting anger control you. Don't let the sun go down while you are still angry, for anger gives a foothold to the devil.*

ROMANS 12:19, 21 • *Dear friends, never take revenge. Leave that to the righteous anger of God. . . .* ***Don't let evil conquer you, but conquer evil by doing good.***

PRAY GOD'S PROMISE

God, I come to you today because I am filled with anger toward someone. I know this is not good for either one of us, and it might lead to behavior you don't want from me. I pray for your help in dealing with this problem. ⚘ I receive your wisdom that this anger I feel could give a foothold to the enemy. I ask you to settle me and reassure me. ⚘ Lord God, this is difficult, but *I will claim your promise that it's possible to conquer evil with acts of goodness.* I pray right now that you will help me turn this around by finding better ways of dealing with this bad situation.

Tell God about the nature of your anger and the specific situation it comes out of. Listen for his response to you.

———————————— ⟨◦⟩ ————————————

ANGUISH • CONFESSING A SIN THAT GRIEVES GOD

Come close to God, and confess to him your sin. The passages below address the ache and anguish regretful sinners feel. But there is a promise here as well. So, enter into the presence of God . . .

GOD'S PROMISE

JAMES 4:8 • *Come close to God, and God will come close to you. Wash your hands, you sinners; purify your hearts, for your loyalty is divided between God and the world.*

JAMES 4:9 • *Let there be tears for what you have done. Let there be sorrow and deep grief. Let there be sadness instead of laughter, and gloom instead of joy.*

JAMES 4:10 • **Humble yourselves before the Lord, and he will lift you up in honor.**

PRAY GOD'S PROMISE

Lord, I am feeling deep grief over what I have done and how I have sinned against you. I know that for some time I have led a divided life, caught between serving you and serving the world. And I confess to you now that in my sin I have given myself to the world instead of to you. ❧ I pray for your forgiveness, Lord. I pray that you will come close to me in my anguish and regret. I humble myself before you right now, realizing that in trying to live life under my own power, in seeking what I think is best for me, I fail and stumble. ❧ *You promise that you will lift me up in honor—honor I do not deserve. I pray, Lord, that you might once again honor this humble spirit.*

In further moments of prayer, engage with God about how to reorder your priorities so that your life is pleasing to him.

ANIMOSITY · DISCOVERING THE POWER OF FORGIVENESS

Spend some time talking with God about the negative feelings you have toward a certain person in your life. Open your heart to God's wisdom and direction for overcoming this hostility . . .

GOD'S PROMISE

MATTHEW 7:1-5 · *Do not judge others, and you will not be judged. For you will be treated as you treat others. The standard you use in judging is the standard by which you will be judged. And why worry about a speck in your friend's eye when you have a log in your own? How can you think of saying to your friend, "Let me help you get rid of that speck in your eye," when you can't see past the log in your own eye? Hypocrite! First get rid of the log in your own eye; then you will see well enough to deal with the speck in your friend's eye.*

EPHESIANS 4:31-32 · *Get rid of all bitterness, rage, anger, harsh words, and slander, as well as all types of evil behavior. Instead, be kind to each other, tenderhearted, forgiving one another, just as God through Christ has forgiven you.*

MARK 11:25 · **When you are praying, first forgive anyone you are holding a grudge against, so that your Father in heaven will forgive your sins, too.**

PRAY GOD'S PROMISE

Father, I come to you today knowing that I have an issue with someone in my life. But while this person is responsible for causing me some trouble and spurring this ill feeling in me, I also confess that I have allowed myself to become bitter and angry. It's hard to admit I'm wrong when I feel I have been wronged, and yet I do confess this. Forgive me, Lord. ❧ Help me to recognize my own shortcomings. Help me to see the ways I have hurt others—others who may be bitter toward me as well. I need to see the log in my own eye. ❧ *Father, I want right now to embrace this connection—that when I forgive another's sins, you forgive my sins.* Help me, for this is hard to do.

In the next moments with God, dwell on these truths from Scripture. Listen for his words of instruction about how you might go to this person and forgive the wrong that you feel has been done to you.

ANXIETY · RESTING IN GOD'S PROVISION

For a few moments right now, quiet yourself. Shut out the distractions of your life. Step away from anxious thoughts and open yourself to God's voice. Dare to trust and believe as you hear what he says to you . . .

GOD'S PROMISE

LUKE 12:25 • *Can all your worries add a single moment to your life?*

MATTHEW 6:25-26 • *That is why I tell you not to worry about everyday life—whether you have enough food and drink, or enough clothes to wear. Isn't life more than food, and your body more than clothing? Look at the birds. They don't plant or harvest or store food in barns, for your heavenly Father feeds them. And aren't you far more valuable to him than they are?*

LUKE 12:31 • *Seek the Kingdom of God above all else, and he will give you everything you need.*

PRAY GOD'S PROMISE

Father in heaven, I do believe that you love me, but even so, it's difficult for me to trust that you will take care of the many things I'm fretting about. I suppose I think that if I fail to worry about all these things, they will turn out badly. I know this is a lack of trust in you. ❦ Help me to know how valuable I really am to you. Oh Father, I long to experience this in a tangible way! ❦ *And I do indeed claim your promise that if I seek you and your Kingdom, you will provide everything I need.*

Take some additional moments to consider this promise from God more deeply. Allow time for him to speak to you about what it means to seek his Kingdom.

BAD HABITS • OVERCOMING UNHEALTHY LIVING

Let go of your frustration and let God help you with the specific habits you're struggling with. Spend time with him in these next moments . . .

GOD'S PROMISE

ROMANS 12:1 • *I plead with you to give your bodies to God because of all he has done for you. Let them be a living and holy sacrifice—the kind he will find acceptable. This is truly the way to worship him.*

ROMANS 12:2 • *Don't copy the behavior and customs of this world, but let God transform you into a new person by changing the way you think. Then you will learn to know God's will for you, which is good and pleasing and perfect.*

1 CORINTHIANS 10:13 • *The temptations in your life are no different from what others experience. And God is faithful.* **He will not allow the temptation to be more than you can stand.** *When you are tempted, he will show you a way out so that you can endure.*

PRAY GOD'S PROMISE

Lord God, you know how I am trying to live for you. I want to please you, but there are some bad habits that keep creeping into my life. I try to resist them, but I cannot. I need your help. ❦ You speak to me about being transformed by changing the way I think. I know I need to do that, God. I don't think I have fully understood what you say about worshiping you with my body. I need to offer it up to you as a living sacrifice—not just on special occasions, but as a regular practice. ❦ Oh God, I know you are faithful, and *I speak forth your promise that you will not allow the temptation to be more than I can stand.* I trust that you will be with me, Lord, and will help me to endure and resist. Thank you, God.

As you continue in prayer, tell God specifically what your struggle is. Tell him what you've done to try resisting these unhealthy habits.

Then let him speak into this part of your life. Let him share with you his wisdom and help.

———————————————— ❖ ————————————————

BATTLING EVIL · WINNING THE WAR WITH GOD
AT YOUR SIDE

As you come to God at this time of spiritual attack, let him prepare you for the battle ahead . . .

GOD'S PROMISE

EPHESIANS 6:12 · *We are not fighting against flesh-and-blood enemies, but against evil rulers and authorities of the unseen world, against mighty powers in this dark world, and against evil spirits in the heavenly places.*

REVELATION 17:14, NIV · *They will wage war against the Lamb, but the Lamb will triumph over them because he is Lord of lords and King of kings—and with him will be his called, chosen and faithful followers.*

ISAIAH 58:8-9, NIV · **Your light will break forth like the dawn, and your healing will quickly appear; then your righteousness will go before you, and the glory of the LORD will be your rear guard.** *Then you will call, and the LORD will answer; you will cry for help, and he will say: Here am I.*

PRAY GOD'S PROMISE

Lord, evil forces are amassing all around me these days— surrounding my work, my friends, and even my family in personal and frightening ways. ❦ It thrills me to read these words that in the end times the Lamb—Jesus—will overcome evil (thank you, Lord!) and that I will, as one of his followers, be with him when he wins this great victory. ✦ *I claim his promise that as the light will break forth like the dawn, the glory of the Lord will be my rear guard.* You have my back, Lord! Thank you for being there when I call. The most beautiful words of all are when you say, "Here am I."

In this time of quiet with God, know that he will overcome the evil that is manifesting in your life right now. Call on him each day when you feel under attack. He will respond, "Here am I." Watch him overcome.

BATTLING FOR TRUTH · THE ULTIMATE ANSWER IS CHRIST

Bring to God the circumstance you're in that has you waging an intellectual battle over the truth of the gospel. Let his words strengthen you . . .

GOD'S PROMISE

ISAIAH 55:8-9, NIV • *"My thoughts are not your thoughts, neither are your ways my ways," declares the LORD. "As the heavens are higher than the earth, so are my ways higher than your ways and my thoughts than your thoughts."*

2 CORINTHIANS 10:3-4 • *We are human, but we don't wage war as humans do. We use God's mighty weapons, not worldly weapons, to knock down the strongholds of human reasoning and to destroy false arguments.*

ISAIAH 9:6, NIV • *To us a child is born, to us a son is given, and the government will be on his shoulders. And he will be called Wonderful Counselor, Mighty God, Everlasting Father, Prince of Peace.*

PRAY GOD'S PROMISE

Father, I feel so inadequate trying to argue with others on an intellectual level. And yet I know what I believe, and I believe in the power of the gospel. But I still need your help. ❧ I truly pray for those who are opposing me. I pray that they would come to believe—that they would let go, at some point, of all their self-important philosophies and come face-to-face with you. ❧ *And thank you for the greatest promise of all, Father—I hold on to it tightly: that you sent your Son, the Prince of Peace, who saves us from our sins.* I know that this simple truth trumps all arguments and all philosophies. I praise you, my Father and God!

In silence, let God speak to you. Listen for his words, his advice about how to wage this kind of battle going forward.

BEING BULLIED · RELYING ON GOD'S POWER

At some point in life, even in adulthood, most everyone experiences bullying from an enemy—whether in school or at the office or even in a church group. God has surprising advice for successfully facing this trial. Come to God in prayer about this situation in your life . . .

GOD'S PROMISE

2 TIMOTHY 1:7 • *God has not given us a spirit of fear and timidity, but of power, love, and self-discipline.*

ISAIAH 41:11-13, ESV • *Behold, all who are incensed against you shall be put to shame and confounded; those who strive against you shall be as nothing and shall perish. You shall seek those who contend with you, but you shall not find them; those who war against you shall be as nothing at all.* **For I, the LORD your God, hold your right hand; it is I who say to you, "Fear not, I am the one who helps you."**

ROMANS 12:19-20 • *Dear friends, never take revenge. Leave that to the righteous anger of God. For the Scriptures say, "I will take revenge; I will pay them back," says the LORD. Instead, "If your enemies are hungry, feed them. If they are thirsty, give them something to drink."*

PRAY GOD'S PROMISE

Lord God, you know how I have been hurt and made fun of. It shames me. I feel hesitant, troubled, even scared. And in other moments it makes me angry. Yet I don't know what to do. ⚜ I embrace these encouraging words of Scripture; they remind me that you give me a spirit of power and love—not fear. And I am reassured that there will be justice in some way at some point. Help me trust that you are protecting me, Lord. ⚜ I thank you for the promise *that you will hold me by the hand and say to me that I am not to fear—that you are the one who helps me.* I claim that promise and will make it mine.

Keep talking with God and ask him what it might look like to "feed your enemies." How would you repay their wrongdoing with good?

———————— ◇ ————————

BITTERNESS · REDISCOVERING GOD'S PEACE

As you step into prayer with God, focus on the effects of bitterness upon your life and the lives of others around you. Listen to his words and counsel . . .

GOD'S PROMISE

HEBREWS 12:14-15 · *Work at living in peace with everyone, and work at living a holy life, for those who are not holy will not see the Lord. Look after each other so that none of you fails to receive the grace of God. Watch out that no poisonous root of bitterness grows up to trouble you, corrupting many.*

MATTHEW 6:14-15 · *If you forgive those who sin against you, your heavenly Father will forgive you. But if you refuse to forgive others, your Father will not forgive your sins.*

PHILIPPIANS 4:8-9 · *Fix your thoughts on what is true, and honorable, and right, and pure, and lovely, and admirable. Think about things that are excellent and worthy of praise. **Keep putting into practice all you learned and received from me—everything you heard from me and saw me doing. Then the God of peace will be with you.***

PRAY GOD'S PROMISE

Lord God, I know in coming to you right now that I have feelings of bitterness toward a particular person. These verses reinforce what I already know—that this bitterness will only hurt me further and eventually rot my heart and spirit from the inside out. ‡ I want to be focused on you, Lord. I want to pursue those positive things that please you and build me up . . . those things that will help me to help others. ‡ *Lord, I long for your promise that you, the God of peace, will be with me.* I know that means I need to let go of these bitter feelings and focus my thoughts on what is true and good. Help me, Lord, to shed my bitterness. Fill my heart with your goodness.

Allow yourself to sit with God in silence. Listen for his whisper. Let his peace fill you.

———————————— ‹◇› ————————————

BOREDOM · GETTING OUT OF A RUT

The door is open. Enter in. Have a conversation with God about how listless and bored you have become of late. Let him know the feelings you have about your job, your life, your future. Allow him to speak into your current situation . . .

GOD'S PROMISE

PROVERBS 13:12 · *Hope deferred makes the heart sick, but a dream fulfilled is a tree of life.*

JAMES 1:2-4 · *When troubles of any kind come your way, consider it an opportunity for great joy. For you know that when your faith is tested, your endurance has a chance to grow. So let it grow, for when your endurance is fully developed, you will be perfect and complete, needing nothing.*

ISAIAH 40:31 · **Those who trust in the LORD will find new strength. They will soar high on wings like eagles. They will run and not grow weary. They will walk and not faint.**

PRAY GOD'S PROMISE

Lord, I need your help in getting out of this rut. I am discouraged. I have no energy and no passion for most things in my life these days. Help me, Lord. ‡ I realize I am lacking joy in my life. I don't know how to regain that, and I am wary of fake, false, artificial means of manufacturing "joy." I trust that you are the source of renewed passion in me, Lord. I pray that you will help reenergize me in a way that is authentic and real and true. ‡ *I love this verse about soaring high on wings like eagles. I want this for my life, Lord.* Help me embrace this promise, and I pray it will manifest in my life in the coming days.

Talk with God about the people, interests, and activities that really mean something to you these days. Ask him what life change he might be leading you into.

BREAKING UP · COMING TO GOD WITH THE LOSS OF LOVE

Come to God at this difficult time in your life. The loss of a relationship is heartbreaking. Bring your feelings and tears to God. Share with him from the depths of your heart . . .

GOD'S PROMISE

1 CORINTHIANS 13:4-7 · *Love is patient and kind. Love is not jealous or boastful or proud or rude. It does not demand its own way. It is not irritable, and it keeps no record of being wronged. It does not rejoice about injustice but rejoices whenever the truth wins out. Love never gives up, never*

loses faith, is always hopeful, and endures through every circumstance.

PSALM 37:4, ESV • *Delight yourself in the LORD, and he will give you the desires of your heart.*

JEREMIAH 29:11-12, NIV • *"I know the plans I have for you," declares the LORD, "plans to prosper you and not to harm you, plans to give you hope and a future. Then you will call on me and come and pray to me, and I will listen to you."*

PRAY GOD'S PROMISE

Oh Father God! I am so discouraged. My heart is broken. I feel hopeless about the possibility of loving and being loved. Be with me, Father. Hold me right now. ‡ I'm not sure I am in a place where I can fully appreciate these words from Scripture, but I do hear them—that love never gives up and never loses faith. Are you speaking to me, Father, through these words? Help me to trust you with my life and my relationships. What do you have for me? Who do you have for me? ‡ *Your promise here is that you have a plan and a future for me. I want to embrace that, Father.* Help me to trust you for that hope.

Take time with God. Pour out to him the ache of your heart. Allow him to speak into your hurt and your life.

BROKENNESS · THE PROMISE OF LIVING WATER

Broken and dry . . . come into the presence of God in this moment, even if you aren't feeling worthy to do so. Let his words rain refreshment upon you . . .

GOD'S PROMISE

HOSEA 10:12, ESV • *Sow for yourselves righteousness; reap steadfast love; break up your fallow ground, for it is the time to seek the LORD, that he may come and rain righteousness upon you.*

JOHN 15:1-4 • *I am the true grapevine, and my Father is the gardener. He cuts off every branch of mine that doesn't produce fruit, and he prunes the branches that do bear fruit so they will produce even more. You have already been pruned and purified by the message I have given you. Remain in me, and I will remain in you. For a branch cannot produce fruit if it is severed from the vine, and you cannot be fruitful unless you remain in me.*

LEVITICUS 26:4 • **I will send you the seasonal rains. The land will then yield its crops, and the trees of the field will produce their fruit.**

PRAY GOD'S PROMISE

My Lord, I am feeling so broken, so dry right now. Nothing I do seems to work. My efforts have shriveled up. My dreams have faded and disappeared. I don't have anything left. ‡ I look to you to pick me up again, to give me—somehow—new life. And Lord, your words here tell me that you tend and prune branches so the vine can produce more fruit. If I am in that pruning phase, I will embrace that reality and trust it to bring forth a better season. ‡ *Lord God, I come to you now and claim your promise: Please send me the seasonal rains. Let my life yield new crops and new fruit.*

In the next few minutes, converse with God. Tell him about your broken-
ness, how dry you've become inside. Listen for him to speak to you in
these minutes and in the days and weeks to come. Let his voice and
presence stir refreshment in you. New growth will spring up in due time.

———————————— ‹◇› ————————————

BROKENNESS · GOD RESCUES THE BROKENHEARTED

Enter into God's presence and open up your troubled heart to him.
Understand that when we become broken, that's when God starts
to do great things . . .

GOD'S PROMISE

MATTHEW 5:3, MSG · *You're blessed when you're at the end of*
your rope. With less of you there is more of God and his rule.

2 CORINTHIANS 1:9 · *As a result, we stopped relying on ourselves*
and learned to rely only on God, who raises the dead.

PSALM 34:18 · *The LORD is close to the brokenhearted;* ***he***
rescues those whose spirits are crushed.

PRAY GOD'S PROMISE

Lord God, I am brokenhearted over many things right
now. So many things have gone wrong in my life. And
I have done wrong myself. I've brought this on my own
head. ⚜ Please come close to me, as you promise in these
words. I'm at the end of my rope, and I need your presence right now. Thank you for being with me. ⚜ Please
know I come to you now in confession and repentance
and brokenness. *I claim your promise that you will rescue*
those whose spirits are crushed. I give myself to you for
your blessing, which I surely need.

In these moments, unburden your heart before God by saying out loud to him the things that have gone wrong and the things you have done wrong. Ask for his forgiveness. Listen for his guidance. Experience his presence.

———————————— ❖ ————————————

BROKENNESS FROM SIN · RECOVERY THAT STARTS WITH CONFESSION

In the depths of your sin and brokenness, you know it is time to talk with God. Come into his presence right now to do so. Quiet yourself. Prepare your heart to be honest and truthful before him . . .

GOD'S PROMISE

PSALM 51:1-2 • A psalm of David, regarding the time Nathan the prophet came to him after David had committed adultery with Bathsheba: *Have mercy on me, O God, because of your unfailing love. Because of your great compassion, blot out the stain of my sins. Wash me clean from my guilt. Purify me from my sin.*

PSALM 51:9-10 • *Don't keep looking at my sins. Remove the stain of my guilt. Create in me a clean heart, O God.*

ISAIAH 66:2, ESV • **This is the one to whom I will look: he who is humble and contrite in spirit and trembles at my word.**

PRAY GOD'S PROMISE

Lord God, I confess that I have sinned against you—in thought, word, and deed. I have done wrong, and my wrongs have been hurtful to others. Most importantly, they have separated me from you. Forgive me, Lord.

I regret my sin and repent of my wrongdoing. ⸸ *I claim your promise, Lord God, that as I come to you in a contrite spirit, you will see me and be with me.* ⸸ I take comfort from the example of David, who sinned greatly, but came to you broken and repentant. And look at what you did with his remarkable life! Redeem my life, Lord, and make it worth something again.

In these next moments, humble yourself before God. Tell him about your sins and failures. Like David, cry out for forgiveness. Rest in God's promise to restore and redeem.

CANCER · FINDING GOD IN THE MIDST OF SUFFERING

Although many illnesses can be successfully treated these days, the diagnosis of cancer is often still devastating. God can and does work healing miracles. But if illness remains, such a difficult circumstance can draw us into deeper intimacy with God. Right now, bring your troubled heart to God and enter into his presence . . .

GOD'S PROMISE

PSALM 34:18-19 · *The LORD is close to the brokenhearted; he rescues those whose spirits are crushed. The righteous person faces many troubles, but the LORD comes to the rescue each time.*

ROMANS 5:3-5, ESV · *We rejoice in our sufferings, knowing that suffering produces endurance, and endurance produces character, and character produces hope, and hope does not put us to shame, because God's love has been poured into our hearts through the Holy Spirit who has been given to us.*

PSALM 73:26 • *My health may fail, and my spirit may grow weak, but God remains the strength of my heart; he is mine forever.*

PRAY GOD'S PROMISE

Oh Lord Jesus, I am in deep distress. I can't even think clearly. I am coming to you bearing this immense and impossible burden. I need your calming voice and your healing touch. ❧ I believe you can heal, and I know of the many miracles you have worked in people's lives. I believe you can rescue me as well. I pray for that, Lord. But I also pray that in this season of my life, I can grow closer to you. ❧ In reading these words from Psalms, I receive their promise—*that even should my health continue to fail, you, God, remain the strength of my heart.* I know I can continue to persevere with your strength, and in all of it I am reassured that you are indeed mine forever.

Spend some time reading about the miracles of Jesus in the Gospels—Matthew, Mark, Luke, and John. Pay attention to the way Jesus heals spiritually as he heals physically.

CAR ACCIDENT • GOD'S PURPOSE IN THE WORLD'S RANDOMNESS

When a random, tragic event hits, pause to refocus on God and consider who he is in the midst of the crisis . . .

GOD'S PROMISE

LUKE 12:6-7 • *What is the price of five sparrows—two copper coins? Yet God does not forget a single one of them. And the very hairs on your head are all numbered. So don't be afraid; you are more valuable to God than a whole flock of sparrows.*

1 CHRONICLES 29:11 • *Everything in the heavens and on earth is yours, O LORD, and this is your kingdom. We adore you as the one who is over all things.*

REVELATION 21:4 • ***He will wipe every tear from their eyes, and there will be no more death or sorrow or crying or pain. All these things are gone forever.***

PRAY GOD'S PROMISE

Lord, as I come to you right now, I can hardly find any words. What has happened is senseless. It's difficult to even know how to pray. I read this verse about how everything in the heavens and earth is yours—so why did you let this happen, God? ⚡ And yet I do believe you are still "over all" when bad things happen—even an accident such as this. Oh Lord, I need your presence right now. Help me to have your perspective. ⚡ Your promise is one that looks to the future, and even as I struggle in this current situation, *I claim your promise that there will someday be no more death or sorrow or pain*. I ask that you will help me get through this. Help me to embrace this promise in these hours and coming days.

In these moments, pour out your hurt and how this has shaken you. Let God's words speak to you. Allow his loving embrace to comfort you.

———————————— ❖ ————————————

THE CHALLENGE OF BEING A DAD

• RESTRAINT IN PARENTAL DISCIPLINE

Come into God's presence to tell him about this challenging matter of disciplining your child. First, listen to his words . . .

GOD'S PROMISE

EPHESIANS 6:4 • *Fathers, do not provoke your children to anger by the way you treat them. Rather, bring them up with the discipline and instruction that comes from the Lord.*

PSALM 103:13, ESV • **As a father shows compassion to his children, so the LORD shows compassion to those who fear him.**

LUKE 15:20 • *He returned home to his father. And while he was still a long way off, his father saw him coming. Filled with love and compassion, he ran to his son, embraced him, and kissed him.*

PRAY GOD'S PROMISE

Father God, I want my child to succeed and do well. I know that one has to push himself in life in order to achieve. But I confess that I go overboard sometimes—I can be really hard on my kid. I feel guilty. Father, I'm sorry for my actions. ❧ I don't want my child to become angry and bitter toward anyone, and certainly not toward me. I know that the way I reprimand might have that effect. ❧ And so I pray for you to help me in this area. ***Thank you for your promise to show compassion toward me, your son.*** I ask for your help to do likewise with my own child. Instruct me in how to do this better, Father.

Talk with God about how you might share with your child what these verses mean to you.

———————— ◇ ————————

THE CHALLENGE OF BEING A DAD

• WISDOM FROM THE FATHER

Come to God to ask for his wisdom about being a good father. He happens to know something about that. Listen to his words . . .

GOD'S PROMISE

PSALM 103:13-14 • *The LORD is like a father to his children, tender and compassionate to those who fear him. For he knows how weak we are; he remembers we are only dust.*

PROVERBS 3:12 • *The LORD corrects those he loves, just as a father corrects a child in whom he delights.*

1 THESSALONIANS 2:11-12, NIV • *You know that we dealt with each of you as a father deals with his own children, encouraging, comforting and urging you to live lives worthy of God, who calls you into his kingdom and glory.*

PRAY GOD'S PROMISE

Lord God, I come to you for wisdom about how to be a good father. I really don't know if I am capable of doing this. I don't have the best example from my own father to follow. I am praying for your help. ⚜ It's so comforting to read your words about how *you* are a father to *us*—treating us with tenderness and compassion, even properly disciplining us. I pray that you would give me what it takes to do those same things so I become the father I should be. *Lord, I want to be a father who encourages and comforts my children—who shows them how to live in a manner that is worthy of your blessing.* I look forward to the day when my children and I will together know the joy of reigning with you in your Kingdom.

Purpose in your heart to come to God each day and ask for his father-wisdom.

—————————— ❖ ——————————

THE CHALLENGE OF BEING A MOM • EXCHANGING ANXIETY FOR THE PEACE OF GOD

As you try to survive the beautiful mess of raising children, come to God and enjoy a few moments of quiet. Let him come alongside and wrap you in his comforting peace . . .

GOD'S PROMISE

2 THESSALONIANS 3:16, ESV • *May the Lord of peace himself give you peace at all times in every way.*

1 PETER 3:4 • *You should clothe yourselves instead with the beauty that comes from within, the unfading beauty of a gentle and quiet spirit, which is so precious to God.*

PHILIPPIANS 4:4-7, NIV • *Rejoice in the Lord always. I will say it again: Rejoice! Let your gentleness be evident to all. The Lord is near. Do not be anxious about anything, but in everything, by prayer and petition, with thanksgiving, present your requests to God. **And the peace of God, which transcends all understanding, will guard your hearts and your minds in Christ Jesus.***

PRAY GOD'S PROMISE

Lord, I'm a mess—oh-so-weary and on edge. I love my kids, but they have been too much for me to handle today. I need your comfort, Lord. I need some peace of mind. ✦ Thank you for these words that remind me of the rewards of being a godly woman and mother. ✦ I know I need to let go of my anxieties and trust you. I do rejoice in being your child, Lord. Though I wonder—*Am I as much trouble to you as my kids are to me?!* **But most of all I claim your promise that your peace will protect my heart and mind as I journey through these difficult days.** Thank you, Lord.

Let God speak to you in this quiet time. Tell him about your day—your anxieties and frustrations—and let him speak to you about how precious you are to him. Let his peace wash over you.

THE CHALLENGE OF BEING A MOM • REFRESHMENT IN THE MIDST OF FRAZZLE

As you're overwhelmed by exhaustion and the relentless demands of being a mom, come to God with your tired heart. Let his words wash over you . . .

GOD'S PROMISE

2 CORINTHIANS 4:17-18 • *Our present troubles are small and won't last very long. Yet they produce for us a glory that vastly outweighs them and will last forever! So we don't look at the troubles we can see now; rather, we fix our gaze on things that cannot be seen. For the things we see now will soon be gone, but the things we cannot see will last forever.*

1 THESSALONIANS 2:7, NIV • *We were gentle among you, like a mother caring for her little children.*

PROVERBS 31:28-31, NKJV • *Her children rise up and call her blessed; her husband also, and he praises her: "Many daughters have done well, But you excel them all." Charm is deceitful and beauty is passing,* **but a woman who fears the LORD, she shall be praised.** *Give her of the fruit of her hands, and let her own works praise her in the gates.*

PRAY GOD'S PROMISE

Oh Lord, I am tired and frazzled—and the day isn't over yet! I have doubts about whether what I do in life matters or counts for anything. It's so hard these days to even have the time to gain perspective on who I am as a woman and as a mother. ‡ Lord, I thank you that these verses from the Bible clarify my calling. I accept that my day-to-day exhaustion is temporary (I pray that's so!), and I will set my hopes on the glory that you assure me lies ahead. ‡ *Lord, I also thank you for this truth that in your eyes, the woman who is to be admired and praised is the one who lives in obedience to you.* I want that promise for my own life, Lord.

Let God speak to you in this quiet time. Think about how you might rearrange your schedule so that spending time in his refreshing presence is no longer a wish but a reality.

―◇―

THE CHALLENGE OF BEING A PARENT

• ONE OF GOD'S BEST GIFTS

Sometimes in the midst of the frenzy of raising children, we forget about how precious they are and what a blessing they bring. Quiet your heart and mind in these moments and let God speak to you . . .

GOD'S PROMISE

JEREMIAH 1:5 • *I knew you before I formed you in your mother's womb. Before you were born I set you apart.*

PSALM 139:13-16 • **You made all the delicate, inner parts of my body and knit me together in my mother's womb.** *Thank you for making me so wonderfully complex! Your workmanship is marvelous—how well I know it. You watched me as I was being formed in utter seclusion, as I was woven together in the dark of the womb. You saw me before I was born.* **Every day of my life was recorded in your book.** *Every moment was laid out before a single day had passed.*

PSALM 127:3-5, MSG • *Don't you see that children are God's best gift? The fruit of the womb his generous legacy? Like a warrior's fistful of arrows are the children of a vigorous youth. Oh, how blessed are you parents, with your quivers full of children!*

PRAY GOD'S PROMISE

Lord, I am frazzled. Exhausted. At the end of my rope. I need a time-out. I need you to whisper encouragement to me. Allow me to sit for a moment in your rest. ❧ I need these scriptural reminders of how you have brought blessings to me through my children. Thank you, Lord. There are times most days when that blessing becomes apparent and shines through the squeals and messes, but it's easy to miss them. ❦ *I claim your promise, Lord, of your intimate presence in each of my children's lives—as they were delicately formed in the womb and as they live out each day you've ordained for them. I thank you for them, my very best gifts from you.*

Pray for each of your children, being mindful of how God formed them with specific gifts, talents, and purposes. Thank God for those unique traits.

———————————— ❖ ————————————

THE CHALLENGE OF BEING A PARENT

• TEACHING THE WONDER OF GOD'S GREAT WORKS

Sometimes it's hard to know how to talk with our kids about God, especially when they aren't receptive. Open your heart to God's words and wisdom . . .

GOD'S PROMISE

PSALM 78:4, ESV • *We will not hide them from their children, but tell to the coming generation the glorious deeds of the LORD, and his might, and the wonders that he has done.*

DEUTERONOMY 11:18-21 • *Commit yourselves wholeheartedly to these words of mine. Tie them to your hands and wear them on your forehead as reminders.* **Teach them to your children.** *Talk about them when you are at home and when you are on the road, when you are going to bed and when you are getting up.* **Write them on the doorposts of your** *house and on your gates, so that as long as the sky remains above the earth, you and your children may flourish in the land the LORD swore to give your ancestors.*

PSALM 103:13, 17-18 • *The LORD is like a father to his children, tender and compassionate to those who fear him. His salvation extends to the children's children of those who are faithful to his covenant, of those who obey his commandments!*

PRAY GOD'S PROMISE

Lord God, I want to raise my kids to know you as I know you. I'm afraid, however, that I'm not doing such a good job of that. They're not always open to listening to me when I try to talk about you. I pray for your guidance and help. ❧ I think you are telling me that simply pointing out to them what you have done in my life and the lives of others around us might be a good place to start. ❧ *Lord, I claim your promise that as I tell my children about the wisdom of your ways and the great things you have done, they will flourish.* I commit them to your care, Lord.

Pray for each of your children right now. Think about how you might tell each one about God, not by preaching, but by simply recounting to them real-life stories of his miraculous provision.

—◆—

THE CHALLENGE OF BEING A PARENT

• TRAINING CHILDREN IN THE WAY THEY SHOULD GO

You have questions about some of your strategies in raising your kids. Come talk with God about the challenges you face with your children. Listen to his words to you . . .

GOD'S PROMISE

HEBREWS 12:11, ESV • *For the moment all discipline seems painful rather than pleasant, but later it yields the peaceful fruit of righteousness to those who have been trained by it.*

PROVERBS 29:17 • *Discipline your children, and they will give you peace of mind and will make your heart glad.*

PROVERBS 22:6, ESV • ***Train up a child in the way he should go; even when he is old he will not depart from it.***

PRAY GOD'S PROMISE

Lord God, I come to you with concerns about my children. I want to be careful about how I raise them. I want to do the right thing as a parent. Most of all, I want to raise my kids to love and worship you. ❧ Your words point me to your wisdom about these things. I've read several of the latest parenting books, but they make me crazy with theories and statistics. Your words cut through all of that. Thank you. ❧ *I embrace your promise that if I am faithful in training my children, pointing them in the right direction, and most of all leading them to acknowledge you, then in their later years they will stay with you.* I pray for that kind of good result, Lord. Help me to do my best and trust that you will keep them safe in your arms.

Take some moments to pray for each of your children individually. Ask God to keep them safe in his care.

———————— ❖ ————————

THE CHALLENGE OF BEING A SINGLE MOM · GOD'S GIFT, YOUR BLESSING

Your child is a gift from God. Let God's words assure you in this time of feeling overwhelmed and at loose ends . . .

GOD'S PROMISE

1 SAMUEL 1:27-28, NIV · *I prayed for this child, and the LORD has granted me what I asked of him. So now I give him to the LORD. For his whole life he will be given over to the LORD.*

DEUTERONOMY 6:7-9, ESV · *You shall teach them diligently to your children, and shall talk of them when you sit in your house, and when you walk by the way, and when you lie down, and when you rise. You shall bind them as a sign on your hand, and they shall be as frontlets between your eyes. You shall write them on the doorposts of your house and on your gates.*

PSALM 127:3-5, MSG · **Don't you see that children are GOD's best gift? The fruit of the womb his generous legacy? Like a warrior's fistful of arrows are the children of a vigorous youth. Oh, how blessed are you.**

PRAY GOD'S PROMISE

Lord God, I am alone in caring for my child. I don't know how I can make this work, but I trust you will continue to be there for me, just as I know you are now. ❦ Sometimes I also struggle with making sense of all that's happened to me. Lord, I ask for strength and encouragement. ❦ You remind me that my child is a precious gift from you. *I receive your promise that my child is—and always will be—a very special blessing to me.* Thank you, Lord.

In these next minutes, be still and silent. Let God speak to you about the blessing you are to him, and the gift your child is to you.

—·—◇—·—

CHRONIC PAIN · FINDING STRENGTH IN GOD

Often life involves physical hardship, sometimes in the form of chronic pain. Come boldly to God in these moments and ask for relief. But also simply seek him in the midst of these challenges . . .

GOD'S PROMISE

JOB 30:17 · *At night my bones are filled with pain, which gnaws at me relentlessly.*

JOB 33:19, ESV · *Man is also rebuked with pain on his bed and with continual strife in his bones.*

2 CORINTHIANS 12:7-10 · *I was given a thorn in my flesh, a messenger from Satan to torment me and keep me from becoming proud. Three different times I begged the Lord to take it away. Each time he said, "My grace is all you need. My power works best in weakness." So now I am glad to boast about my weaknesses, so that the power of Christ can work through me. That's why I take pleasure in my weaknesses, and in the insults, hardships, persecutions, and troubles that I suffer for Christ.* **For when I am weak, then I am strong.**

PRAY GOD'S PROMISE

Oh God, you know the pain I live with. It makes my days difficult and my nights restless. I come to you now to ask of you some measure of comfort in the midst of my hurt. ‡ God, I read these words about a thorn in the flesh, and they point me to a new perspective about my situation. I understand a little better that sometimes because of our difficulties we are forced to rely on you more. Perhaps I need to see things differently. ‡ *God, I embrace your promise that when I am weak, then I am strong.* Through my weakness your power can be seen by others. I pray for you to use my condition and my pain for your glory and the good of others.

In this time of prayer, converse with God about how you might help someone else in pain. Who might that be?

—◇—

CHURCH PROBLEMS · BRINGING COMMUNITY CONFLICTS TO GOD IN PRAYER

Bring to God your prayers for your church. Share with him your love for the people there as well as your concerns for the church in its present state. Pray for God's blessings . . .

GOD'S PROMISE

ROMANS 12:4-5 · *Just as our bodies have many parts and each part has a special function, so it is with Christ's body. We are many parts of one body, and we all belong to each other.*

EPHESIANS 4:16 · *He makes the whole body fit together perfectly. As each part does its own special work, it helps the other parts grow, so that the whole body is healthy and growing and full of love.*

MATTHEW 18:20 • *Where two or three gather together as my followers, I am there among them.*

PRAY GOD'S PROMISE

Lord God, I bring to you some requests and concerns for my church. You know how much I have given myself to this community and how I love the people there. Yet I am concerned that things are not working well. I know some have expressed dissatisfaction. There is an undercurrent of frustration. ❧ I pray that you might remind us all of your words here, about how the body of Christ has many parts, each one having its special work. Speak to me personally about what I need to know and how I might need to change, if that is part of what's needed. ❧ *Lord, I claim the promise of your presence among as few as two or three of us—that in such a small and simple gathering, you are with us.* I pray that you will speak to me and others about how we can more fully realize the beauty of the body of Christ together.

Quiet your heart before God. What other things is he saying to you? Can you sense his great love for your church?

CHURCH PROBLEMS · RECLAIMING THE PROMISE OF OUR FAITH

Settle yourself in the presence of God. Share with him your concerns about your church and your worries that it has fallen away from the true work of the gospel . . .

GOD'S PROMISE

MATTHEW 5:13 • *You are the salt of the earth. But what good is salt if it has lost its flavor? Can you make it salty again? It will be thrown out and trampled underfoot as worthless.*

PHILIPPIANS 2:3-4, ESV • *Do nothing from selfish ambition or conceit, but in humility count others more significant than yourselves. Let each of you look not only to his own interests, but also to the interests of others.*

COLOSSIANS 1:21-23 • *[God] . . . has reconciled you to himself through the death of Christ in his physical body. As a result, he has brought you into his own presence, and you are holy and blameless as you stand before him without a single fault. But you must continue to believe this truth and stand firmly in it. Don't drift away from the assurance you received when you heard the Good News.*

PRAY GOD'S PROMISE

Lord Jesus, yes—I am concerned that my church is no longer the salt for our community. Some people have left, and there is dissension. I grieve over this, as I have dedicated much of myself to this church for so long. ⁑ Help me, Jesus, to receive these Scriptures as applying to both me and the others in my church. Help me to look clearly at my own attitudes and behaviors through this lens. ⁑ *Lord Jesus, I ask that all of us would recall the promise of our faith, that we can stand holy and blameless before God because of your sacrifice on the cross.* Help us to remember and experience your presence. I pray that we will not drift away any further.

In silence, listen to God speak into your church situation and your life. What guidance are you discerning?

———————————— ‹◦› ————————————

COARSE LANGUAGE · FINDING GRACE IN CONVERSATION

Come into God's presence. Be prepared to confess your struggle with the kind of language you use with and toward others . . .

GOD'S PROMISE

ECCLESIASTES 5:2, ESV • *Be not rash with your mouth, nor let your heart be hasty to utter a word before God, for God is in heaven and you are on earth. Therefore let your words be few.*

1 TIMOTHY 4:12 • *Be an example to all believers in what you say, in the way you live, in your love, your faith, and your purity.*

COLOSSIANS 3:8-10 • *Now is the time to get rid of anger, rage, malicious behavior, slander, and dirty language. Don't lie to each other, for you have stripped off your old sinful nature and all its wicked deeds.* **Put on your new nature, and be renewed as you learn to know your Creator and become like him.**

PRAY GOD'S PROMISE

Father, I am coming to you now with a specific issue in mind, for I am convicted about the language I use with and toward others. I confess that too often I do not control my tongue, and I find myself using words that are offensive or hurtful. ⚡ You admonish me in these verses to make sure my language is an example to others in being helpful, not destructive. ⚡ I accept this correction from you, Lord. *And I receive your words to put on my new nature and to be renewed. What a great blessing it is to know my Creator and become like him!* Thank you, Father. Help me today and in coming days to control the language I use with others.

In a deeper time of prayer, think about specific people you may have hurt when you used coarse language. Mention these names to God. Allow him to speak to you about how you might rectify these situations and receive forgiveness for each one.

--- • ---

COMPROMISE · DISCERNING THE WILES OF THE WORLD

You are here because you know, deep down, that you have some things to talk about with God. Open your heart to him. Let him speak into your life choices . . .

GOD'S PROMISE

MATTHEW 6:24 · *No one can serve two masters. For you will hate one and love the other; you will be devoted to one and despise the other.*

JAMES 1:22-24 · *Don't just listen to God's word. You must do what it says. Otherwise, you are only fooling yourselves. For if you listen to the word and don't obey, it is like glancing at your face in a mirror. You see yourself, walk away, and forget what you look like.*

1 JOHN 2:15-17 • *Do not love this world nor the things it offers you, for when you love the world, you do not have the love of the Father in you. For the world offers only a craving for physical pleasure, a craving for everything we see, and pride in our achievements and possessions. These are not from the Father, but are from this world. And this world is fading away, along with everything that people crave.* **But anyone who does what pleases God will live forever.**

PRAY GOD'S PROMISE

Lord God, I have been troubled lately because I know how my life has drifted away from you. I often feel torn between pursuing the worldly things I desire and obediently following you. § You say that I cannot serve two masters, and yet I know I have been trying to. I confess that I am easily tempted to make wrong choices. But I know that when I do, I find myself apart from you, even resenting you. § I confess these things to you, Lord. Strengthen me to make the right choices, to no longer flirt with compromise. *And I hold dear the promise of your words—that in pleasing you, I will live forever.* I know I have the assurance of eternity in Christ. Help me to follow you with my whole heart, mind, and body.

In these moments, think about the Scripture verses from James. What do they say to you?

———————————— <·> ————————————

COMPULSIVE BEHAVIOR · RECOVERING

A LIFE THAT'S BROKEN

Come to God in this moment, honestly confessing to him the state of your life. Know that many others have struggled also—even the apostle Paul. Realize that God specializes in people who are broken. Allow God to be present with you and to encourage you right now. Listen for his words and his direction . . .

GOD'S PROMISE

ROMANS 7:14-15, NIV · *I am unspiritual, sold as a slave to sin. I do not understand what I do. For what I want to do I do not do, but what I hate I do.*

MATTHEW 5:3, MSG · *You're blessed when you're at the end of your rope. With less of you there is more of God and his rule.*

PHILIPPIANS 4:11, 13 · *Not that I was ever in need, for I have learned how to be content with whatever I have. . . . **For I can do everything through Christ, who gives me strength.***

PRAY GOD'S PROMISE

God, I am at the bottom. I struggle with a compulsion I cannot stop. I feel like I'm at the end of my rope. It seems hopeless to me, and I cannot see any way out of this life. I try and try to change, but I always end up in this same place. ⚜ I long for there to be more of you, God, in my life, but I simply do not know how to make that happen. ⚜ *Yet even in this, I want right now to claim your promise that I can do everything through you who strengthens me.* God, help me focus on you when I am tempted.

Spend time now listening to God. Feel his arms around you. Know he isn't condemning you, but also know he wants you back. What is he telling you to do? Who is he telling you to seek out for help?

CONFESSION · ACCEPTING GOD'S SALVATION

Come before God to acknowledge him as God. Confess that you now believe in him and the work of his Son, Jesus Christ, on the cross . . .

GOD'S PROMISE

ROMANS 10:9 · *If you confess with your mouth that Jesus is Lord and believe in your heart that God raised him from the dead, you will be saved.*

LUKE 12:8 · *I tell you the truth, everyone who acknowledges me publicly here on earth, the Son of Man will also acknowledge in the presence of God's angels.*

JOHN 3:16 · *This is how God loved the world: He gave his one and only Son,* **so that everyone who believes in him will not perish but have eternal life.**

PRAY GOD'S PROMISE

God, I enter your presence acknowledging who you are. I confess I have not always believed that you are God, and I've certainly not made you God over my life. ❦ I do claim Jesus Christ as my personal Savior, and I understand that his sacrifice on the cross serves as payment for my sinfulness. ❦ *Lord God, I claim your promise that in confessing these things right now I am saved from eternal death and destruction.* Thank you, Lord, for your grace and love and salvation. Thank you for the gift of eternal life.

Take some more time in prayer. Allow God to speak to you. Know that he loves you and delights in your confession of belief in him today.

————————— ❖ —————————

CONFESSION · COMING CLEAN WITH GOD

Enter into God's presence for a time of confession. He invites you to experience his cleansing, healing forgiveness in exchange for your heartfelt honesty. Listen for his voice as you open yourself to him . . .

GOD'S PROMISE

PROVERBS 28:13 • *People who conceal their sins will not prosper, but if they confess and turn from them, they will receive mercy.*

PSALM 38:18 • *But I confess my sins; I am deeply sorry for what I have done.*

1 JOHN 1:9 • *But if we confess our sins to him,* **he is faithful and just to forgive us our sins and to cleanse us from all wickedness.**

PRAY GOD'S PROMISE

Lord God, I come to you as a sinner. I have done wrong, by choice and intention. I have sinned against you in thought, word, and deed. I have wronged others as well. ❦ I am aware that your rules for life are designed for my benefit and for the lives of others. You want what's best for me. And yet I have chosen to go against that. I am deeply sorry for what I have done. ❧ Lord, I ask you to forgive me. *I claim your promise that you will forgive my sins*. I further commit to obey you in my life and actions.

In the next few minutes, tell God specifically how you have sinned. Ask for his forgiveness, simply and sincerely. Believe by faith that you are cleansed!

CONFESSION · GROWING IN CHRIST BY CONFESSING TO OTHERS

God's Word instructs us to confess our sins to one another. That's often easier said than done, right? But when we take that plunge, we reap a priceless reward. Hear what God has to say about this. Quiet yourself and allow his words to wash over you . . .

GOD'S PROMISE

JAMES 5:16 · *Confess your sins to each other and pray for each other so that you may be healed. The earnest prayer of a righteous person has great power and produces wonderful results.*

EPHESIANS 4:2-3 · *Always be humble and gentle. Be patient with each other, making allowance for each other's faults because of your love. Make every effort to keep yourselves united in the Spirit, binding yourselves together with peace.*

EPHESIANS 4:15-16 · *We will speak the truth in love, growing in every way more and more like Christ, who is the head of his body, the church. He makes the whole body fit together perfectly. As each part does its own special work, it helps the other parts grow, so that the whole body is healthy and growing and full of love.*

PRAY GOD'S PROMISE

Lord God, I know that I have not been open to talking with people about my problems and some of the things I've done. Sometimes I fear the consequences of telling others. And yet I hear your words about how the body of Christ is supposed to work. ❦ Lord, your words about "making allowance for each other's faults" give me hope that my confession to others might be received well. Help me to have courage to share with them. ❦ ***Lord, I claim your promise that speaking the truth will help me grow more and more like you.*** I want that, Lord.

In this time with God, let him speak to you about when and where you might open up and share with other believers.

CONFLICT · OVERCOMING TENSION WITH OTHERS

Talk with God about the situation you're in and the conflicts you're facing with certain people. Pray and listen . . .

GOD'S PROMISE

COLOSSIANS 3:13 · *Make allowance for each other's faults, and forgive anyone who offends you. Remember, the Lord forgave you, so you must forgive others.*

ROMANS 12:17-21, ESV · *Repay no one evil for evil, but give thought to do what is honorable in the sight of all. If possible, so far as it depends on you, live peaceably with all.*

Beloved, never avenge yourselves, but leave it to the wrath of God, for it is written, "Vengeance is mine, I will repay, says the Lord." To the contrary, "if your enemy is hungry, feed him; if he is thirsty, give him something to drink; for by so doing you will heap burning coals on his head." Do not be overcome by evil, but overcome evil with good.

2 CORINTHIANS 7:5-6, NIV • *When we came into Macedonia, we had no rest, but* **we were harassed at every turn— conflicts on the outside, fears within. But God, who comforts the downcast, comforted us.**

PRAY GOD'S PROMISE

Father God, I am anxious about a conflict I have with someone. I feel strongly that in our situation a particular direction is called for, while this other person holds the opposite opinion. As a result, we've been fighting. I ask for your help in resolving this conflict. § I hear your words, Father, about forgiving others and living peaceably with all. I ask for your help in doing that in this situation. § *Father, I also embrace your promise of comfort in this tense personal matter. Just as you comforted the apostle Paul, so I ask you to comfort us as well.*

So often in tense personal situations we tend to charge ahead. Take some time to listen to God. How is he directing you to proceed here?

———————————— ◇ ————————————

CONFRONTATION · SPEAKING THE TRUTH
IN LOVE

Confronting another person is seldom easy. Yet at this time you know it is necessary. Talk with God about the confrontational situation you're facing. Enter his presence with an open ear, listening for his words of advice . . .

GOD'S PROMISE

EPHESIANS 4:26-27, MSG · *Go ahead and be angry. You do well to be angry—but don't use your anger as fuel for revenge. And don't stay angry. Don't go to bed angry. Don't give the Devil that kind of foothold in your life.*

MATTHEW 18:15, NIV · *If your brother or sister sins, go and point out their fault, just between the two of you. If they listen to you, you have won them over.*

1 TIMOTHY 1:5, MSG · **The whole point of what we're urging is simply love—love uncontaminated by self-interest and counterfeit faith, a life open to God.**

PRAY GOD'S PROMISE

God, I am facing this situation in which I need to confront someone who has not only wronged me but who has also been disruptive to others. I need courage to deal with this directly. And I need wisdom in knowing what to say and how to say it. ❧ In reading your words, I hear your voice regarding anger and confession and forgiveness. Thank you for pointing me in this direction. ❧ *God, I receive your words about holding to the main goal of speaking in love, not out of selfish interest, and through it all staying open to you.* Thank you for giving me the wisdom and confidence to do this.

Express to God the specific nature of the conflict and the things you're afraid of in confronting this person. Listen for God's responses.

———————— ❖ ————————

CONFUSION · CLARITY IN GOD'S WISDOM

Right now, things are not falling into place, and you're confused about what you should do. You've decided to seek God's wisdom. Settle your mind and heart as you come into his presence with an expectation for clarity and peace . . .

GOD'S PROMISE

1 CORINTHIANS 14:33, ESV · *God is not a God of confusion but of peace.*

PSALM 119:169 · *O LORD, listen to my cry; give me the discerning mind you promised.*

1 JOHN 5:14-15, NIV · *This is the confidence we have in approaching God: that if we ask anything according to his will, he hears us. And if we know that he hears us— whatever we ask—we know that we have what we asked of him.*

PRAY GOD'S PROMISE

Lord God, I find myself in a place of concern and questioning. I have some decisions to make, and I am unsure of what to do. I'm also confused about certain things, and I need the best choice to be made clear to me. I ask for your help. ❦ I know, Lord, that you can provide a deeper understanding of the issues at hand. I ask for knowledge that will serve me in making a good decision. ⚜ *Lord, I agree with your promise that if I ask for these things, you will hear me and provide the insight I need for the decision at hand.*

Take some more time in silence. Listen to God. Pay attention to his voice. As you proceed through your day, trust that you're hearing from him. He will show you the way.

CRITICIZING OTHERS · OVERCOMING BEING JUDGMENTAL

Come to God in prayer. Ask him to work in you to help you overcome being judgmental and critical in your interactions with others . . .

GOD'S PROMISE

MATTHEW 7:1-5 • *Do not judge others, and you will not be judged. For you will be treated as you treat others. The standard you use in judging is the standard by which you will be judged. And why worry about a speck in your friend's eye when you have a log in your own? How can you think of saying to your friend, "Let me help you get rid of that speck in your eye," when you can't see past the log in your own eye? Hypocrite! First get rid of the log in your own eye; then you will see well enough to deal with the speck in your friend's eye.*

EPHESIANS 4:29 • *Don't use foul or abusive language. Let everything you say be good and helpful, so that your words will be an encouragement to those who hear them.*

GALATIANS 5:16, 22-23 • *So I say, let the Holy Spirit guide your lives. . . . the Holy Spirit produces this kind of fruit in our lives: love, joy, peace, patience, kindness, goodness, faithfulness, gentleness, and self-control.*

PRAY GOD'S PROMISE

Oh Lord, I know I am too often guilty of being critical of others. I tend to judge them harshly, sometimes in spite of doing and saying the very same things myself. Please convict me when you see this hypocrisy occurring in my life. ✦ Lord, I want to speak and act in a way that is helpful to others. Change my character as I cooperate with you. ✦ *I pray right now for your Spirit to be at work inside of me. I ask that the Holy Spirit will guide my life, and I receive the promise that he will produce in me these fruits—character qualities—that you want to grow in me.*

In this quiet time, ask the Lord to speak to you about those you have judged in the past. What is he telling you about seeking their forgiveness?

———————————— ❖ ————————————

CRITICIZING OTHERS · REDISCOVERING KINDNESS IN THE MODEL OF CHRIST

Come to God prepared to confess your struggle with being overly critical of others. Quiet your heart and mind. Allow God to speak into your life . . .

GOD'S PROMISE

MATTHEW 7:1-3, MSG • *Don't pick on people, jump on their failures, criticize their faults—unless, of course, you want the same treatment. That critical spirit has a way of boomeranging. It's easy to see a smudge on your neighbor's face and be oblivious to the ugly sneer on your own.*

ROMANS 14:12-13 • *Yes, each of us will give a personal account to God. So let's stop condemning each other. Decide instead to live in such a way that you will not cause another believer to stumble and fall.*

EPHESIANS 4:31-32 • *Get rid of all bitterness, rage, anger, harsh words, and slander, as well as all types of evil behavior. Instead, be kind to each other, tenderhearted, forgiving one another, just as God through Christ has forgiven you.*

PRAY GOD'S PROMISE

Lord God, I have become aware of late how I often bear a critical spirit toward others. I want to believe it's because I seek something better from myself and other people. That I desire for us all to live up to those standards. But perhaps I am simply wanting to grab attention and seem important. I come to you, Lord, in a spirit of confession. ‡ I ask you to work in my spirit and character. I need to be more aware of how my criticisms can be hurtful to other people. ‡ *I embrace your words here that I need to show kindness and forgiveness, like the example Jesus showed us all.* Help me to be like Christ in this way.

In a deeper time of prayer, think about specific people you may have hurt through your critical words. Mention these names to God. Allow him to speak to you about how you might seek forgiveness for each situation.

DANGEROUS TIMES · PEACE IN A WORLD
OF WORRY

You are troubled by terrible events that are happening around the world. Unload your worries and place them at God's feet. Listen to his words . . .

GOD'S PROMISE

1 PETER 4:12-13 · *Dear friends, don't be surprised at the fiery trials you are going through, as if something strange were happening to you. Instead, be very glad—for these trials make you partners with Christ in his suffering, so that you will have the wonderful joy of seeing his glory when it is revealed to all the world.*

PSALM 9:9, ESV · *The LORD is a stronghold for the oppressed, a stronghold in times of trouble.*

PHILIPPIANS 4:7, ESV · **The peace of God, which surpasses all understanding, will guard your hearts and your minds in Christ Jesus.**

PRAY GOD'S PROMISE

Lord God, I watch the news and see such awful things occurring everywhere. And sometimes the terror strikes close. It fills me with anxiety and fear. I need to know you are here, Lord—present with me, protecting me. ❦

I know that we are to expect trials and tribulations on earth; I know that our world eats and drinks sin, giving the enemy a foothold for violence. ❧ Oh Lord, I pray for your protection and comfort. I want to be kept safe inside the stronghold that is you. *I claim your promise of peace. I know this is not just a temporary peace, but a sense of tranquility that surpasses all understanding.* Help me to rest in that, Lord.

Spend some more quiet time with God. Let him speak to your heart and soothe your soul.

———————— ⋖⋅⋗ ————————

DANGEROUS TIMES · THE SOVEREIGN LORD
WILL SURROUND AND PROTECT

Bring your worried heart to the one who knows all, is over all, and controls all. In the midst of these turbulent world events, listen for God's reassuring comfort . . .

GOD'S PROMISE

1 CORINTHIANS 15:30-31, MSG · *Why do you think I keep risking my neck in this dangerous work? I look death in the face practically every day I live. Do you think I'd do this if I wasn't convinced of your resurrection and mine as guaranteed by the resurrected Messiah Jesus?*

PSALM 5:11 · *Let all who take refuge in you rejoice; let them sing joyful praises forever.*

PSALM 5:11-12 · *Spread your protection over them, that all who love your name may be filled with joy. For you bless the godly, O LORD; you surround them with your shield of love.*

PRAY GOD'S PROMISE

It seems, Lord, that we face some threat or danger or terror every hour of the day and night. It rattles me. I need your comfort. ⚜ Help me find refuge in you, Lord. It's difficult to bring myself to a point of joy in all this, to see my way toward rejoicing and singing. But with your help, I can look beyond the turmoil of this world and see the great salvation that I have in you. ⚜ *Thank you for spreading your protection over me and filling me with joy. Surround me, I pray, with your shield of love.*

Talk with God about some of the specific events that have most troubled you. Pray for those who have been in the midst of those events. Thank God for his power and ultimate triumph over the tragedies in this world.

DATING · FINDING THE ONE GOD HAS FOR YOU

Make some time for God in your life right now. Share with him your thoughts and concerns about finding the right relationship in your life . . .

GOD'S PROMISE

GENESIS 2:18 · *The LORD God said, "It is not good for the man to be alone. I will make a helper who is just right for him."*

ROMANS 12:9, ESV · *Let love be genuine. Abhor what is evil; hold fast to what is good.*

JEREMIAH 29:11-12, NIV • *"I know the plans I have for you,"* *declares the LORD, "plans to prosper you and not to harm you, plans to give you hope and a future. Then you will call on me and come and pray to me, and I will listen to you."*

PRAY GOD'S PROMISE

Father God, I find myself despairing that I may never find a good romantic relationship with someone I love . . . and who loves me. I feel that I've tried so many times and have been disappointed so often. I open up my heart to you about this now. ♦ I hear your words, Father, that love needs to be genuine—not forced, not fake, not false. I ask for your help in being genuine in that way, and I pray I would find someone who also demonstrates such real love. ♦ Father, *thank you for this promise that you have plans for me—plans to prosper me. I embrace that.* Help me entrust to you my future and the romantic relationship I desire. Thank you, Father.

Spend more time with God and talk with him about the good relationships he has provided in your life—with parents, siblings, friends, coworkers.

—◇—

DATING · OVERCOMING SEXUAL TEMPTATION

Come into God's presence prepared to pour out to him the concerns of your heart regarding the relationship you're in . . .

GOD'S PROMISE

1 CORINTHIANS 6:18-20 • *Run from sexual sin! No other sin so clearly affects the body as this one does. For sexual*

immorality is a sin against your own body. Don't you realize that your body is the temple of the Holy Spirit, who lives in you and was given to you by God? You do not belong to yourself, for God bought you with a high price. So you must honor God with your body.

2 TIMOTHY 2:22 • *Run from anything that stimulates youthful lusts. Instead, pursue righteous living, faithfulness, love, and peace. Enjoy the companionship of those who call on the Lord with pure hearts.*

1 THESSALONIANS 4:3-4 • *God's will is for you to be holy, so stay away from all sexual sin. Then each of you will control his own body and live in holiness and honor.*

PRAY GOD'S PROMISE

Lord God, you know my heart and my life. You know my sexual struggles in this relationship. I know your Word and your warnings about sexual sin. And I need to confess these things to you. ⸰ I pray that you will help me be pure in this relationship. I want to honor you with my heart and my life and my body. ⸰ *And Lord, I do claim your words. Make them true in my life—that both of us will control ourselves sexually so that we might live in holiness and honor.*

In the next few minutes, take time to talk with God specifically about this relationship you're in. Listen to his response. Open your heart to what he is telling you.

———————— ❖ ————————

DEATH · GOD'S PRESENCE IN THE ACHE OF LOSS

In this time of mourning a loved one, know that God has answered the sting of death with the truth of the Resurrection . . .

GOD'S PROMISE

JOHN 11:26 · *Everyone who lives in me and believes in me will never ever die. Do you believe this?*

1 THESSALONIANS 4:14, NIV · *We believe that Jesus died and rose again, and so we believe that God will bring with Jesus those who have fallen asleep in him.*

REVELATION 21:4 · **He will wipe every tear from their eyes, and there will be no more death or sorrow or crying or pain. All these things are gone forever.**

PRAY GOD'S PROMISE

Father God, I have lost someone in my family, someone I've been close to. I need your comfort, your touch, your whispers. Help me understand, Father. Give me some assurance that all of this has meaning and purpose. ⚜ Yes, I believe that the sacrifice of your Son on the cross has overcome death. And yet, I need more. I need to know what a life stands for, what it means, how it matters. ⚜ Father, help me to hold close the promise you have given us—*that you will wipe these tears from my eyes* and ease the ache of my heart.

In these next moments, quiet your heart and listen to God respond to your heart's questions.

———————— ◆ ————————

DEATH · THE HOPE OF ETERNAL LIFE

In this time of grieving the loss of a friend, enter God's presence, knowing that in Christ, death has been overcome . . .

GOD'S PROMISE

1 CORINTHIANS 15:26 · *The last enemy to be destroyed is death.*

ROMANS 5:17 · *The sin of this one man, Adam, caused death to rule over many. But even greater is God's wonderful grace and his gift of righteousness, for all who receive it will live in triumph over sin and death through this one man, Jesus Christ.*

JOHN 11:25-26, NIV · ***I am the resurrection and the life****. The one who believes in me will live, even though they die; and whoever lives by believing in me will never die.*

PRAY GOD'S PROMISE

Lord Jesus, I come to you right now experiencing the loss of someone close. This has been difficult for me. ❧ I know that through you we have triumph over death, but the loss is still there, and I ache. I pray for you to fill that ache. ❧ ***I thank you for this hope and promise—that you are the resurrection and the life, and that through you, death no longer reigns****.* I embrace that hope, even in the midst of my sorrow and loss.

In these minutes with God, tell him about the friend who has passed away. What about that person will you dearly miss? Share your grief with God and turn to him for comfort.

——————————— ❖ ———————————

DEATH · THE PROMISE OF A LIFE TRANSFORMED

Listen to God's words and whispers as you share with him the loss that you're experiencing in the passing of someone close . . .

GOD'S PROMISE

1 CORINTHIANS 15:51 · *Let me reveal to you a wonderful secret. We will not all die, but we will all be transformed!*

1 CORINTHIANS 15:52 · *It will happen in a moment, in the blink of an eye, when the last trumpet is blown. For when the trumpet sounds, those who have died will be raised to live forever. And we who are living will also be transformed.*

1 CORINTHIANS 15:54-55 · **When our dying bodies have been transformed into bodies that will never die, this Scripture will be fulfilled: "Death is swallowed up in victory. O death, where is your victory? O death, where is your sting?"**

PRAY GOD'S PROMISE

Father God, I know that in death we have triumphed through your Son, Jesus Christ. And I rejoice that even in this circumstance, we have reason to be hopeful. Thank you for the promise of overcoming and the hope of heaven. ⚜ I long for the day when our bodies will be transformed and we will all be clothed in your righteousness. ⚜ *And Father, I claim your wonderful promise that death is indeed swallowed up in victory.* Thank you, Lord, for your deliverance!

In a period of quiet, let your heart praise God for the remarkable work of his Son on the cross.

DEBT · OVERCOMING THE IMPOSSIBLE

You come before God today with a financial debt weighing heavily on your mind and heart. Still yourself in God's presence . . .

GOD'S PROMISES

PHILIPPIANS 4:19 · *This same God who takes care of me will supply all your needs from his glorious riches, which have been given to us in Christ Jesus.*

ROMANS 13:7 · *Give to everyone what you owe them: Pay your taxes and government fees to those who collect them.*

2 CORINTHIANS 9:10-11 · *God is the one who provides seed for the farmer and then bread to eat. **In the same way, he will provide and increase your resources and then produce a great harvest of generosity in you.** Yes, you will be enriched in every way so that you can always be generous.*

PRAY GOD'S PROMISE

Lord, you know the weight and worry of the debts I owe. They overwhelm me these days. I don't even know how I got into this mess. I need your help. ⸙ Your words remind me that you are a God who takes care of me. How easy it is for me to forget that and fail to trust you! I thank you for your promises to provide all my needs. ⸙ I don't know how that will happen, but I know you are a great God. ***And so right now I claim your promise to provide and increase my resources.*** And I trust you to fulfill your promise, even as I vow to be generous to others in ways that I can.

Think of someone you can help. You may not be able to offer financial help, but you could meet some other need. Bring this opportunity to God and promise him you will do it.

⟨◦⟩

DEBT · DISCOVERING WHERE YOUR TREASURE IS

Enter right now into a prayer time with God. Bring to him your concerns about your financial debts. God will supply your needs. Listen to his words . . .

GOD'S PROMISE

1 CORINTHIANS 7:30-31 • *Those who weep or who rejoice or who buy things should not be absorbed by their weeping or their joy or their possessions. Those who use the things of the world should not become attached to them. For this world as we know it will soon pass away.*

MATTHEW 6:21 • *Wherever your treasure is, there the desires of your heart will also be.*

2 CORINTHIANS 9:8 • **God will generously provide all you need.** *Then you will always have everything you need and plenty left over to share with others.*

PRAY GOD'S PROMISE

Lord God, I hear your words in this quiet moment today. You assure me that you will provide what I need but also remind me that perhaps my priorities aren't where they should be. Yes, I confess that might be true. ⚜ Lord God, I ask for your help financially. I have such large debts, and I don't know how to repay them. However, I do know that you can and will provide for me. ⚜ ***Right now, in this***

moment, I claim your promise to supply all that I need.
You say I will even have enough left over to share. I pray
right now that you would work that miracle in my life.

In this personal time with God, consider what your priorities are. Confess to God, if you are led to do so, ways in which you've pursued financial interests that don't matter or possessions that are temporal. Listen for God's response.

———————— ❖ ————————

DEJECTION · HOPE THAT OVERCOMES DISCOURAGEMENT

In the midst of feeling discouraged about how things are going in
your life, quiet your heart in preparation for this time with God . . .

GOD'S PROMISE

PSALM 42:11 · *Why am I discouraged? Why is my heart so
sad? I will put my hope in God! I will praise him again—
my Savior and my God!*

ROMANS 8:26-27, ESV · *Likewise the Spirit helps us in
our weakness. For we do not know what to pray for as
we ought, but the Spirit himself intercedes for us with
groanings too deep for words. And he who searches hearts
knows what is the mind of the Spirit, because the Spirit
intercedes for the saints according to the will of God.*

1 CHRONICLES 28:20 · *Be strong and courageous, and do the
work. **Don't be afraid or discouraged, for the LORD God,
my God, is with you. He will not fail you or forsake you.***

PRAY GOD'S PROMISE

Oh Lord, I come to you right now in prayer for deliverance

from a general season of discouragement I've been in for a while. It isn't coming from one specific hurt, but from lots of little arrows that have stung me over time. I feel like everything I do is challenged and becomes so difficult. ✦ I like the verse that speaks of "groanings too deep for words." That's how I feel right now. I'm groaning from life. ✦ Lord, I pray to you to lift me up, to give me new strength. And I ask for some specific positive things in my life to help me go on. *Your promise is that you, Lord, are with me and will not fail me or forsake me. I believe that is true, and I claim that promise for my life right now.*

Think of one particular situation or area of your life that is causing you discouragement. How might God's intervention make a big difference? Ask him to help you in that specific thing.

◇

DEMENTIA · THE PROMISE OF THE FUTURE

Quiet your troubled heart in these moments with God. He knows how heartbreaking it is when someone close to you begins to mentally decline and can no longer remember certain aspects of life, whether big or small. It's painful that you can no longer share your special memories. Bring your sorrow to him . . .

GOD'S PROMISE

MATTHEW 15:4 · *God says, "Honor your father and mother."*

1 CORINTHIANS 15:51-52 · *Let me reveal to you a wonderful secret. We will not all die, but we will all be transformed! It will happen in a moment, in the blink of an eye, when the last trumpet is blown. For when the trumpet sounds, those*

who have died will be raised to live forever. And we who are living will also be transformed.

PSALM 34:17-18, ESV • *When the righteous cry for help, the LORD hears and delivers them out of all their troubles. **The LORD is near to the brokenhearted and saves the crushed in spirit.***

PRAY GOD'S PROMISE

Lord God, my heart is breaking for someone close to me who has been diagnosed with a form of dementia, and the symptoms are so very apparent. It's a scary time for all of us, and it's almost more than I can bear. Lord, see my tears. ✤ I am touched by the verse that refers to your return, when our bodies and minds will be restored. Though time on earth seems to take so long, I know that to you, it's all happening in the blink of an eye. ✤ I need your comfort, Lord. I am crying to you for help. I claim your promise that somehow, through all the mental decline, *my loved one will know you are near and that you will hold him in your arms until the time of your return.*

In silence, listen to what God says to you. Think about sharing these words with this special person you are close to.

———————— ‹◆› ————————

DEPRESSION · GOD HEALS THE WOUNDS OF YOUR LIFE

The best thing you can do when you're feeling down is to seek time with God. Lean on him in this time of turmoil. Cast your cares on him, and listen as he speaks to you . . .

GOD'S PROMISE

1 PETER 5:7 • *Give all your worries and cares to God, for he cares about you.*

PSALM 143:11-12 • *For the glory of your name, O LORD, preserve my life. Because of your faithfulness, bring me out of this distress. In your unfailing love, silence all my enemies and destroy all my foes, for I am your servant.*

ISAIAH 53:4-5, ESV • *Surely he has borne our griefs and carried our sorrows; yet we esteemed him stricken, smitten by God, and afflicted. But he was pierced for our transgressions; he was crushed for our iniquities; upon him was the chastisement that brought us peace, and **with his wounds we are healed**.*

PRAY GOD'S PROMISE

Lord Jesus, I am hard-pressed these days to find much to give me joy. So many things in life are pushing in on me. I feel pressure and am hopeless as to how to get through it all. ❧ I pray to you, Lord, for some deliverance from all these worries. I pray to you for some light and hope. ❧ Your promise is that you have carried these very feelings of mine on your back and in your heart. You have been crucified to deliver us all from the discouragements and disappointments of life. *I speak forth your promise that you have healed my wounds of sadness and depression.* Be with me, Jesus. Lift me up, I pray.

Let God speak to you. Talk with him, as in a conversation, about how you feel. Let him lift these weights off your back and onto his shoulders.

❖

DEPRESSION · GOD'S STRENGTH TO SHOULDER YOUR BURDENS

In the midst of so many things you're dealing with right now, all the current struggles that seem so overwhelming, ask God for comfort. Let him lift you up in these next moments . . .

GOD'S PROMISE

2 TIMOTHY 1:7, ESV · *God gave us a spirit not of fear but of power and love and self-control.*

JAMES 5:13-15 · *Are any of you suffering hardships? You should pray. Are any of you happy? You should sing praises.*

2 CORINTHIANS 1:4 · *He comforts us in all our troubles so that we can comfort others.*

PRAY GOD'S PROMISE

God, I am struggling with so many things in life right now, and it seems they all are getting me down. It just feels like the simple act of living, of getting up in the morning, is overwhelming to me. I need your help. ❧ I am praying to you, God, for the spirit of power. I pray to you for strength and encouragement. ❧ Dear God, *I hear your words that in comforting me, you equip me to comfort others. I claim that promise, and I ask that you would connect me to others who need my comfort and help and encouragement.*

Spend time right now with God and speak to him the names of people who are special to you. What are their needs? How can you comfort them?

DEPRESSION · TURNING SADNESS INTO DANCING

Quiet your heart before God. Let him speak to you now and remind you of the hope that is in him . . .

GOD'S PROMISE

PSALM 143:7 · *Come quickly, LORD, and answer me, for my depression deepens. Don't turn away from me, or I will die.*

PSALM 34:18, ESV · *The LORD is near to the brokenhearted and saves the crushed in spirit.*

PSALM 30:11-12, ESV · **You have turned for me my mourning into dancing; you have loosed my sackcloth and clothed me with gladness, that my glory may sing your praise and not be silent.** *O LORD my God, I will give thanks to you forever!*

PRAY GOD'S PROMISE

Lord, I am really down right now. Not much has gone well for me in recent days or weeks, and I am struggling to remain above water. I need your help, love, and encouragement. ❧ I look to you for comfort as well as some answers to the burdens I face. Lord, please help me. I ask that you might change something in my life right now to make this better. ❧ I receive these words of encouragement from you. This hope. *Yes, I believe you can turn my depression into dancing. I trust that you can do all things—and even perform a miracle within me right now.*

In quiet time with God, ask him specifically about the things in your life that discourage you.

———— ❖ ————

DESPAIR · GOD'S LEADING THROUGH TOUGH TIMES

Settle into this private time with God. Shut out distractions. Let him speak to you about how he is present with you through everything . . .

GOD'S PROMISE

PSALM 61:1-2 · *O God, listen to my cry! Hear my prayer! From the ends of the earth, I cry to you for help when my heart is overwhelmed.*

PSALM 42:9-10, ESV · *I say to God, my rock: "Why have you forgotten me? Why do I go mourning because of the oppression of the enemy?" As with a deadly wound in my bones, my adversaries taunt me, while they say to me all the day long, "Where is your God?"*

DEUTERONOMY 31:8, NIV · **The LORD himself goes before you and will be with you; he will never leave you nor forsake you. Do not be afraid; do not be discouraged.**

PRAY GOD'S PROMISE

Oh God, I come to you just completely overwhelmed by so many things in my life. I am drowning in despair. I don't even know where to start in doing things that I'm supposed to do, as there's just so much to attend to. And there are those who question me. I need your help, God. ⚜ I long for some direction and organization and sense of priority in my life. I need your assurance, God, about the big things I'm supposed to do. ⚜ *God, I hear your words that you will go before me, and I cherish that. I hold to the promise that you will walk in front of me and show me the path where I should walk.* Please help me to focus,

and give me strength to push through all of the stuff that
fills my life and overwhelms me.

*Why not take some time with God right now and list for him the big
things in your life that need to be done? Pause after each one, listening
for God's words to you and his advice about each one.*

———————— ❖ ————————

DIETING · GOD'S HELP FOR DIFFICULT TASKS

God speaks to any issue you're facing. Come into his presence and
share with him your struggles with weight and dieting . . .

GOD'S PROMISE

1 CORINTHIANS 6:19-20 · *Don't you realize that your body is
the temple of the Holy Spirit, who lives in you and was
given to you by God? You do not belong to yourself, for God
bought you with a high price. So you must honor God with
your body.*

PSALM 139:13-14 · *You made all the delicate, inner parts
of my body and knit me together in my mother's womb.
Thank you for making me so wonderfully complex! Your
workmanship is marvelous—how well I know it.*

1 JOHN 5:14-15 · **We are confident that he hears us
whenever we ask for anything that pleases him. And
since we know he hears us when we make our requests,
we also know that he will give us what we ask for.**

PRAY GOD'S PROMISE

Lord God, you know how I have struggled for quite
a while with my weight. I've tried so many diets, and

some seem to work for a while . . . but then I fall off the program. I need your help. ❧ I understand that my body belongs to you, Lord, and that it is the temple of your Holy Spirit. Thank you for these words that remind me I am wonderfully made by you. I want to be content in who you made me to be. ❧ *Thank you for hearing me as I ask for your help in my efforts to lose weight. And since you hear me, I trust your promise to give me what I'm requesting.* Help me to be strong in this, Lord. Stay by my side as I seek the healthy lifestyle you want for me.

Commit to making prayer time a regular part of your diet program going forward.

—————————————— ❖ ——————————————

DIFFICULTIES · OVERCOMING ADVERSITY

Sometimes you find yourself lifting your face toward heaven and yelling, "God, I can't take any more!" Perhaps this is a time for you to do that. God will understand. Once you do, then settle into some quiet listening, keeping your ears and heart attentive to what God has to say about his sustenance in times of overwhelming adversity . . .

GOD'S PROMISE

PSALM 69:1-2 • *Save me, O God, for the floodwaters are up to my neck. Deeper and deeper I sink into the mire; I can't find a foothold. I am in deep water, and the floods overwhelm me.*

PSALM 23:2-3, ESV • *He makes me lie down in green pastures. He leads me beside still waters.*

PSALM 34:19, NIV • *The righteous person may have many troubles, but the LORD delivers him from them all.*

PRAY GOD'S PROMISE

Lord, I feel like the psalmist who cried out that he was drowning. The waters of life have risen up to *my* neck, too. I had all that I could handle this past week, and then there was that new problem, which lifted the water level even higher. ❦ Lord, I need your calming hand on my life. I need mental strength to keep track of everything and to follow through as I need to. I ask you for a time of respite, a time when I can lie down in a green pasture beside still—not rising—waters. ❦ So, Lord, *I claim your promise that although I may have lots to do and face many troubles, you will come to the rescue.* Deliver me from this time I'm going through. I will trust you for that, Lord.

Make a mental list of all the things that are overwhelming you right now. Take each one to the Lord. Allow him to speak to you as you do this. Feel his soothing touch on your life.

————————— ⟨◊⟩ —————————

DISABILITY · GOD'S POWER IN DIFFICULT CIRCUMSTANCES

Why are some blessed with perfectly healthy lives, coasting through their days and thriving in the seemingly limitless opportunities available to them? And why must others suffer the hindrances and heartaches of a disability? As you look to God for answers, open your heart and listen to his words . . .

GOD'S PROMISE

LUKE 13:11-13, ESV • *There was a woman who had had a disabling spirit for eighteen years. She was bent over and could not fully straighten herself. When Jesus saw her, he called her over and said to her, "Woman, you are freed from your disability." And he laid his hands on her, and immediately she was made straight, and she glorified God.*

JOHN 9:1-3 • *As Jesus was walking along, he saw a man who had been blind from birth. "Rabbi," his disciples asked him, "why was this man born blind? Was it because of his own sins or his parents' sins?" "It was not because of his sins or his parents' sins," Jesus answered. "This happened so the power of God could be seen in him."*

PSALM 147:3 • **He heals the brokenhearted and bandages their wounds.**

PRAY GOD'S PROMISE

Lord God, I don't understand sometimes why things are the way they are. Why do you allow such things to happen in this world? I believe that you have the power to heal, but often you don't. Why? ❧ But your words in these verses lead me to see something new. Sometimes a disability allows you to show your power and grace—sometimes through healing, sometimes not—but always by simply shining through the afflicted person. ❧ *I embrace your promise that you heal the brokenhearted, that you bandage all our wounds, and that your power can be seen in whatever our situation might be.* Thank you, Lord. Help me hold on to these words in the days to come.

In these quiet minutes with God, pray for someone who is dealing with a disability. How can you personally reach out to that person?

------------ ◦❖◦ ------------

DISAPPOINTING GOD · RETURNING TO HIS FAVOR

The apostle Paul speaks of a time when the church at Corinth had disappointed God. As a result, the Corinthians were filled with anguish and sorrow regarding their failure. Is that a place you're in now? Have you, too, fallen short, and now you feel deep regret? Come to God in prayer and confession . . .

GOD'S PROMISE

2 CORINTHIANS 7:8-9 · *I am not sorry that I sent that severe letter to you, though I was sorry at first, for I know it was painful to you for a little while. Now I am glad I sent it, not because it hurt you, but because the pain caused you to repent and change your ways.*

2 CORINTHIANS 7:9 · *It was the kind of sorrow God wants his people to have, so you were not harmed by us in any way.*

2 CORINTHIANS 7:10 · ***The kind of sorrow God wants us to experience leads us away from sin and results in salvation.*** *There's no regret for that kind of sorrow. But worldly sorrow, which lacks repentance, results in spiritual death.*

PRAY GOD'S PROMISE

Father God, I feel deep regret that I have disappointed you in my behavior, my priorities, and my failure to spend time with you. ❧ I regret that I haven't acted differently. I am sorry I have let you down. ❧ Father, forgive me. Help me to change my ways in the coming days. I want to please you, follow you, and be close to you. *I embrace this sorrow I feel right now—as your promise to me reveals that through it you will lead me away from sin.* Thank you, Father God.

In these moments of quiet, talk with God about how you want to be pleasing to him. Know that God is extending his arms toward you.

———————————— ◁◇▷ ————————————

DISAPPOINTMENT · PEACE IN THE MIDST OF SETBACKS

Some things haven't worked out as you had expected. You're despondent over what didn't happen. You're worried about how to cope. Bring to God the recent experiences that have disappointed you . . .

GOD'S PROMISE

PSALM 34:18 · *The LORD is close to the brokenhearted; he rescues those whose spirits are crushed.*

ISAIAH 55:8-9 · *My thoughts are nothing like your thoughts, says the LORD. And my ways are far beyond anything you could imagine. For just as the heavens are higher than the earth, so my ways are higher than your ways and my thoughts higher than your thoughts.*

PHILIPPIANS 4:6-7 · *Don't worry about anything; instead, pray about everything.* ***Tell God what you need, and*** *thank him for all he has done. Then you will experience God's peace, which exceeds anything we can understand.* His peace will guard your hearts and minds as you live in Christ Jesus.

PRAY GOD'S PROMISE

Lord, I come to you with a downcast heart. Some things I had counted on have fallen through. I was sure these hopes I had would work out and take care of the needs I have. ♦ I am struggling to make sense of what has happened, Lord. And I am worrying now about how these needs will be taken care of. I know you are over all, and I thrill to be reminded that your ways are beyond what I can imagine. Yet I struggle. ♦ You tell me not to worry, and instead to pray. Well, I am praying, Lord. *I will tell you of the needs I have and embrace your promise that I will experience your peace.* Thank you, Lord. Let your peace guard my heart.

Take this time to tell God the specific needs you are worrying over. Then listen to him speak to you about his greatness and provision and love.

DISAPPOINTMENT · STRENGTH TO WEATHER
A CRUSHING BLOW

When we set our hearts on meeting certain goals, it is easy to feel discouraged if they fall through. In this time of deep disappointment, open your heart to God and listen to his words . . .

GOD'S PROMISE

PSALM 55:22 • *Give your burdens to the LORD, and he will take care of you. He will not permit the godly to slip and fall.*

PSALM 30:5 • *Weeping may last through the night, but joy comes with the morning.*

ISAIAH 40:28-31 • *Have you never heard? Have you never understood? The LORD is the everlasting God, the Creator of all the earth. He never grows weak or weary. No one can measure the depths of his understanding. He gives power to the weak and strength to the powerless. Even youths will become weak and tired, and young men will fall in exhaustion.* **But those who trust in the LORD will find new strength.** *They will soar high on wings like eagles. They will run and not grow weary. They will walk and not faint.*

PRAY GOD'S PROMISE

God, you know what has happened, and I want to tell you how devastated I am by it. I had so wanted it, and I had counted on it. I was so sure. And now it has fallen through and is gone. It hurts so much. I want to embrace your promise that joy will come with the morning, but I don't know if I can. Right now, I only have tears. ❦ But I will give my burdens to you, God. I will tell you of my worries and troubles, especially now. ❦ *I will hold close your promise that you will help me find new strength and that I can make it through this.* I know you are a great God, the Creator of all. Help me to trust you in the wake of what has happened and in the events that are yet to come.

Follow through on telling God about your worries and burdens. Allow him to whisper to you the promises of his love and provision.

DISCERNMENT · GUIDANCE FOR A COMPLEX DECISION

As you consider the pros and cons of the issue at hand, bring them to God. Listen to his advice about discerning the truth . . .

GOD'S PROMISE

1 JOHN 4:1, 6 · *Dear friends, do not believe everyone who claims to speak by the Spirit. You must test them to see if the spirit they have comes from God. For there are many false prophets in the world. . . . But we belong to God, and those who know God listen to us. If they do not belong to God, they do not listen to us. That is how we know if someone has the Spirit of truth or the spirit of deception.*

ROMANS 12:2, ESV · *Do not be conformed to this world, but be transformed by the renewal of your mind, that by testing you may discern what is the will of God, what is good and acceptable and perfect.*

2 TIMOTHY 3:16-17 · *All Scripture is inspired by God and is useful to teach us what is true and to make us realize what is wrong in our lives.* **It corrects us when we are wrong and teaches us to do what is right. God uses it to prepare and equip his people to do every good work.**

PRAY GOD'S PROMISE

Lord God, I am in a place in life where I have to discern the truth about this matter at hand. I need your wisdom, and I seek your counsel. I want to do your will in this. ⚜ God,

I hear your words regarding false spirits, and I sure don't want to be misled by a spirit of deception. Help me to listen only to you, the true God. ❧ *I embrace your promise, Lord, that through your Word you correct me when I am wrong and teach me to do what is right. Thank you that you will use this to prepare and equip me for your work.* I trust you, Lord, to help me make the right decision.

In this time with God, lay out for him the issue you are wrestling with. Then, in silence, listen to his voice of instruction.

DISCERNMENT · WISDOM TO MAKE THE BEST DECISION

You've come to the right place. God is the source of all wisdom. Clear your mind of outside distractions. Prepare your heart to receive God's words speaking into the decision you're facing . . .

GOD'S PROMISE

1 CORINTHIANS 14:33 · *God is not a God of disorder but of peace.*

1 THESSALONIANS 5:21-22 · *Test everything that is said. Hold on to what is good. Stay away from every kind of evil.*

PROVERBS 2:3-6, 9-11 · *Cry out for insight, and ask for understanding. Search for them as you would for silver; seek them like hidden treasures. Then you will understand what it means to fear the LORD, and you will gain knowledge of God. For the LORD grants wisdom! . . . Then you will understand what is right, just, and fair, and you will find the right way to go. For wisdom will enter your heart, and knowledge will fill you with joy. Wise choices will watch over you. Understanding will keep you safe.*

PRAY GOD'S PROMISE

Father God, I am indeed crying out to you for insight and understanding. Thank you that you are a God of order and stability and truth. Help me to discern the best way to approach this decision. ✟ I ask for your wisdom, Lord. Grant me your knowledge, especially in this matter at hand. ✟ *Right now, I am taking hold of the promise that in searching for your wisdom, you will grant it and give me new joy.* Thank you, Lord.

In the coming days, pay attention to the things God brings across your path. He has a way of speaking to us through daily events.

DISCONNECTION · GOD'S PRESENCE WHEN FRIENDS ARE FAR AWAY

Sometimes we go through a period in life when relationships aren't working well, and we feel far apart from others. Come to God with your concerns about this and let his voice speak to you . . .

GOD'S PROMISE

PROVERBS 18:24, MSG · *Friends come and friends go, but a true friend sticks by you like family.*

HEBREWS 13:2-3 · *Don't forget to show hospitality to strangers, for some who have done this have entertained angels without realizing it! Remember those in prison, as if you were there yourself. Remember also those being mistreated, as if you felt their pain in your own bodies.*

PSALM 27:10 • *Even if my father and mother abandon me, the LORD will hold me close.*

PRAY GOD'S PROMISE

Lord, I have been feeling that so many who have previously been close to me are now so far away. I feel distant, disconnected, even lonely. I wonder if I have done something to offend them, but I think it's just the circumstances of life I'm in right now. We're all so busy. ❦ But whether I'm feeling disconnected from family or friends or coworkers, I will still trust in you, Lord. *I embrace your promise that even if my very own parents were to abandon me, you would hold me close.* ❦ And I also hear your words of instruction, Lord, that reaching out to others is something I need to consider. I realize that I perhaps expect the opposite—for people to come to me, to do things for me, to reach out to me. Instead of dwelling on my loneliness, help me to focus on others. Thank you, Lord.

Talk with God about others around you who have needs. Ask him how you might be able to help them. Listen to God speak to you about reaching out to others.

———————— ❖ ————————

DISCOURAGEMENT • PEACE IN THE FACE OF REJECTION

Rejection is never easy, especially after you've devoted time and energy to something you care about. Bring your discouragement to God, and allow his words to comfort you . . .

GOD'S PROMISE

PSALM 42:6-8 • *Now I am deeply discouraged, but I will remember you—even from distant Mount Hermon, the source of the Jordan, from the land of Mount Mizar. I hear the tumult of the raging seas as your waves and surging tides sweep over me. But each day the LORD pours his unfailing love upon me, and through each night I sing his songs, praying to God who gives me life.*

2 THESSALONIANS 3:13 • *As for the rest of you, dear brothers and sisters, never get tired of doing good.*

PHILIPPIANS 4:6-7 • *Don't worry about anything; instead, pray about everything.* **Tell God what you need, and thank him for all he has done. Then you will experience God's peace,** *which exceeds anything we can understand. His peace will guard your hearts and minds as you live in Christ Jesus.*

PRAY GOD'S PROMISE

Father, I am deeply discouraged by so many things. I am trying so hard to do your will and to serve others, but doors seem to be shutting, and I am suffering rejection after rejection. ‡ I don't doubt you, Father, or your desire to provide for me, but I am struggling with worry about how things will turn out. I need your help. I pray to you right now for some glimmer of a positive development in my life. ‡ *I hear your promise of peace, Father. Yes, I will right now tell you my needs and thank you for the provision you've granted so many times throughout my life.* I pray that your peace will indeed guard my heart and mind in this tough time I'm facing.

Tell God the specific needs you have. Recount for him your praises for specific things he has done for you.

———————————— ◆ ————————————

DISCOURAGEMENT · STRENGTH TO OVERCOME OBSTACLES

For a few moments, unload the setbacks and frustrations you're experiencing, and listen to God's words of encouragement and hope . . .

GOD'S PROMISE

JOB 4:5, NIV · *Now trouble comes to you, and you are discouraged; it strikes you, and you are dismayed.*

GALATIANS 6:9 · *Let's not get tired of doing what is good. At just the right time we will reap a harvest of blessing if we don't give up.*

ISAIAH 41:10 · *Don't be discouraged, for **I am your God. I will strengthen you and help you.** I will hold you up with my victorious right hand.*

PRAY GOD'S PROMISE

Lord, I am so down right now. So much has been difficult and disappointing of late. I keep running into obstacles and barriers, and it seems nothing is going well. I need your help. I need your encouragement. ❧ I feel that I am working hard to do good things for my work, my family, and my friends. And yet it seems so many forces are working against me. Help me, Lord. ❧ I need you to hold me up in this tough time. I embrace your words, Lord, not to be discouraged, as hard as that is right now. *You are my God, and in you I will find strength and victory.* I believe your words, Lord, and I will look for your work in my life in the days to come. Thank you, Lord.

Tell God about the specific discouragements you've experienced. Ask him to speak into each one. Be attentive to his response.

DISMAY · PEACE IN GOD'S PRESENCE

Something is troubling you. Perhaps it's a circumstance you find yourself in or a decision you made. Whatever it is, you are deeply troubled about it. Bring your concern to God. Listen to his voice . . .

GOD'S PROMISE

PSALM 143:4-6, NIV • *My spirit grows faint within me; my heart within me is dismayed. I remember the days of long ago; I meditate on all your works and consider what your hands have done. I spread out my hands to you; I thirst for you like a parched land.*

DEUTERONOMY 31:6 • *Be strong and courageous! Do not be afraid and do not panic before them. For the LORD your God will personally go ahead of you. He will neither fail you nor abandon you.*

JOHN 14:27 • *The peace I give is a gift the world cannot give. So don't be troubled or afraid.*

PRAY GOD'S PROMISE

Lord God, I am disturbed by recent events in my life and in the world. I feel that some things just aren't right. They seem out of control, and I fear that the enemy is taking over. ❧ I am praying to you for some assurance that you are in charge after all. I need to know you are present within events that have transpired in the world. I also long to feel your presence and stability in my life. Lord God, help me. ❧ *I claim your promise, Lord, that you offer a peace the world will never be able to give. I claim your promise that you will go before me on this path and be present with me personally.* Thank you, Lord.

Tell God your specific fears about what's going on in the world. Let him speak to you in these next moments of silence.

DISOBEDIENCE • CLAIMING GOD'S MERCY

You know you have gone against God's will. Enter into his presence prepared to confess that your actions followed your own path instead of his. Listen to his words to you . . .

GOD'S PROMISE

JAMES 1:14, ESV • *Each person is tempted when he is lured and enticed by his own desire.*

2 TIMOTHY 3:2-5, ESV • *People will be lovers of self, lovers of money, proud, arrogant, abusive, disobedient to their parents, ungrateful, unholy, heartless, unappeasable, slanderous, without self-control, brutal, not loving good, treacherous, reckless, swollen with conceit, lovers of pleasure rather than lovers of God, having the appearance of godliness, but denying its power.*

ROMANS 11:32, NIV · *God has bound everyone over to disobedience so that he may have mercy on them all.*

PRAY GOD'S PROMISE

Lord God, I come to you with apologies and sincere regrets. In certain matters of late, I have pursued my own direction, by going against what I knew was your will for me. ⚜ I ask you to forgive me, Lord. I pray for your mercy. Most of all, I want to be reconnected with you once more. ⚜ Lord, you speak of mercy, and I know that's what I'm asking for. *I claim your promise, coming from your endless grace, that you will have mercy on me.* Lord God, I ask that as I move forward, you would help me to follow your path. I want to be on the journey you have for me.

In a deeper time with God, listen to him speaking to you. How can you avoid making this same error again?

———————— ◇ ————————

DISTANCE FROM GOD · FINDING GOD AGAIN

Sometimes we feel distant from God. At times we even feel abandoned by him in the midst of circumstances, messes, and troubles. He is always with us, but we often don't have time for him in our busy days. In these moments, make some space for God to enter into your life . . .

GOD'S PROMISE

PSALM 22:1 · *My God, my God, why have you abandoned me? Why are you so far away when I groan for help?*

ISAIAH 49:15-16, MSG • *Can a mother forget the infant at her breast, walk away from the baby she bore? But even if mothers forget, I'd never forget you—never. Look, I've written your names on the backs of my hands.*

JOSHUA 1:9 • *Be strong and courageous! Do not be afraid or discouraged.* **For the LORD your God is with you wherever you go.**

PRAY GOD'S PROMISE

Father, I have felt far away from you in recent days and weeks. I struggle to feel worthwhile, valued, and truly loved by you. ¶ I know that I haven't made time for you in my busy life. I confess I've drifted from you in certain ways. ¶ Your words remind me that you created me and will never forget me. You even say that my name is engraved on your hands. ¶ Father, I just long to be closer to you. *I claim this promise that you are with me wherever I go.* I trust that you will be present with me today.

Make a daily appointment with God. Come to him each day in quiet, listening prayer.

———————— <·> ————————

DISTANCE FROM GOD • FINDING A DEEPER RELATIONSHIP WITH HIM

God wants to be close to you. If you are feeling alienated from him, it's because you've allowed something to get in the way. In this time of prayer, be honest with God about your life and this distance you feel. Be open to what God has to say to you . . .

GOD'S PROMISE

COLOSSIANS 1:20-21 • *Through him [Christ] God reconciled everything to himself. He made peace with everything in heaven and on earth by means of Christ's blood on the cross. This includes you who were once far away from God.*

EPHESIANS 4:18, ESV • *They are darkened in their understanding, alienated from the life of God because of the ignorance that is in them, due to their hardness of heart.*

COLOSSIANS 1:21-22, NKJV • *And you, who once were alienated and enemies in your mind by wicked works,* ***yet now He has reconciled in the body of His flesh through death, to present you holy, and blameless, and above reproach in His sight.***

PRAY GOD'S PROMISE

God, I am facing so many things right now. I turn to you, but you seem so far from me. I feel separated from you. ❖ In reading these verses, I realize that what I feel has much to do with things in my life that are keeping me from the closeness I desire. ❖ *God, your promise here is that in Christ I am reconciled with you, and I claim that promise.* I believe that Christ died so that I would no longer be separated from you. Through him, I realize I can be blameless and above reproach in your sight. Thank you, Jesus. Thank you, God.

As you continue in prayer with God, confess to him the things in your life that have gotten in the way of a close relationship with him.

———————————— ❖ ————————————

DISTANCE FROM GOD • WALKING WITH GOD DAY BY DAY

Invite God to spend time with you right now. He'll be there. Open up your heart to him about your fear that he will be far away when you need him . . .

GOD'S PROMISE

PSALM 31:22 • *In panic I cried out, "I am cut off from the LORD!" But you heard my cry for mercy and answered my call for help.*

LEVITICUS 26:11, MSG • *I'll set up my residence in your neighborhood; I won't avoid or shun you.*

DEUTERONOMY 31:8, ESV • **It is the LORD who goes before you. He will be with you; he will not leave you or forsake you. Do not fear or be dismayed.**

PRAY GOD'S PROMISE

Father God, I have been panicking of late about certain things that are happening in my life. I'm afraid, and I need your help. I confess I have not trusted in you as I should, and I fear you and I will be far apart when I need you most. ❦ I have been distant from you in recent weeks and months—I just haven't made much time for you. I regret that I only come to you when I face intense challenges and have significant, urgent needs. ❦ God, help me to walk with you on a regular basis, not just from time to time. *I thank you and praise you for your promise to me here and now. I thank you for going before me, being with me, and not leaving me.*

In these quiet moments, allow God to speak to your specific needs. And promise to him a time each day when you will come to him in prayer.

———————————— ‹·› ————————————

DISTRESS · ENCOURAGEMENT FOR TENSE TIMES

The setbacks and hurdles you're facing right now are pressing on you. Take a deep breath, quiet your mind, and settle into God's presence . . .

GOD'S PROMISE

PSALM 42:5 · *Why am I discouraged? Why is my heart so sad?*

2 CORINTHIANS 4:17 · *Our present troubles are small and won't last very long. Yet they produce for us a glory that vastly outweighs them and will last forever!*

2 CORINTHIANS 4:18 · **We don't look at the troubles we can see now; rather, we fix our gaze on things that cannot be seen. For the things we see now will soon be gone, but the things we cannot see will last forever.**

PRAY GOD'S PROMISE

Lord God, I am struggling with deep discouragement. I'm facing relationship troubles, some hurdles in my daily life, and even some challenges financially. I sometimes feel I'll never overcome these things and will need to live like this forever. I need your help, Lord. ⚜ I pray for your perspective, for your vision about the big picture of my life. I need to know that all this is worth it. ⚜ I hear your words of encouragement that my present troubles are small, and won't last very long. *I claim your even bigger promise,*

Lord, that by refraining from dwelling on my troubles now, I will see the things that cannot be seen, those more important things that will last forever. Thank you, Lord, and help me to keep my eyes focused on the reality of my eternal life that is to come.

In these moments with God, think about the bigger things in your life that he has already provided for.

———————————— ‹◇› ————————————

DOUBT · COMING TO GOD THROUGH AN ACT OF FAITH

One of the great Bible passages depicting doubt is the story of Thomas's encounter with Jesus after the Resurrection. In Thomas, you may find some comfort. See if you can identify with him as you read about his experience . . .

GOD'S PROMISE

JOHN 20:24-25, NIV · *Thomas (also known as Didymus), one of the Twelve, was not with the disciples when Jesus came. So the other disciples told him, "We have seen the Lord!"*

JOHN 20:25, NIV · *But he said to them, "Unless I see the nail marks in his hands and put my finger where the nails were, and put my hand into his side, I will not believe."*

JOHN 20:26-28, NIV · *Though the doors were locked, Jesus came and stood among them and said, "Peace be with you!" Then he said to Thomas, "Put your finger here; see my hands. **Reach out your hand and put it into my side. Stop doubting and believe."** Thomas said to him, "My Lord and my God!"*

PRAY GOD'S PROMISE

God, I am struggling to believe. Many around me are believers in you, but it's harder for me. Like Thomas, I need more proof, I guess. ❧ I am praying to you, yes, even though I'm not sure I believe in you. That sounds crazy, but it's true. I think it's because I want to have the hope that others have. ❧ *And so I speak over myself what is, for me, the promise in this story: "Reach out your hand and put it into my side. Stop doubting and believe."* I want that, even though I can't believe that as of yet. Help me believe, God.

Are there other things you believe in that you don't have physical proof for? Keep listening and watching for evidence of God working in your life.

EMOTIONAL FATIGUE • PARTAKING
OF GOD'S REFRESHMENT

You may be emotionally spent from all the people and needs and issues you've had to attend to in recent days and weeks. Let it all go for a few minutes so that God can refresh you emotionally . . .

GOD'S PROMISE

PROVERBS 4:23, NIV • *Above all else, guard your heart, for everything you do flows from it.*

PHILIPPIANS 4:7, NIV • *The peace of God, which transcends all understanding, will guard your hearts and your minds in Christ Jesus.*

ACTS 2:26-28, NIV • *My heart is glad and my tongue rejoices; my body also will rest in hope, because you will not abandon me to the realm of the dead, you will not let your holy one see decay. You have made known to me the paths of life;* **you will fill me with joy in your presence.**

PRAY GOD'S PROMISE

Father God, I am at the end of my capacity to serve people and come alongside their needs. Now I need you to come alongside *me* and replenish my soul. § I hear your advice to guard my heart, and I know I've allowed my heart to ache for so many people and for so many needs. I have no more capacity. § *I cherish your promise here to fill me with joy once again.* I ask for your peace, your comfort, your precious presence in my life.

Recount for God each of the people you've had to help in recent days and weeks. Turn their care over to him. Let him care for you.

—————————— ‹·› ——————————

EMOTIONAL PAIN • REST FOR THE TORTURED SOUL

Through the weariness of all this hurt you've carried around, let God speak to you personally in these next few minutes . . .

GOD'S PROMISE

PSALM 56:8, ESV • *You have kept count of my tossings; put my tears in your bottle.*

MATTHEW 5:8, MSG • *You're blessed when you get your inside world—your mind and heart—put right. Then you can see God in the outside world.*

MATTHEW 11:28-29, ESV • **Come to me, all who labor and are heavy laden, and I will give you rest.** *Take my yoke upon you, and learn from me, for I am gentle and lowly in heart, and you will find rest for your souls.*

PRAY GOD'S PROMISE

Lord Jesus, I'm kind of a mess inside. I'm struggling through my days. I'm struggling through my nights. ⚜ I'm torn up inside by recent events, things that have hurt me. I know I need to get my mind and heart sorted out and made right. I pray that you would do that for me, Lord. ⚜ *I pray your promise that in coming to you now, you will provide rest for my soul.* I ask that you would bring order to my private, inside world. I pray for peace and rest. Thank you, Jesus.

Tell God about the events of late that have become emotional hurts for you. Listen for his responses to each one.

———————— ❖ ————————

EMOTIONAL PAIN • SOOTHING THE HURTS OF LIFE

You're struggling with some deep emotions—pains and hurts that haunt you. Rest your mind and heart in these next moments. Come to God, prepared to listen to his voice . . .

GOD'S PROMISE

JOB 30:17, ESV • *The night racks my bones, and the pain that gnaws me takes no rest.*

PSALM 119:50, MSG • *These words hold me up in bad times; yes, your promises rejuvenate me.*

ROMANS 8:26-27, NIV • **In the same way, the Spirit helps us in our weakness.** *We do not know what we ought to pray for, but the Spirit himself intercedes for us with wordless groans. And he who searches our hearts knows the mind of the Spirit, because the Spirit intercedes for God's people in accordance with the will of God.*

PRAY GOD'S PROMISE

Father, I don't even know what to pray for. I hurt so much inside. My pain comes from different sources, but really, I'm not sure what the main cause is. I am just suffering inside. ❧ You say that your Spirit intercedes for us. And I pray for your Spirit to be present in my life right now. ❧ No, I don't know what to pray for, but your Spirit will pray for me with groans that words cannot express. ***And so I claim your promise that the Spirit will help me in my weakness, in this emotional turmoil, in this anguish I'm feeling.*** Take this from me, I pray.

Give God's Spirit some time with you. Release your pain. Be silent. Be still. Listen to the whispers of his Spirit in these moments.

—◇—

EMPTINESS · DISCOVERING THE FULLNESS OF GOD

Sometimes schedules, circumstances, and our busyness keep us from God. In the absence of time spent with him, we feel lost, and life is empty. Come into his presence now and fill yourself . . .

GOD'S PROMISE

ECCLESIASTES 2:11, NIV · *When I surveyed all that my hands had done and what I had toiled to achieve, everything was meaningless, a chasing after the wind; nothing was gained under the sun.*

PSALM 63:1, NIV · *You, God, are my God, earnestly I seek you; I thirst for you, my whole being longs for you, in a dry and parched land where there is no water.*

PSALM 81:16, ESV · **He would feed you with the finest of the wheat, and with honey from the rock I would satisfy you.**

PRAY GOD'S PROMISE

God, I recently realized that my life has become more futile, and my days feel empty. Now I know why. I've been distant from you. ❧ This is a good reminder about the importance of making time for you each day. It's true that I had been seeking you before, God, because without you I would become dry. Even so, I got distracted; life got in the way. ❧ But there is no life without you. Not really. *I long for your promise here that you will feed me and satisfy me with the wheat and honey of your presence.* I come to you now and thank you, God, for the richness of time spent with you. I praise you indeed.

Talk with God about what you will do to make more time for him each day.

———————————— ❖ ————————————

EMPTINESS · THE FULFILLING MEANING OF THE EMPTY TOMB

Jesus' empty tomb equals the potential for a full life. By sharing in the resurrection life of Christ, you can find the fullness of life you long for . . .

GOD'S PROMISE

LUKE 24:22-24, MSG · *Early this morning they were at the tomb and couldn't find his body. They came back with the story that they had seen a vision of angels who said he was alive. Some of our friends went off to the tomb to check and found it empty just as the women said, but they didn't see Jesus.*

PHILIPPIANS 3:10 · *I want to know Christ and experience the mighty power that raised him from the dead.*

COLOSSIANS 2:8-9 · *Don't let anyone capture you with empty philosophies and high-sounding nonsense that come from human thinking and from the spiritual powers of this world, rather than from Christ. **For in Christ lives all the fullness of God in a human body.***

PRAY GOD'S PROMISE

Lord Jesus, I come to you feeling empty and lost. I've been apart from you for so long, and I've been distracted by some of those empty philosophies and that high-sounding nonsense. I know my sense of emptiness means I need more of you in my life. ⚘ I am struck by the idea of an empty tomb representing the beginning of a full life. ⚘ *And so I want to embrace the promise of this phrase—that "in Christ lives all the fullness of God."* Lord, I want my life to be about your fullness shining through me each day.

How might you invite the fullness of Christ into your life today?

---◇---

ENEMIES · COURAGE IN THE FACE OF OPPOSITION

You face some difficult conversations ahead with people who stand against you. Come into God's presence and ask him for strength and courage in facing your enemies . . .

GOD'S PROMISE

PSALM 102:8, NIV • *All day long my enemies taunt me; those who rail against me use my name as a curse.*

EPHESIANS 6:10-12, NIV • *Be strong in the Lord and in his mighty power. Put on the full armor of God so that you can take your stand against the devil's schemes. For our struggle is not against flesh and blood, but against the rulers, against the authorities, against the powers of this dark world and against the spiritual forces of evil in the heavenly realms.*

DEUTERONOMY 31:6, NIV • *Be strong and courageous. Do not be afraid or terrified because of them, for the LORD your God goes with you; he will never leave you nor forsake you.*

PRAY GOD'S PROMISE

Lord, I come to you feeling weak and powerless in the midst of people who are opposing me. I know I need to stand up to them in some way, but I lack the right words to say. I ask for your help, Lord. ⚘ I'm wanting to act on your words to be strong in you and your mighty power. Help me do that, Lord. ⚘ *And help me to claim your promise that you will go with me and that you will never leave me.* Help me not to be afraid, but to wear the armor you have provided.

As you think about confronting your adversaries, imagine that God is standing right next to you.

ENEMIES • GRACE WITH THOSE WHO ARE AGAINST YOU

People in your life are against you, testing you not only in your work but also in your faith. As you face opposition, calm your heart and mind before God . . .

GOD'S PROMISE

PSALM 71:10, ESV • *My enemies speak concerning me; those who watch for my life consult together.*

PSALM 138:7, ESV • *Though I walk in the midst of trouble, you preserve my life; you stretch out your hand against the wrath of my enemies, and your right hand delivers me.*

LUKE 6:35, NIV • *Love your enemies, do good to them, and lend to them without expecting to get anything back.*

Then your reward will be great, and you will be children of the Most High.

PRAY GOD'S PROMISE

Father, you know how I am being oppressed by people around me who are opposing me in my life, work, and faith. This is difficult for me and fills me with hopelessness. I need your intervention. ❧ I trust you to help me in the midst of this. I pray that you would take this oppression from me. ❧ *And Father, I claim your promise that if I love my enemies, my reward will come from you.* But I need your help in loving those who are against me. Help me to do that, Father, I pray.

Spend some time with God praying about how you might show love to your enemies.

ENTITLEMENT · YOUR NEED FOR GOD IS ALL YOU NEED

We sometimes find ourselves wrestling with feelings such as jealousy and envy because we feel we deserve the best that life has to offer. Come to God right now and let him speak to your sense of entitlement . . .

GOD'S PROMISE

GENESIS 3:6 · *The woman was convinced. She saw that the tree was beautiful and its fruit looked delicious, and she wanted the wisdom it would give her. So she took some of the fruit and ate it. Then she gave some to her husband, who was with her, and he ate it, too.*

MATTHEW 5:3 • *God blesses those who are poor and realize their need for him, for the Kingdom of Heaven is theirs.*

PHILIPPIANS 2:3-4, ESV • *Do nothing from selfish ambition or conceit, but in humility count others more significant than yourselves. Let each of you look not only to his own interests, but also to the interests of others.*

PRAY GOD'S PROMISE

Lord God, I come to you and confess that I've allowed jealousy to influence my actions. I realize that I nurse a sense of deserving certain things. I know this is wrong, and I ask for your forgiveness. ❧ Show me a better way, Lord. Help me to overcome this jealousy through your promise that *you will bless those who realize their need for you.* ❧ I want to be one of those people, Lord, who expects little and simply cherishes the majesty of who you are.

Talk with God about your sense of entitlement. Let him satisfy you instead with his overwhelming greatness, abounding provision, and perfect love for who you are.

———————————— ❖ ————————————

ENVY • DISCOVERING GOD'S SUFFICIENCY

Come to God and open your heart to him about that person in your life whom you compare yourself to and find yourself envying. Listen to God's words . . .

GOD'S PROMISE

TITUS 3:3 • *Once we, too, were foolish and disobedient. We were misled and became slaves to many lusts and pleasures.*

Our lives were full of evil and envy, and we hated each other.

1 PETER 2:1-2, MSG • *Clean house! Make a clean sweep of malice and pretense, envy and hurtful talk. You've had a taste of God.*

PSALM 73:21-25, MSG • *When I was beleaguered and bitter, totally consumed by envy, I was totally ignorant, a dumb ox in your very presence. **I'm still in your presence, but you've taken my hand. You wisely and tenderly lead me, and then you bless me.** You're all I want in heaven! You're all I want on earth!*

PRAY GOD'S PROMISE

Lord God, I confess to you that I've been guilty of envying a particular person. I confess that I've thought too much about what that person owns, the job that person has, and the talents that person seems to possess. I compare myself, and I feel inferior. I find myself wishing I had those same things. ❧ I know this is wrong, and I come to you with sorrow for allowing envy to rule my life. ❧ Lord, I need your help to overcome this. ***I pray your promise that you will take my hand and bless me.*** Help me remember that you are all I need and nothing else matters. Help me to live in the riches of your presence, Lord.

Talk with God specifically about why you envy this person. Let him speak to you about your own unique talents and gifts and how valuable you are to him.

———————— ❖ ————————

FACING A CROSSROAD · GOD HAS PLANS
FOR YOU

As you leave the old and approach the new, free yourself from the uncertainties of your life. Let God whisper to you . . .

GOD'S PROMISE

PSALM 40:13 · *Please, LORD, rescue me! Come quickly, LORD, and help me.*

ISAIAH 43:19 · **I am about to do something new. See, I have already begun! Do you not see it? I will make a pathway through the wilderness. I will create rivers in the dry wasteland.**

PSALM 22:23-24, MSG · *Shout Hallelujah, you God-worshipers; give glory, you sons of Jacob; adore him, you daughters of Israel. He has never let you down, never looked the other way when you were being kicked around. He has never wandered off to do his own thing; he has been right there, listening.*

PRAY GOD'S PROMISE

Lord God, I am at a crossroads where I'm finished with something that has been my endeavor for so long, and I'm needing help for this next chapter of my life. I am hopeful. Yet I know whatever I do will require a lot, and I have so little with which to carry it out. ❧ Father, I pray to you right now for direction, wisdom, and strength. Show me your plans for me. ❧ And Lord, *your promise that you are about to do something new in my life fills me with excitement. Make a pathway through the wilderness ahead! Thank you for the rivers you will create!* Hallelujah!

In the next few minutes, go ahead and praise God for specific things he has done in your life. Hallelujah!

———————— ◈ ————————

FACING SPIRITUAL ATTACK

• OVERCOMING THE ENEMY'S DISCOURAGEMENTS

God's enemy, Satan, sometimes throws obstacles across our paths to discourage us. Resist him by stepping into the shelter of God's presence. Sit with Jesus for these next moments and wait for him to strengthen you . . .

GOD'S PROMISE

PSALM 55:2-3, ESV • *Attend to me, and answer me; I am restless in my complaint and I moan, because of the noise of the enemy, because of the oppression of the wicked.*

1 PETER 5:8-9 • *Stay alert! Watch out for your great enemy, the devil. He prowls around like a roaring lion, looking for someone to devour. Stand firm against him, and be strong in your faith. Remember that your family of believers all over the world is going through the same kind of suffering you are.*

JOHN 16:33 • *I have told you all this so that you may have peace in me. Here on earth you will have many trials and sorrows.* **But take heart, because I have overcome the world.**

PRAY GOD'S PROMISE

Lord Jesus, I am feeling attacked and oppressed by others in my life, and I know it's coming from the enemy. It has left me deeply discouraged. I need your help, Lord. ❧ I pray to you for deliverance from these assaults. I need your strength and encouragement. ❧ You are reminding me that I am not alone, and that many others in the faith are facing similar hurdles. ***And you give me this promise, that you have overcome the world.*** I claim that promise, Lord Jesus, knowing that you can and will overcome these setbacks in my life. Thank you, Jesus.

Spend some further moments in silence with God. Let him reassure you of his power and protection over your life at this difficult time.

———————————— ❖ ————————————

FACING SPIRITUAL ATTACK

• THE PROMISE OF REFUGE FROM THE ENEMY

As you feel vulnerable in an environment of spiritual attacks, come to God for his protection . . .

GOD'S PROMISE

EPHESIANS 6:10-11 • *Be strong in the Lord and in his mighty power. Put on all of God's armor so that you will be able to stand firm against all strategies of the devil.*

PSALM 91:1-2 • *Those who live in the **shelter** of the Most High will find rest in the shadow of the Almighty. This I declare about the LORD: He alone is my **refuge**, my place of **safety**; he is my God, and I trust him.*

PSALM 91:7, ESV • *A thousand may fall at your side, ten thousand at your right hand, but it will not come near you.*

PRAY GOD'S PROMISE

Lord God, I am feeling under attack from the enemy. A number of events of late seem as if they are coming from dark places. ‡ I am afraid, Lord. I am in need of strength and help and protection as these attacks seem to be hitting me from all different sides. ‡ *I claim your promise that you are my refuge, my shelter, and my place of safety.* Cover me, Lord, with your presence. Keep the enemy out of my life, I pray.

Listen for God's voice. In silence, let him speak to you.

FAILURE • EMBRACING THE DISCIPLINE OF HARDSHIP

Come to God and share with him your recent situation. He wants to encourage you to keep going in the race . . .

GOD'S PROMISE

HEBREWS 12:7, NIV • *Endure hardship as discipline; God is treating you as his children.*

HEBREWS 12:1-2, MSG • *Strip down, start running—and never quit! No extra spiritual fat, no parasitic sins. Keep your eyes on Jesus, who both began and finished this race we're in. Study how he did it. Because he never lost sight of where he was headed—that exhilarating finish in and with God—he could put up with anything along the way: Cross, shame, whatever.*

PSALM 73:26, ESV • *My flesh and my heart may fail, but God is the strength of my heart and my portion forever.*

PRAY GOD'S PROMISE

Lord, I am reeling right now over this recent failure. I was so sure I was doing well, that I was on the right track. It's disappointing to me. And it's also embarrassing that I didn't do better than this. I need your encouragement. ❧ I accept your truth that hardship is a discipline. I need to look for the lessons I can learn through this experience. And then move on. ❧ *You offer me this promise—that even if my flesh and heart fail, you are my strength.* Lord, I ask that you would give me your wisdom, your encouragement, and your help to continue this race we're in together.

Give yourself time with God to talk through the circumstances of your failure. Listen for his wisdom and reassurance.

———————————— ⟨◇⟩ ————————————

FATIGUE • RELIEF FOR THE WEARY

You are down because you are so tired and exhausted. Take a deep breath. Calm your heart. Lay down your troubles before God. Let him shoulder your burdens . . .

GOD'S PROMISE

PSALM 127:2, MSG • *It's useless to rise early and go to bed late, and work your worried fingers to the bone. Don't you know he [God] enjoys giving rest to those he loves?*

PSALM 77:6, ESV • *Let me remember my song in the night; let me meditate in my heart.*

MATTHEW 11:28 • *Come to me, all of you who are weary and carry heavy burdens, and I will give you rest.*

PRAY GOD'S PROMISE

Oh Lord, I am tired and exhausted. In some ways, I am so tired I cannot fall asleep. I need your hand to calm me, steady me, and relax me. I need your presence in my life. ❧ Lord, I have so many things running through my head at night when I lay down to sleep. My worries and anxieties conspire to keep me awake. And in my lack of rest I have become depressed about everything. I look to you, Lord, for help. I pray for some relief from this. ❧ *Lord, I claim this familiar verse as a promise—that you will give me rest by taking on my weariness and concerns.* Thank you, Lord. Thank you.

Next time you find yourself awake at night, think of a song or hymn and sing it to the Lord.

FEAR · TRIUMPH IN EVERY SITUATION

As you approach a difficult situation and are feeling fearful about how it will play out, come to God with your apprehension and let him speak to your heart and mind . . .

GOD'S PROMISE

HEBREWS 13:6, NIV • *We say with confidence, "The Lord is my helper; I will not be afraid. What can mere mortals do to me?"*

PSALM 27:1, NIV • *The Lord is my light and my salvation—whom shall I fear? The Lord is the stronghold of my life—of whom shall I be afraid?*

EXODUS 14:13, NIV • *Do not be afraid.* ***Stand firm and you will see the deliverance the LORD will bring you today.***

PRAY GOD'S PROMISE

Lord God, I face a difficult and complicated situation coming up. It requires me to say some unpopular things. I am afraid about how my words will be taken. I'm fearful of people's reactions. I need your help. ❧ I want to enter into this confidently, but my inner strength is failing me. I welcome the words that you, Lord, are my helper. I cherish the thought that if you are my stronghold, there is no one I should fear. ❧ *Most of all, I claim your promise that if I stand firm, I will see you at work in this situation and will experience your deliverance.* Thank you, Lord.

Talk with God about the things you need to say in this coming situation. Listen to him speak to you.

———————— ❖ ————————

FEAR • FINDING ASSURANCE IN GOD'S LOVE

Come to God right now and open up to him about the many different things you live in fear of. Allow him to speak to you and comfort you . . .

GOD'S PROMISE

2 TIMOTHY 1:7 • *God has not given us a spirit of fear and timidity, but of power, love, and self-discipline.*

1 JOHN 4:18, MSG • *There is no room in love for fear. Well-formed love banishes fear. Since fear is crippling, a fearful life—fear of death, fear of judgment—is one not yet fully formed in love.*

ISAIAH 41:10, ESV • **Fear not, for I am with you; be not dismayed, for I am your God; I will strengthen you, I will help you, I will uphold you with my righteous right hand.**

PRAY GOD'S PROMISE

Lord, I pray to you right now because I fear so many things. Dangers from the world around me, circumstances in my daily life, concerns about my job and even my family. I have become a fearful person, Lord. I ask you to help me. ❧ I want to embrace your words here that you have not given me a spirit of fear but of power. I want to, but that's difficult for me. I need you to help me with this. ❧ *And so, Lord, I ask you to fulfill in me your promise of upholding me with your right hand.* I need your presence to comfort me. I need your hand to sustain me. Thank you, Lord.

Tell God about the various fears you have. As you share them with him, listen for his words of response.

———————————— ‹◦› ————————————

FEAR OF DYING · FREEDOM FROM WORRY ABOUT DEATH

Christ died so you can be set free from the fear of death. Let him reassure you about how he has liberated you from this bondage . . .

GOD'S PROMISE

ISAIAH 25:8 • *He will swallow up death forever! The Sovereign LORD will wipe away all tears.*

PSALM 23:4, MSG • **Even when the way goes through Death Valley, I'm not afraid when you walk at my side.**

HEBREWS 2:14-15 • *Because God's children are human beings—made of flesh and blood—the Son also became flesh and blood. For only as a human being could he die, and only by dying could he break the power of the devil, who had the power of death. Only in this way could he set free all who have lived their lives as slaves to the fear of dying.*

PRAY GOD'S PROMISE

Lord Jesus, more and more often I find myself facing the reality of my own mortality. These thoughts roll around in my mind, and I have doubts and fears of what might be in store for me. ☙ I need your help, comfort, and assurance. I thank you for these Bible verses, and I will wrap my mind and my arms around them. ☙ I believe that you rose from the dead, Jesus, and I accept that you conquered death for us all. *I will claim your promise that even as I may go through the experience of death, you are walking by my side, and I need not be afraid.* Thank you, Jesus.

Talk with Jesus right now about your specific fears. Hear him speak to you about each one.

FEAR OF DYING · GOD'S GOT A PLACE FOR YOU

The great overarching message of the gospel is that Christ conquered death. Step into God's presence right now and hear his hopeful words. Then share with him your heart pangs and fears . . .

GOD'S PROMISE

JOSHUA 1:9, NIV · *Have I not commanded you? Be strong and courageous. Do not be afraid; do not be discouraged, for the LORD your God will be with you wherever you go.*

ROMANS 6:5, NIV · *If we have been united with him in a death like his, we will certainly also be united with him in a resurrection like his.*

JOHN 14:1-3, NIV · *Do not let your hearts be troubled. You believe in God; believe also in me. My Father's house has many rooms; if that were not so, would I have told you that **I am going there to prepare a place for you?** And if I go and prepare a place for you, I will come back and take you to be with me that you also may be where I am.*

PRAY GOD'S PROMISE

Lord, I am thinking about death more often these days. I confess that I am afraid of what might happen to me at the end of my life. I need to hear your assurances, Lord, about life, death, and heaven. ⚜ Help me to be strong and courageous as I deal with these matters in my own life and as I think about how they'll play out in the lives of my family and friends. ⚜ *And help me hold close to this promise of your provision for me in heaven—that you will prepare a place for me.* Give me courage and confidence to face what's ahead, Lord.

Can there be any greater promise in God's Word than this—that he will prepare a place for you? Talk with God about how you feel about this kind of reassurance.

———————— ◇ ————————

FEAR OF DYING • THE PROMISE OF ETERNITY WITH GOD

In Christ, we are promised that death has been defeated through the gift of eternal life. Come to God right now and let him speak to you about your life to come . . .

GOD'S PROMISE

2 CORINTHIANS 3:5-6 • *He has enabled us to be ministers of his new covenant. This is a covenant not of written laws, but of the Spirit. The old written covenant ends in death; but under the new covenant, the Spirit gives life.*

1 CORINTHIANS 15:54-55 • *When our dying bodies have been transformed into bodies that will never die, this Scripture will be fulfilled: "Death is swallowed up in victory. O death, where is your victory? O death, where is your sting?"*

REVELATION 21:4 • *He will wipe every tear from their eyes, and **there will be no more death** or sorrow or crying or pain. All these things are gone forever.*

PRAY GOD'S PROMISE

Father God, I struggle when it comes to thinking about matters of life and death. I have fears about what happens to me after I die. I ask for your assurance and comfort about these things. ⚜ I thrill to read these verses about how our bodies will be transformed and death will be conquered. You speak about bodies that will never die. Is that possible? Yes it is, through your power and the work of Christ on the cross. ⚜ *I claim your beautiful promise that in the life to come there will be no more death or sorrow or pain.* I need your help to truly believe this, Father, but I thank you for this promise and will hold to it dearly.

Spend some deeper time in conversation with God. Reread these verses and memorize the promise so you can always have it with you.

FEELING ADRIFT · GOD'S GUIDANCE FOR THE JOURNEY

Sometimes we're left wondering if we've ventured too far away from everything and everyone. Or maybe we're still on the right track, but we feel we're all alone on the path. In the next few minutes, bring these fears and concerns to God . . .

GOD'S PROMISE

JEREMIAH 30:10-11, NIV · *Do not be afraid, Jacob my servant; do not be dismayed, Israel, declares the LORD. I will surely save you out of a distant place, your descendants from the land of their exile. Jacob will again have peace and security, and no one will make him afraid. I am with you and will save you, declares the LORD.*

ISAIAH 41:10 · *Don't be afraid, for I am with you. Don't be discouraged, for I am your God. I will strengthen you and help you. I will hold you up with my victorious right hand.*

DEUTERONOMY 31:8 • *It is the LORD who goes before you. He will be with you; he will not leave you or forsake you. Do not fear or be dismayed.*

PRAY GOD'S PROMISE

Father, I am feeling very alone these days, and it troubles me. I'm walking along on the journey I believe you have ordained for me, but it concerns me that I am so much on my own in this. ✹ I need to have some assurance that I'm on the right track. Father, I want to have a deeper sense of your presence in my life. ✹ I hear your voice, Father, through your words. *I cherish your promise that you will strengthen me and help me and hold me up.* I find so much comfort in knowing that you are with me and will walk before me, leading me. Thank you, Father, for being with me on this journey.

Do you talk with God every day of your journey? Pledge to him to do so, even if it's just a few minutes each day.

FEELING LOST • GOD WILL RESCUE YOU

You may feel as if God has lost track of you, but God has a different take. Come and confess your heart to him. He will open his arms to you . . .

GOD'S PROMISE

PSALM 119:176, NIV • *I have strayed like a lost sheep.*

LUKE 6:20, MSG • *You're blessed when you've lost it all. God's kingdom is there for the finding.*

LUKE 15:4-7, NIV • *Suppose one of you has a hundred sheep and loses one of them. **Doesn't he leave the ninety-nine in the open country and go after the lost sheep until he finds it? And when he finds it, he joyfully puts it on his shoulders and goes home.** Then he calls his friends and neighbors together and says, "Rejoice with me; I have found my lost sheep." I tell you that in the same way there will be more rejoicing in heaven over one sinner who repents than over ninety-nine righteous persons who do not need to repent.*

PRAY GOD'S PROMISE

Dear God, I haven't talked to you in a very long while. I've never been one to diligently seek you, and yet I find myself eagerly seeking you at this moment. I ask that you would hear my prayer. ❧ I'm at a point where I feel lost and finally recognize my need for your help. ❧ Your words speak of a shepherd who is looking for his lost sheep. Well, God, I am certainly one very lost sheep. *I wish to claim this promise that you will find me and rescue me.* I ask that you would bring me back into your sheepfold. I'm ready to come in. Thank you, God.

What are some things you can do to make time for God in your life? Reading the Bible will help you learn about his plans for you. Listen as he speaks to you through his words.

———————————— ❖ ————————————

FEELING LOW IN SPIRIT · REAPING GOD'S NEW HARVEST

Perhaps as you approach God today it's a time when you feel as low as you've ever felt. Know that whatever has happened, God will triumph, and he will bring new growth out of fallow ground. Come before him. Give yourself to him right now . . .

GOD'S PROMISE

PSALM 31:12, ESV · *I have been forgotten like one who is dead; I have become like a broken vessel.*

JOHN 12:24 · *I tell you the truth, unless a kernel of wheat is planted in the soil and dies, it remains alone. But its death will produce many new kernels—a plentiful harvest of new lives.*

GALATIANS 6:9 · *Let's not get tired of doing what is good. **At just the right time we will reap a harvest of blessing if we don't give up.***

PRAY GOD'S PROMISE

God, I have fallen to a very low spot in my life. I have failed, and my heart and soul are broken. I do not know how I can come out of this, recover, become whole again. I fear I will never again be productive and healthy. ‖ But your words, they comfort me. I hear your voice right now telling me that even in my failure, you can redeem my life for your purposes, and that somehow a harvest can still come from my fruitless efforts. ‖ *Father God, I claim your promise that if I keep going, I will reap a harvest of blessing in my life.* I don't know how that can happen, but I know one thing—I need your strength.

Spend some time thinking about how you can approach God at the beginning of each day, enabling you to embrace his promises and discover his helping hand.

————————— ◈ —————————

FEELING OFF TRACK · GOD LEADS YOU WHEN YOU'RE LOST

Know that God hears your cries for help. Trust him to rescue you from your predicament. Enter God's presence prepared to listen for his direction . . .

GOD'S PROMISE

PSALM 18:6, NIV • *In my distress I called to the LORD; I cried to my God for help. From his temple he heard my voice; my cry came before him, into his ears.*

HEBREWS 10:35-36, ESV • *Do not throw away your confidence, which has a great reward. For you have need of endurance, so that when you have done the will of God you may receive what is promised.*

PROVERBS 3:5-6, ESV • *Trust in the LORD with all your heart, and do not lean on your own understanding. In all your ways acknowledge him, and he will make straight your paths.*

PRAY GOD'S PROMISE

Lord, I've gotten off track, and I need your help. I had thought I was doing well, but things got messed up, and I've lost my way. I'm looking to you for a way out. ✦ Fill me with your strength, Lord. I'm tired, exhausted, and I need you to hold me up. I pray for energy, for health, for physical well-being. ⚘ *Lord, this familiar verse is something I claim as a promise from you: that if I trust in you and let go of trying to figure out my life on my own, then you will make my path straight.* Show me a new direction, Lord.

So, now, keep an open ear to God's voice. He'll show you the way.

FEELING ON EDGE · GOD'S CARE IN ANXIOUS MOMENTS

In this time of anxiety, take time to be quiet and still in God's presence. Hear his voice speaking to you . . .

GOD'S PROMISE

JOHN 14:1, NIV • *Do not let your hearts be troubled. You believe in God; believe also in me.*

JOHN 17:11 • *Now I am departing from the world; they are staying in this world, but I am coming to you. Holy Father, you have given me your name; now protect them by the power of your name so that they will be united just as we are.*

JOHN 17:9, NIV • *I am not praying for the world, but for those you have given me, for they are yours.*

PRAY GOD'S PROMISE

Lord Jesus, I find myself on edge these days. Maybe it's because of uncertainties in my life or that I'm distressed about what's happening in the world. I ask for your help discerning the source of my anxiety. *And I claim this promise as a comfort to my heart—that you, Jesus, are praying for me.* I read these words as if for the first time, and I see now that you are talking about all believers— about me—in your prayer to the Father. ⚜ You are entrusting me into his care. ⚜ I can have peace knowing that no matter what happens in this world, God my Father will protect me and provide what I need. Thank you, Lord.

Continue in prayer, thanking Jesus for the good things in your life. Let his promises sink in, and feel his peace envelop you.

FEELING OUT OF CONTROL

• OVERCOMING ADDICTION

You know, God wants what's good for you. He isn't wanting to punish you for seeking pleasure and joy. But he wants you to be truly alive, not simply lurching from experience to experience in your addiction. He wants you—heart, body, and soul. Come to him, and open your life to him . . .

GOD'S PROMISE

1 PETER 4:3 • *You have had enough in the past of the evil things that godless people enjoy—their immorality and lust, their feasting and drunkenness and wild parties, and their terrible worship of idols.*

ROMANS 8:37, NIV • *In all these things we are more than conquerors through him who loved us.*

ROMANS 8:38 • *I am convinced that nothing can ever separate us from God's love. **Neither death nor life, neither*** *angels nor demons, neither our fears for today nor our worries about tomorrow—not even the powers of hell can separate us from God's love.*

PRAY GOD'S PROMISE

I confess I'm not in control, Lord. I do things I know are wrong, but I can't help myself. I wake up the next day loathing myself for what I've done. And I vow to stop and to pull myself out of this pit, but then it just starts over. ❧ I do believe that you can help me overcome this lifestyle. And I need even more than just "help," God, because I know I can do so little of this myself. I need you to do the heavy lifting here. ❧ I hear these words—that through Christ I can be rescued from this. ❧ *Right now I claim your promise, Lord, that not even the powers of this kind of hell can separate me from your love. I believe that, and I will hold on to it dearly.*

Think about the things God has done for you in recent days and weeks and months. Be specific. After you reflect on each one, tell God, "Thank you for loving me." Do you believe he can also pull you out of your addiction?

———————— ❖ ————————

FEELING OVERWHELMED · GOD'S

DELIVERANCE WHEN LIFE IS TOO MUCH

God hears you when you're "up to here" with life. Right now, come to God and share with him the weight of your responsibilities . . .

GOD'S PROMISE

PSALM 55:2 • *Please listen and answer me, for I am overwhelmed by my troubles.*

PSALM 143:4, NKJV • *My spirit is overwhelmed within me; my heart within me is distressed.*

2 CORINTHIANS 1:8-10 • *We were crushed and overwhelmed beyond our ability to endure. . . . As a result, we stopped relying on ourselves and learned to rely only on God, who raises the dead. And he did rescue us . . . and he will rescue us again. We have placed our confidence in him, and **he will continue to rescue us**.*

PRAY GOD'S PROMISE

God, I come to you right now with so many things crowding my mind and heart. I cannot do this anymore. My life is overwhelming on all fronts. ❧ Your words here comfort me as they remind me that even David was overwhelmed at times. Yet you also bring me face-to-face with the possibility that I've been relying on myself for too much—too often. ❧ I need your help to do this, but *here and now I claim your promise to rescue me.* I lay all that overwhelms me at your feet.

Take a further moment to tell God the specific things that overwhelm you. Literally bring all of your worries to him.

—◈—

FEELING OVERWHELMED · SEEING

GOD'S BIG PICTURE FOR YOU

You're stressed and exasperated, but make time to come to God right now. In these moments, tell God how overwhelmed you are—by tasks, people, expectations . . .

GOD'S PROMISE

PSALM 61:2 · *From the ends of the earth, I cry to you for help when my heart is overwhelmed.*

MARK 4:18-19, MSG · *The seed cast in the weeds represents the ones who hear the kingdom news but are overwhelmed with worries about all the things they have to do and all the things they want to get. The stress strangles what they heard, and nothing comes of it.*

MATTHEW 10:41, MSG · *Accepting a messenger of God is as good as being God's messenger. Accepting someone's help is as good as giving someone help. **This is a large work I've called you into, but don't be overwhelmed by it.** It's best to start small.*

PRAY GOD'S PROMISE

Father, like the psalm says, my heart is overwhelmed, and I cry out to you today. The stress of all that I have to do is strangling me and the work that I'm doing. I receive your words and your advice today. ❧ I'm not sure I've thought about that before—how accepting someone's help is as good as giving someone help. Help me to be open to others who can help me. Help me to start small so that I can accomplish great things through you. ❧ And yes,

I claim your promise, Father, about the large work you have called me into, and I receive your comforting instructions to not be overwhelmed by it.

In this quiet moment, silently listen for God to whisper to you. Wait for him to show you the person or persons he has made available to help you. Listen for his focused direction on small steps you can take today.

---- ❖ ----

FINANCIAL GIVING · PRAISING GOD WITH YOUR MONEY

God longs for you to give back to him—and not because you may gain some reward, but because you want to—because you love him. Open your mind to him and listen to his words . . .

GOD'S PROMISE

2 CORINTHIANS 8:3-5, ESV · *They gave according to their means, as I can testify, and beyond their means, of their own accord, begging us earnestly for the favor of taking part in the relief of the saints—and this, not as we expected, but they gave themselves first to the Lord and then by the will of God to us.*

MALACHI 3:8-10, MSG · *Begin by being honest. Do honest people rob God? But you rob me day after day. You ask, "How have we robbed you?" The tithe and the offering— that's how! And now you're under a curse—the whole lot of you—because you're robbing me. Bring your full tithe to the Temple treasury so there will be ample provisions in my Temple. Test me in this and see if I don't open up heaven itself to you and pour out blessings beyond your wildest dreams.*

PROVERBS 3:9-10, NIV • *Honor the LORD with your wealth, with the firstfruits of all your crops; then your barns will be filled to overflowing, and your vats will brim over with new wine.*

PRAY GOD'S PROMISE

Lord God, I know I've been holding onto my income and not giving back to you. I don't tithe, and I really don't give much else of what I have to your work—to ministries or to the church. ❧ I ask that you would help me in this matter, Lord. Open my eyes to your provision and your heart of generosity. ❧ I want to give out of the right spirit, Lord. *I embrace your promise here that you will provide for me abundantly. But I also want to be sure I'm doing this because I wish to honor and praise and love you for who you are.*

During these moments, what is God whispering to you about generosity and giving?

———————————— ❖ ————————————

FINANCIAL IRRESPONSIBILITY

• REDISCOVERING TRUE CONTENTMENT

Come into God's presence with a humble heart. Let him speak to you about this problem you are facing . . .

GOD'S PROMISE

ISAIAH 55:2 • *Why spend your money on food that does not give you strength? Why pay for food that does you no good?*

LUKE 12:15, MSG • *Take care! Protect yourself against the least bit of greed. Life is not defined by what you have, even when you have a lot.*

HEBREWS 13:5, ESV • **Keep your life free from love of money, and be content with what you have, for he has said, "I will never leave you nor forsake you."**

PRAY GOD'S PROMISE

Lord God, I have been made aware of a chronic problem I have with money. Specifically, that I spend it and spend it. I sometimes don't even feel in control of what I buy. I don't understand it, Lord, except that I know I need help. ⚜ I realize my spending may come from a place of deep greed or covetousness. Or it may manifest from a desire to satisfy myself in some way. In any case, these are wrong motivations, I know, and they've thrown my life off kilter. ⚜ *Please help me to claim and incorporate into my life your promise that if I keep myself free from the love of money and learn to be content with what I have, you will not leave me or forsake me.* I pray for these priorities in my life, Lord.

Try an experiment: Go for a few days without spending a single cent. Live simply on just what you have. Each day, pray for and watch for God's provision.

———————— ❖ ————————

FINANCIAL NEED · GOD'S PROVISION IN TIMES OF NEED

You face some challenges in making ends meet, and you worry frequently about how to provide for your family and yourself. In this time of financial need, let God's words of provision speak to you and reassure you . . .

GOD'S PROMISE

ECCLESIASTES 5:19, NIV · *When God gives someone wealth and possessions, and the ability to enjoy them, to accept their lot and be happy in their toil—this is a gift of God.*

LUKE 6:38, ESV · *Give, and it will be given to you. Good measure, pressed down, shaken together, running over, will be put into your lap. For with the measure you use it will be measured back to you.*

PHILIPPIANS 4:19, ESV · **My God will supply every need of yours according to his riches in glory in Christ Jesus.**

PRAY GOD'S PROMISE

Lord God, I am praying to you because I'm in financial need. I'm doing what I can to bring money in. I'm careful about spending. But I have to provide for others as well. And my ends just don't meet. ❧ Lord, I also need your help in finding some peace in this period of financial stress. ❧ *I sure want to embrace your promise that you will supply my every need.* I thank you in faith for taking care of me and supplying what is necessary for me to make this work. Thank you, Lord.

Throughout the following days and weeks, bring each of your financial needs to God in prayer. Pay attention to what he says to you about each one. Watch for things to happen. He will provide.

---<·>---

FINANCIAL PREOCCUPATION

• DISCOVERING GOD'S FINANCIAL PLAN

Clear your mind of budget sheets and income numbers. Pay attention to God's voice in these next few minutes . . .

GOD'S PROMISE

LUKE 12:16-21, MSG • *The farm of a certain rich man produced a terrific crop. He talked to himself: "What can I do? My barn isn't big enough for this harvest." Then he said, "Here's what I'll do: I'll tear down my barns and build bigger ones. Then I'll gather in all my grain and goods, and I'll say to myself, Self, you've done well! You've got it made and can now retire. Take it easy and have the time of your life!" Just then God showed up and said, "Fool! Tonight you die. And your barnful of goods—who gets it?" That's what happens when you fill your barn with Self and not with God.*

LUKE 12:29, MSG • *What I'm trying to do here is get you to relax, not be so preoccupied with* getting *so you can respond to God's giving.*

LUKE 12:31, MSG • **Steep yourself in God-reality, God-initiative, God-provisions. You'll find all your everyday human concerns will be met.**

PRAY GOD'S PROMISE

God, I pray to you today because I have become pre-occupied with money and budgets, and I know this isn't the right focus I should have. I need to be more focused on you and how you provide. ❧ I think part of my pre-occupation is that it gives me a sense of control over things I worry about. But I realize that sometimes it gives me a false sense of security. ❧ God, I ask for your help in this. I want to refocus on you. *Help me to claim this promise that if I immerse myself in you instead of spreadsheets, you will provide for my everyday needs and take care of my concerns and worries.*

Purpose in your heart that over these next days and weeks you'll lift your eyes up out of the numbers and refocus them on what God is doing in your life and the lives of others.

FINANCIAL WOES · GOD WILL PROVIDE

You're facing mounting debts with little income—in part because you haven't managed your money well. Come to God humbly in confession and faith. Step into God's loving and providing presence . . .

GOD'S PROMISE

ACTS 20:35, ESV · *In all things I have shown you that by working hard in this way we must help the weak and remember the words of the Lord Jesus, how he himself said, "It is more blessed to give than to receive."*

PHILIPPIANS 4:11-13 • *I have learned how to be content with whatever I have. I know how to live on almost nothing or with everything. I have learned the secret of living in every situation, whether it is with a full stomach or empty, with plenty or little. For I can do everything through Christ, who gives me strength.*

PHILIPPIANS 4:19 • **This same God who takes care of me will supply all your needs** *from his glorious riches, which have been given to us in Christ Jesus.*

PRAY GOD'S PROMISE

Lord Jesus, I'm in a place where I have little left and some significant debts. Financially, I'm a mess. I need you to help me and rescue me. ❧ I know I haven't done well in managing my finances. I realize that I've spent too much at times. I have much to learn and much to be accountable for. ❧ Lord, I hear these words about learning to be content with what I have and giving to others in need, and I hold on to them. *I will claim your promise that you will take care of me and supply all my needs.* I know this doesn't come without responsibility, but I trust you, Lord, to help me, even with that.

Talk with God about some things you will do differently going forward. Watch for his provision in the upcoming days and weeks.

FORGIVING · FINDING GRACE IN DEALING WITH OTHERS

Sometimes we hold grudges against others, and it's difficult for us to let go and forgive. But God has another model for us to follow. Enter his presence and listen to what he tells you . . .

GOD'S PROMISE

PROVERBS 19:11 · *Sensible people control their temper; they earn respect by overlooking wrongs.*

COLOSSIANS 3:13 · *Make allowance for each other's faults, and forgive anyone who offends you.* **Remember, the Lord forgave you, so you must forgive others.**

MARK 11:25 · *When you are praying, first forgive anyone you are holding a grudge against, so that your Father in heaven will forgive your sins, too.*

PRAY GOD'S PROMISE

Lord, I come to you with regret that I have held back from forgiving this person. I know I should, but I'm harboring ill feelings. ⸙ I pray that you would help me to do what is right in this situation. ⸙ I know your model for forgiving others is the example I need to follow—*that since you forgave our sins, how much more should we forgive others' sins against us.* I will embrace your promise in that, Lord, thanking you for forgiving me. I ask that your presence would guide me as I approach this other person.

Talk to God about this person who wronged you. Then let him speak to you about that person. Listen for God's direction.

FORGIVING · FOLLOWING THE EXAMPLE OF CHRIST

Sometimes the hurts we suffer at the hands of others are deep and so very difficult to forgive. Come into God's presence prepared to listen to his words about forgiveness . . .

GOD'S PROMISE

LUKE 17:3-4 · *If another believer sins, rebuke that person; then if there is repentance, forgive. Even if that person wrongs you seven times a day and each time turns again and asks forgiveness, you must forgive.*

MATTHEW 18:21-22 · *Peter came to him and asked, "Lord, how often should I forgive someone who sins against me? Seven times?" "No, not seven times," Jesus replied, "but seventy times seven!"*

EPHESIANS 4:32 · **Be kind to each other, tenderhearted, forgiving one another, just as God through Christ has forgiven you.**

PRAY GOD'S PROMISE

Father God, I come before you with some hard feelings. The person who hurt me has apologized, but the sin against me is so difficult to forgive. Help me in this situation, I pray. ❦ I am chastised by the account of Peter asking Jesus how many times he should forgive. I know it is my responsibility as a Christian not only to forgive but also to forgive abundantly. ❦ I pray for your help in this, Father. This is not easy for me. *But I claim your words—just as you have forgiven me for so much, so I should forgive this person.* Father, help me to carry this out in this situation in my life.

Ask God for his wisdom in how to approach this person and offer forgiveness.

———————— ◇ ————————

FORGIVING · GRACE IN CONFRONTING ANOTHER'S WRONGS

It's hard when a brother or sister in the body of Christ hurts us. We tend to have higher expectations for other believers, don't we? We think that since they are God's children, they will always treat us fairly. But the truth is that they are fallible human beings, just as we are. Open your heart to God. Share with him your struggles in dealing with this difficult situation . . .

GOD'S PROMISE

2 CORINTHIANS 2:5-8 • *I am not overstating it when I say that the man who caused all the trouble hurt all of you more than he hurt me. Most of you opposed him, and that was punishment enough. Now, however, it is time to forgive and comfort him. Otherwise he may be overcome by discouragement. So I urge you now to reaffirm your love for him.*

JAMES 5:19-20 • *My dear brothers and sisters, if someone among you wanders away from the truth and is brought back, you can be sure that whoever brings the sinner back will save that person from death and bring about the forgiveness of many sins.*

2 CORINTHIANS 2:10, MSG • *If you forgive him, I forgive him. Don't think I'm carrying around a list of personal grudges. The fact is that I'm joining in with your forgiveness, as* **Christ is with us, guiding us.**

PRAY GOD'S PROMISE

Lord Jesus, I pray to you right now asking for wisdom. This is a difficult situation—a person in my midst has committed some wrongs. I want to give the benefit of the doubt, but this has gone on too long, and something needs to be done. ⚹ I confess that confronting someone isn't an easy task for me, and I ask for your help. But I also know that in addressing this offense, I may be able to help this person. ⚹ *Your promise here is that in this process, you, Jesus, will be here guiding us.* I need your direction and wisdom. And I need your help to forgive.

Take some moments with God to listen to him and discern his instruction for you in this matter.

———————————— ◇ ————————————

FRUSTRATION · ENCOURAGEMENT FOR GETTING
THROUGH THE DAY

Sometimes life just seems way too hard. Sometimes every simple action we try to take feels overwhelming. Open your heart to God in the next few minutes . . .

GOD'S PROMISE

PSALM 88:8-9, MSG • *I'm caught in a maze and can't find my way out, blinded by tears of pain and frustration.*

PHILIPPIANS 4:6-7 • *Don't worry about anything; instead, pray about everything.* **Tell God what you need, and thank him for all he has done. Then you will experience God's peace,** *which exceeds anything we can understand. His peace will guard your hearts and minds as you live in Christ Jesus.*

JOHN 16:33 • *Here on earth you will have many trials and sorrows. But take heart, because I have overcome the world.*

PRAY GOD'S PROMISE

Lord, I am struggling right now with life in general. Everything I do seems to be difficult in some way. Nothing seems to be going well. I feel "caught in a maze." I'm crying out to you, Lord, for help. ❧ I accept the reality of your words—that life is hard and I will have trials and sorrows. And I will embrace the truth that you have overcome the world. There certainly is great hope in that. ❧ *So I claim the promise that you are there, and that if I tell you what I need and thank you for what you have done, I will experience your peace.* Thank you, Lord.

Now spend some time telling God about specific needs you have today. Thank him for his provision in the past. Listen to his words of peace and let them cover you.

———————— ‹·› ————————

FRUSTRATION WITH GOD • GROWING

FAITH IN GOD'S PLANS AND PURPOSES

As in the biblical story of Mary and Martha, we can occasionally find ourselves being frustrated by God. *Why won't God solve my problem? Why doesn't he intervene?* And yet God knows us better than we know ourselves. He has his plans and purposes . . .

GOD'S PROMISE

LUKE 10:40-42, NIV • *Martha was distracted by all the preparations that had to be made. She came to him and asked, "Lord, don't you care that my sister has left me to do the work by myself? Tell her to help me!" "Martha, Martha," the Lord answered, "you are worried and upset about many things, but few things are needed—or indeed only one. Mary has chosen what is better, and it will not be taken away from her."*

ROMANS 8:27-28, MSG • *He knows us far better than we know ourselves. . . . That's why we can be so sure that every detail in our lives of love for God is worked into something good.*

PROVERBS 3:5-7, NIV • **Trust in the LORD with all your heart and lean not on your own understanding; in all your ways submit to him, and he will make your paths straight.** *Do not be wise in your own eyes; fear the LORD and shun evil.*

PRAY GOD'S PROMISE

Lord, forgive me, but I have been frustrated of late that you haven't taken care of things as I was hoping and expecting. I have worries and needs, and I feel that you haven't answered those concerns. ❧ But I listen to these words, and they caution me that I probably am not seeing what's ultimately important. I ask you to show me the bigger picture. ❧ And I also ask that you would help me to trust you. I am impatient, I know, because I lack trust in what you will do in my life. Help me to claim your promise that *if I trust in you, you will make my paths straight.*

Consider the words "do not be wise in your own eyes." Do you think you have in some ways done that, and consequently you've become impatient with God?

———————————— ◆ ————————————

GOSSIP · LIVING OUT THE GOSPEL IN KINDNESS

Perhaps someone has said something to you about this habit. You often talk about others behind their backs in ways that are critical and hurtful. Open your heart in the presence of God. Be honest and truthful with yourself and with him . . .

GOD'S PROMISE

1 TIMOTHY 5:13, NIV · *They get into the habit of being idle and going about from house to house. And not only do they become idlers, but also busybodies who talk nonsense, saying things they ought not to.*

EPHESIANS 5:4, MSG · *Though some tongues just love the taste of gossip, those who follow Jesus have better uses for language than that. Don't talk dirty or silly. That kind of talk doesn't fit our style. Thanksgiving is our dialect.*

PHILIPPIANS 1:27, ESV · **Only let your manner of life be worthy of the gospel of Christ. . . . that you are standing firm in one spirit, with one mind striving side by side for the faith of the gospel.**

PRAY GOD'S PROMISE

Father, I come to you to confess a bad habit I've become aware of in myself. I know I talk about others in gossipy ways. This is not the kind of person you want me to be. I come to you expressing sorrow for these actions and also asking for your help. ♪ I realize my actions may result from needing others to think I'm important. But I should be content knowing that I'm important to you. Help me in this, Lord. ♪ *And Lord, I claim your picture here of the me I could be—one who is worthy of your gospel.* I pray that my mouth might from now on be speaking the good news *to* others and not the gossipy news *about* others.

Spend some quiet moments with God. Allow his words to sink in to your heart.

———————————— ❖ ————————————

GREED · TRADING THE LOVE OF MONEY FOR CONTENTMENT IN GOD

For so long you've had a preoccupation with money and things. You seem to never have enough. But recently you've become aware of how empty your life is. Prepare your heart and mind for this time with God. Be honest with yourself and allow him to speak to you . . .

GOD'S PROMISE

ECCLESIASTES 5:10, ESV · *He who loves money will not be satisfied with money, nor he who loves wealth with his income; this also is vanity.*

LUKE 12:15, MSG · *Take care! Protect yourself against the least bit of greed. Life is not defined by what you have, even when you have a lot.*

HEBREWS 13:5, ESV • *Keep your life free from love of money, and be content with what you have, for he has said, "I will never leave you nor forsake you."*

PRAY GOD'S PROMISE

God, I've become aware that my life has been built on a love for money and things. Having stuff has become all-important to me. And I know this is the wrong track for my life. ❦ I am beginning to understand these words— that life is not defined by what you have, even when you have a lot. I'm beginning to see what is really important in life. ❦ Lord, *I claim your promise that you will never leave me nor forsake me.* That is what's important. Thank you that I no longer need money or possessions in order to feel secure. Help me to be content in you, and you only.

Talk with God about how you might start on this new track regarding your money and possessions. What is one idea for how you could do things differently? Let it be the beginning of a new lifestyle for you.

———————————— ‹◇› ————————————

GRIEF • HOPE FOR THE BROKENHEARTED

Pain from the loss of a loved one cannot be easily or quickly healed. Grieving takes time. But even in the midst of deep loss, there is hope. Come to the Lord right now with your anguish and hurt . . .

GOD'S PROMISE

JEREMIAH 8:18 • *My grief is beyond healing; my heart is broken.*

PSALM 147:3 • *He heals the brokenhearted and bandages their wounds.*

REVELATION 21:4 • ***He will wipe every tear from their eyes, and there will be no more death or sorrow or crying or pain.***

PRAY GOD'S PROMISE

Lord Jesus, oh, how I am hurting right now. My loss is so immense, I can hardly even manage to live. I am numb, and I am full of despair. Yes, my heart is broken. I need you now so much. Please come close and hold me, Lord Jesus. ⚜ I don't know if I can adequately embrace your words here. I do believe in you—that you heal the brokenhearted. That you bind up their wounds. But will you heal *me* and bind up *my* wounds? ⚜ ***Help me to claim your promise, Lord, that in time you will wipe the tears from my eyes.*** And thank you for the hope of heaven. Help me to imagine what it will be like to live in a place where there is no more death or sorrow or crying or pain.

In this time with God, open your heart to him. Pour out your anguish and grief. Let yourself cry with him. He will catch your tears.

———————————— ❖ ————————————

GUILT · CLAIMING THE FORGIVENESS OF THE CROSS

Come into God's presence and share with him your feelings of guilt. Know that in Christ your sins are forgiven. Listen to his words of comfort . . .

GOD'S PROMISE

PSALM 51:2-3, MSG • *Scrub away my guilt, soak out my sins in your laundry. I know how bad I've been; my sins are staring me down.*

ROMANS 3:23, ESV • *All have sinned and fall short of the glory of God.*

HEBREWS 10:2, 10 • *If they could have provided perfect cleansing, the sacrifices would have stopped, for the worshipers would have been purified once for all time, and their feelings of guilt would have disappeared. . . . **For God's will was for us to be made holy by the sacrifice of the body of Jesus Christ, once for all time.***

PRAY GOD'S PROMISE

Lord God, I am experiencing feelings of guilt that I cannot explain. These are general emotions of feeling ashamed for doing wrong—not feelings that result from any of my specific sinful actions. I relate to the verse that speaks of my sins staring me down. ❧ Lord, I am a believer, but I need reassurance that I am forgiven. ❧ I ask for your help. *I want to embrace your promise that once and for all, I am made holy by the sacrifice of Jesus.* Help me to believe this deeply. Take away my feelings of guilt, I pray, Lord.

Just allow God some quiet time with you. Let him whisper to you his love and acceptance. Listen for his reassurance that you belong to him.

———————————— ‹·› ————————————

HARDSHIP · GROWING THROUGH ADVERSITY

The things you are going through these days might, in fact, be a way in which God is preparing you for a great work. That possibility perhaps doesn't make you feel better now, but know that God has his purposes for you, even in this current hardship. Be still right now and let God's words wash over you . . .

GOD'S PROMISE

ISAIAH 30:20-21, NIV · *Although the Lord gives you the bread of adversity and the water of affliction, your teachers will be hidden no more; with your own eyes you will see them. Whether you turn to the right or to the left, your ears will hear a voice behind you, saying, "This is the way; walk in it."*

JAMES 1:2-4, ESV · *Count it all joy, my brothers, when you meet trials of various kinds, for you know that the testing of your faith produces steadfastness. And let steadfastness have its full effect, that you may be perfect and complete, lacking in nothing.*

JAMES 1:12 · **God blesses those who patiently endure testing and temptation.** *Afterward they will receive the crown of life that God has promised to those who love him.*

PRAY GOD'S PROMISE

Lord God, I come to you so challenged by the troubles I've been facing of late. It feels like I've been taking one step forward, then one step back. I'm almost ready to give up. ⚜ But I hear these words that you allow these trials in my life so that you can teach me. They haven't been pleasant, but I concede that there is a purpose to the struggles I've been going through. I pray that I will be able to hear your direction—I'm asking for you to tell me which way I should go. ❦ And Lord, *I cherish this promise you've provided me here—that you bless those who endure.* Help me to listen for your teaching voice in my life through whatever obstacles I face.

Ask yourself what God might be teaching you in these recent experiences that have been so difficult.

HATE · OVERCOMING THE EMOTION THAT DESTROYS

Hate—it's a strong emotion. Left unchecked, it can lead to destruction. Release your anger to God and let him help you with your feelings toward this other person . . .

GOD'S PROMISE

1 JOHN 4:20-21 · *If someone says, "I love God," but hates a fellow believer, that person is a liar; for if we don't love people we can see, how can we love God, whom we cannot see? And he has given us this command: Those who love God must also love their fellow believers.*

HEBREWS 12:14-15 · *Work at living in peace with everyone, and work at living a holy life, for those who are not holy will not see the Lord. Look after each other so that none of you fails to receive the grace of God. Watch out that no poisonous root of bitterness grows up to trouble you, corrupting many.*

MARK 11:25 • *When you are praying, first **forgive anyone you are holding a grudge against**, so that your Father in heaven will **forgive your sins**, too.*

PRAY GOD'S PROMISE

Father in heaven, I pray for your help in dealing with someone in my life. I've developed strong feelings against this person, and this is beginning to affect me in a deeper way. I don't want to feel this way. ⚜ I know that you want us—you want me—to love others, and that hatred should have no place between myself and a brother or sister. I can tell that bitterness is becoming a problem within. ⚜ *Father, I understand that you set an example for me by forgiving my own sins. How much more should I then forgive this other person in my life?* Father, please help me to approach this other person properly. Lead me to do the right thing.

Quiet yourself and listen to God speak into your life about this other person.

———————— ◇ ————————

HEARTBREAK • BLESSING IN THE WAKE OF A LOST OPPORTUNITY

You were turned down, and something you thought was going to come your way hasn't materialized. Bring this situation to God in prayer. Quiet your troubled heart and busy mind. Let him speak to you . . .

GOD'S PROMISE

1 JOHN 5:14, ESV • *This is the confidence that we have toward him, that if we ask anything according to his will he hears us.*

ROMANS 8:28, NIV • *We know that in all things God works for the good of those who love him, who have been called according to his purpose.*

PSALM 126:6, MSG • *Those who went off with heavy hearts will come home laughing, with armloads of blessing.*

PRAY GOD'S PROMISE

Father God, I am shattered that this latest opportunity didn't fall my way. I was practically counting on it, so this news is really difficult. I pray for your presence in my heart and life right now, Lord. ❦ I believe that you may have better opportunities for me ahead, Father. I believe that things really do work together for good, and this situation will be no exception. ❦ *And I love this promise, Father, that you can turn my heavy heart into a laughing heart, and that you will give me armloads of blessings.* I believe that promise, Lord. Thank you for being with me through this.

Tell God about what you are hoping for in a new opportunity. Listen to him speak to you. And watch how he provides in coming days.

———————————— ‹◇› ————————————

HEARTBREAK • GOD'S EMBRACE IN THE LOSS OF LOVE

A once close relationship has dissolved away, and you're left with deep hurt. Come to God in the midst of your heartbreak. Let him wipe away your tears . . .

GOD'S PROMISE

PSALM 34:18, MSG • *If your heart is broken, you'll find GOD right there.*

JAMES 1:2-4 • *Dear brothers and sisters, when troubles of any kind come your way, consider it an opportunity for great joy. For you know that when your faith is tested, your endurance has a chance to grow. So let it grow, for when your endurance is fully developed, you will be perfect and complete, needing nothing.*

1 PETER 5:7 • **Give all your worries and cares to God, for he cares about you.**

PRAY GOD'S PROMISE

Lord God, I come to you after someone I love has left me. I am heartbroken, deeply hurt, and crying inside and out. ❧ I want to take your words here to heart, although it's still too soon for me to think of this pain as having any purpose or value, much less as being a reason for joy. Still I pray that I will understand more about myself and you, Lord, through this experience. ❧ *Lord, I will try to give you my worries and cares and heartbreak. I embrace your promise that you care about me.* Help me through this, Lord.

Let God wrap his arms around you. Let him see your tears.

❖

HEARTBREAK · TURNING TO GOD AFTER
A SUDDEN LOSS

You've just gotten some difficult news. Take this unexpected set-back to God in prayer. Listen to him speak to you . . .

GOD'S PROMISE

PSALM 43:5, ESV · *Why are you cast down, O my soul, and why are you in turmoil within me?*

1 THESSALONIANS 5:18, ESV · *Give thanks in all circumstances; for this is the will of God in Christ Jesus for you.*

1 JOHN 5:14-15 · **We are confident that he hears us whenever we ask for anything that pleases him. And since we know he hears us when we make our requests, we also know that he will give us what we ask for.**

PRAY GOD'S PROMISE

Lord, I've just gotten this news, and it's pretty devastating. I am filled with worry and dismay and heartbreak. What I thought was a good situation is suddenly no more. ❧ Help me, Lord, to understand your purposes in this. Reassure me of what value I have. Come alongside me during this time, I pray. ❧ *I embrace this promise that when I ask you for a solution and a hopeful future beyond this problem, you hear me.* I trust that you will provide what I need, Lord.

Talk with God about this loss. But also express to him your hopes and wishes. He may want to speak to you about a bigger and better opportunity he has for you.

HOMELESSNESS · GOD WILL SUPPLY ALL
YOUR NEEDS

In a time of deep need like this one, these moments in God's presence are a source of comfort and reassurance. Right now, let his words shelter you . . .

GOD'S PROMISE

LAMENTATIONS 3:19-23 · *The thought of my suffering and homelessness is bitter beyond words. I will never forget this awful time, as I grieve over my loss. Yet I still dare to hope when I remember this: The faithful love of the LORD never ends! His mercies never cease. Great is his faithfulness; his mercies begin afresh each morning.*

PHILIPPIANS 4:19 · *This same God who takes care of me will supply all your needs from his glorious riches, which have been given to us in Christ Jesus.*

MATTHEW 6:31-34 · *Don't worry about these things, saying, "What will we eat? What will we drink? What will we wear?" These things dominate the thoughts of unbelievers, but your heavenly Father already knows all your needs.* **Seek the Kingdom of God above all else, and live righteously, and he will give you everything you need.** *So don't worry about tomorrow, for tomorrow will bring its own worries. Today's trouble is enough for today.*

PRAY GOD'S PROMISE

Lord God, I am in a strange place of life these days. I literally have nowhere to live. You know my circumstances, and you also know those friends and family who have provided as much as they can. Yet I am facing a very uncertain future. I bring all these things to you, Lord. ❧ I pray that this time will become one in which I can experience you in a new way. ❧ *Lord, I claim your promise here that you will take care of me and provide all my needs.* Help me to trust you for that, Lord. And help me to walk with you more closely.

Pay attention to those people whom God puts in your path during these next few days. Be open to his provision for you.

HOPELESSNESS · FINDING LIFE IN THE PRESENCE OF GOD

When the future is unclear, it's easy to spiral downward into feelings of hopelessness. Know that God desires to remove you from this entrapment. Settle your mind and come into his presence in these next few moments . . .

GOD'S PROMISE

PSALM 13:2 · *How long must I struggle with anguish in my soul, with sorrow in my heart every day? How long will my enemy have the upper hand?*

LAMENTATIONS 3:20-24 · *I will never forget this awful time, as I grieve over my loss. Yet I still dare to hope when I remember this: The faithful love of the LORD never ends! His mercies never cease. Great is his faithfulness; his mercies begin afresh each morning. I say to myself, "The LORD is my inheritance; therefore, I will hope in him!"*

HEBREWS 6:18-19 • *We who have fled to him for refuge can have great confidence as we hold to the hope that lies before us. This hope is a strong and trustworthy anchor for our souls. It leads us through the curtain into God's inner sanctuary.*

PRAY GOD'S PROMISE

Father God, I am tired and in despair about life, my future, and if it all adds up to anything. It's been a deeply challenging period of time. I feel hopeless about anything really working out well right now. ⚜ However, I am lifted up by these words that say that your faithful love never ends. I think maybe I need to let go of my expectations for myself in this world and focus more on you and your love. ⚜ *Father, I embrace this confidence you offer—that the hope we have in you is an anchor to our souls and is the pathway into your inner sanctuary.* I know that's what really matters. Help me seek that, Father. Help me find that.

In these moments, think about giving God time each day to allow him to draw you into his inner sanctuary. Tell him how you want that for your life going forward.

———————— ⋄ ————————

HOPELESSNESS · EMBRACING GOD'S LARGER PURPOSE

Sometimes we feel hopeless because we aren't seeing the big picture. In these moments with God, step back, look at the larger scope of your life, and listen to him speak to you about the greater work he is doing . . .

GOD'S PROMISE

PSALM 43:5 • *Why am I discouraged? Why is my heart so sad? I will put my hope in God! I will praise him again—my Savior and my God!*

ROMANS 8:24-25, ESV • *Hope that is seen is not hope. For who hopes for what he sees? But if we hope for what we do not see, we wait for it with patience.*

COLOSSIANS 1:4-6 • *We have heard of your faith in Christ Jesus and your love for all of God's people, which come from your confident hope of what God has reserved for you in heaven. . . . **It is bearing fruit everywhere by changing lives,** just as it changed your lives from the day you first heard and understood the truth about God's wonderful grace.*

PRAY GOD'S PROMISE

Lord, I am in this period in which I am discouraged because I don't see anything changing or improving or growing. It seems as if nothing I do will ever be of much use or value. Lord, please help me know what to do. ❧ In reading the verses here, I know I need to reclaim the promises of your Word. I see how I am a part of a process that started at Creation and has continued ever since, with the death of Jesus Christ on the cross marking the turning point of our redemption. ❧ Lord, *I believe your words— that what I am doing is bearing fruit—and I embrace that.* I ask you to show me some evidence of that. Give me encouragement in my work for you, and equip me with the strength to continue on.

Talk with God about the work you are doing for him. Whom have you been in touch with in that work? What is happening in their lives? Do you need to reach out to them?

———————— ❖ ————————

HOPELESSNESS · FINDING STRENGTH TO ENDURE

Sometimes along life's arduous journey, we can lose heart and struggle with thoughts of doubt and feelings of despair. Let God's words wash over you and give you new hope . . .

GOD'S PROMISE

MARK 9:23, ESV · *All things are possible for one who believes.*

HEBREWS 11:1 · *Faith is the confidence that what we hope for will actually happen; it gives us assurance about things we cannot see.*

ROMANS 5:1-5, ESV · *Since we have been justified by faith, we have peace with God through our Lord Jesus Christ. Through him we have also obtained access by faith into this grace in which we stand, and we rejoice in hope of the glory of God. Not only that, but we rejoice in our sufferings, knowing that suffering produces endurance, and **endurance produces character, and character produces hope**, and hope does not put us to shame, because God's love has been poured into our hearts through the Holy Spirit who has been given to us.*

PRAY GOD'S PROMISE

Lord God, I confess to you that I am dealing with doubts and despair. I need to see some more evidence of you in my life. I long for some sign or indication that you are there. ❦ I know faith is believing in things we cannot see. I long to have more confidence in that, more ability to muster a stronger faith. I pray for your assurances, God. ❦ *I embrace your promise that "endurance produces character," and it is through deepened character that I will find new hope and assurance.* Help me to understand that, God. Help me to embrace this for my life right now.

Tell God all of your doubts. Talk them out with him. But then give him time with you so he can whisper to you his reassurances.

HURT BY INFIDELITY · DEALING WITH THE ANGUISH OF ADULTERY

Open your breaking heart to God. Bring to him your anger and hurt. Let him speak to you and comfort you . . .

GOD'S PROMISE

HEBREWS 13:4, NIV · *Marriage should be honored by all, and the marriage bed kept pure, for God will judge the adulterer.*

1 CORINTHIANS 13:7 · *Love never gives up, never loses faith, is always hopeful, and endures through every circumstance.*

COLOSSIANS 3:13 · *Forgive anyone who offends you. Remember, the Lord forgave you, so you must forgive others.*

PRAY GOD'S PROMISE

Oh Father, my heart is broken. I have a hole deep inside. My spouse has committed adultery. It leaves me in tears of anger, hurt, and despair. I need your help and presence. ❧ I don't even know how to pray. Your words are strong in saying you will judge my spouse for this sin. Your words also advise me that love endures through every circumstance. I hear you, Father, but first I need to figure out if I'm even still capable of loving. ❧ I know it will take time. I hear you saying that forgiveness is a process, but even that is hard for me right now. *I embrace your forgiveness of my own shortcomings, Father.* That is the only part of your promise I can hold on to in this moment. Help me, Father. Walk with me through the heartbreak.

Let your tears and thoughts flow out to God. Tell him all of your various feelings about what has been done to you. Listen to his voice. Give yourself to his love and care.

INADEQUACY · FINDING CONFIDENCE IN YOUR GIFTEDNESS

God has given you many gifts and abilities. Consider all the specific resources he has equipped you with to do his will . . .

GOD'S PROMISE

HEBREWS 13:20-21 · *May the God of peace—who brought up from the dead our Lord Jesus, the great Shepherd of the sheep, and ratified an eternal covenant with his blood— may he equip you with all you need for doing his will. May he produce in you, through the power of Jesus Christ, every good thing that is pleasing to him.*

HEBREWS 10:35-36 • *Do not throw away this confident trust in the Lord. Remember the great reward it brings you! Patient endurance is what you need now, so that you will continue to do God's will. Then you will receive all that he has promised.*

1 PETER 4:10 • ***God has given each of you a gift from his great variety of spiritual gifts. Use them well to serve one another.***

PRAY GOD'S PROMISE

Lord Jesus, help me to be more confident in life. Help me to live with greater assurance and resolve. ⚏ I confess that so often I feel weak and incapable of the tasks I'm responsible for. I know that you are a powerful God, but I think I lack faith that you will be there for me. ⚏ Lord, I strongly desire to shed this feeling of inadequacy. Help me trust you for strength, power, and ability to accomplish what you've called me to do. *I claim your promise that I have a gift from you—something I can do well for your Kingdom.* Help me, Lord, to fix my eyes on you, to believe that you will show me that gift, and to boldly live for you in this world.

Continue in prayer and conversation with God. Consider some of the things you've done in the past week that have helped someone else. Talk with God about some of your passions in life. Listen to his voice of wisdom.

INDECISION · SEEKING CLARITY AND CONFIDENCE
IN LIFE'S CHOICES

Difficult decisions often leave us frustrated and unsure of ourselves. Bring your dilemma to God. Seek his wisdom in these next moments . . .

GOD'S PROMISE

JAMES 1:5 · *If you need wisdom, ask our generous God, and he will give it to you.*

PHILIPPIANS 4:6, ESV · *Do not be anxious about anything, but in everything by prayer and supplication with thanksgiving let your requests be made known to God.*

PROVERBS 3:6 · *Seek his will in all you do, and he will show you which path to take.*

PRAY GOD'S PROMISE

Lord, I am unsure about something in my life, and I need to make a difficult decision. I come to you right now to seek your wisdom and direction. I pray for your guidance. ❦ You have said that I should make my requests known to you. And so I pray specifically about this difficult decision. My heart leans one way. My mind leans the other. ❦ I need your wisdom, Lord, and I pray for that now. *You promise that if I seek your will, then you will show me which path to take. I claim that promise now.* I lean on your understanding, Lord. I pray for your will to be done.

In a period of silence, listen for God's direction. What is he telling you?

INFERIORITY · REDISCOVERING HOW GOD HAS GIFTED YOU

God made you, and you know that he does good work. But sometimes it's hard for us to believe that about ourselves. Let God's truth about you wash over your heart . . .

GOD'S PROMISE

JEREMIAH 1:5, MSG · *Before I shaped you in the womb, I knew all about you. Before you saw the light of day, I had holy plans for you.*

1 CORINTHIANS 1:7-9, MSG · *Just think—you don't need a thing, you've got it all!* **All God's gifts are right in front of you as you wait expectantly for our Master Jesus to arrive on the scene for the Finale. And not only that, but God himself is right alongside to keep you steady and on track until things are all wrapped up by Jesus.** *God, who got you started in this spiritual adventure, shares with us the life of his Son and our Master Jesus. He will never give up on you. Never forget that.*

2 CORINTHIANS 5:17, ESV · *If anyone is in Christ, he is a new creation. The old has passed away; behold, the new has come.*

PRAY GOD'S PROMISE

Lord God, thank you for your words. I'm having a hard time finding myself in the world around me. I struggle to know what I'm good at. I'm failing to understand my value. ✦ Yet I know that in Christ I am a new person. I embrace that. I just need to be assured of how that works for me in everyday life. ✦ But I am ready right now to claim the promise that *all God's gifts are in front of me, and that you will be right alongside me for this journey ahead.* Thank you, Lord, for your assurances about myself. Help me to see the specific gifts you've given me and how they can allow me to help others.

Ask God to show you the strengths and skills he's equipped you with. Pay attention to his voice over the next few days.

——————————— ‹◇› ———————————

INJURY · GOD IS IN CHARGE

Sometimes unexpected events can push us into a quiet time with God. Take these next moments with him to begin to refocus your life toward his plan for you . . .

GOD'S PROMISE

PROVERBS 19:21, ESV · *Many are the plans in the mind of a man, but it is the purpose of the LORD that will stand.*

ECCLESIASTES 7:14, MSG · *On a good day, enjoy yourself; on a bad day, examine your conscience. God arranges for both kinds of days so that we won't take anything for granted.*

2 CORINTHIANS 1:4, MSG · *He comes alongside us when we go through hard times, and before you know it, he brings us alongside someone else who is going through hard times so that we can be there for that person just as God was there for us.*

PRAY GOD'S PROMISE

Father, I had so many plans for myself in the days ahead, and now this. I pray for your help in understanding your purpose. And I pray also for healing and recovery. ⚜ I want to make sure I'm focused on you, Father. I don't want to take you for granted in my life, but I confess that sometimes I've allowed that to happen. ⚜ *Thank you for the promise that you come alongside me during hard times.* Help me to think of someone else who needs my help so I can pass along your comfort.

Open your heart to God's leading in the next few days. Be on the lookout for that someone who needs you.

INJURY · A TIME TO REFOCUS

This wasn't what you counted on. Share with God your hurt and frustration. Then let him speak to you about how he already has a plan to cover this unexpected event . . .

GOD'S PROMISE

PROVERBS 16:33 · *We may throw the dice, but the LORD determines how they fall.*

2 CORINTHIANS 4:8-9, ESV · *We are afflicted in every way, but not crushed; perplexed, but not driven to despair; persecuted, but not forsaken; struck down, but not destroyed.*

EPHESIANS 1:11 · *Because we are united with Christ, we have received an inheritance from God, for* **he chose us in advance, and he makes everything work out according to his plan.**

PRAY GOD'S PROMISE

Lord God, I come to you after the accident that's left

me in this condition. I ask, first of all, for your healing touch. I look to you for some sense and meaning in this circumstance. I don't have the patience or resources to deal with a painful injury, especially now. Who has time to be laid up when there's so much work to be done? And did I mention the bills? ⚜ I pray, Lord, for your help in understanding why. ⚜ Lord, I think I need to more fully realize the reality of your power and control over my life. *I accept that you chose me in advance, and I believe you will work even this out according to your plan.* Help me to trust you.

Ask God to show you his purpose in allowing this injury. Open your heart and mind to how he might bring good out of your circumstances in the coming days.

———————— ⬩◇⬩ ————————

INJURY · GOD WILL OVERCOME

Accidents happen, but they don't always make sense. Open your heart to God to discover his purposes. Let him talk with you about what has occurred . . .

GOD'S PROMISE

PHILIPPIANS 4:12-13, ESV · *I know how to be brought low, and I know how to abound. In any and every circumstance, I have learned the secret of facing plenty and hunger, abundance and need. **I can do all things through him who strengthens me.***

JOB 42:2, NIV · *I know that you can do all things; no purpose of yours can be thwarted.*

ROMANS 8:31, MSG • *What do you think? With God on our side like this, how can we lose?*

PRAY GOD'S PROMISE

Lord, I come to you asking for a strong measure of healing. I am hurting, and I face a lengthy time of recovery. Please provide all that I need to get better. ❧ I also know I must trust you during this time. I don't know why this happened, or what your specific purpose is in it. It seems so random and unexpected. But even so, I believe you are in control. ❧ I know I cannot lose with you on my side. *I claim your promise that through you I can do all things, and that you will indeed strengthen me.* Thank you, Lord.

Right now, spend more quiet time with Jesus. Listen for his strategies for overcoming the frustrations you're facing. With God on your side, how can you lose?

INSECURITY • FINDING GOD'S PEACE IN THE MIDST OF WORRY

Come to God in the midst of your insecurity and feelings of vulnerability. Open your heart to him . . .

GOD'S PROMISE

PHILIPPIANS 4:6 • *Don't worry about anything; instead, pray about everything.*

PHILIPPIANS 4:6 • *Tell God what you need, and thank him for all he has done.*

PHILIPPIANS 4:7 • *You will experience God's peace, which exceeds anything we can understand. His peace will guard your hearts and minds as you live in Christ Jesus.*

PRAY GOD'S PROMISE

Lord God, all kinds of insecurities are badgering me right now, from financial fears to safety worries to concerns about health. These have made me anxious and jittery. I need your help. ❦ It's hard for me to obey your command to not worry about anything. But I know I still need to bring all these worries to you in prayer. And I will. ❦ Lord, I thank you for all of the significant and amazing ways you've already worked in my life. *I claim your promise that I can experience your peace.* Thank you that it will guard my heart and my mind from all of these worries.

Take time right now to bring to God each area of your life where you feel insecure. Thank him for the ways he has protected you in the past. Then receive his peace that passes all understanding.

INSECURITY • HOPE IN GOD, NOT IN ABUNDANCE

Even in the midst of surplus and wealth, we sometimes experience profound insecurity. Listen to God's words to you . . .

GOD'S PROMISE

MATTHEW 6:34, ESV • *Do not be anxious about tomorrow, for tomorrow will be anxious for itself. Sufficient for the day is its own trouble.*

1 TIMOTHY 6:17, NIV • *Command those who are rich in this present world not to be arrogant nor to put their hope in wealth, which is so uncertain, but to put their hope in God, who richly provides us with everything for our enjoyment.*

1 CHRONICLES 29:12-13, MSG • *Riches and glory come from you, you're ruler over all; you hold strength and power in the palm of your hand to build up and strengthen all. And here we are, O God, our God, giving thanks to you, praising your splendid Name.*

PRAY GOD'S PROMISE

Lord God, I thank you for the abundant material blessings you've given me. But even though I have so much, I find myself walking tentatively through life, fearful and insecure about so many things. I come to you, Lord, with an open heart. Speak to me about what's going on. ❧ I know that my possessions and financial standing are temporary. I don't really put my trust in them. But I also think I've failed to trust you as fully as I should. ❧ Lord, help me put my hope in you. *Let me claim your promise that you will richly provide for my real needs—those that are unseen but far more important.* Thank you that as I do so, my insecurities will fade away.

Consider how you might use some of your resources to help someone else. See how partnering with God in his Kingdom work takes away your insecurity.

INSECURITY · POWER IN WEAKNESS

Sometimes our insecurity is actually a virtue that makes us more receptive to God's blessings. Open your heart and mind to words of encouragement from your heavenly Father . . .

GOD'S PROMISE

JOHN 12:25, NIV · *Anyone who loves their life will lose it, while anyone who hates their life in this world will keep it for eternal life.*

MATTHEW 5:3-4, MSG · *You're blessed when you're at the end of your rope. With less of you there is more of God and his rule. You're blessed when you feel you've lost what is most dear to you. Only then can you be embraced by the One most dear to you.*

2 CORINTHIANS 12:9 · *Each time he said,* **"My grace is all you need. My power works best in weakness."** *So now I am glad to boast about my weaknesses, so that the power of Christ can work through me.*

PRAY GOD'S PROMISE

Lord Jesus, I come to you with a deep sense of my need for you. I've been struggling with some general insecurities. I want to trust you. Please shine your light into this darkness I'm experiencing. ⚜ I understand your instructions to let go of things in this life, and most of all that we're not to hold on to life itself. I pray for your guidance in releasing whatever I might be clinging to too tightly. ⚜ Jesus, *I want to claim your promise that your grace is all I need.*

I believe that. I ask for your power to work through me in my weakness and need. Thank you, Jesus.

Think of your insecurity as a special blessing from God. In the midst of your need, he can shine through. Talk to him in these next moments about how he might do just that.

JEALOUSY · FINDING EVERYTHING YOU WANT IN GOD

As you wrestle with jealousy in your life, confess the matter to God and let him free you from its bondage . . .

GOD'S PROMISE

1 CORINTHIANS 3:3 • *You are jealous of one another and quarrel with each other. Doesn't that prove you are controlled by your sinful nature?*

ACTS 8:22-23 • *Repent of your wickedness and pray to the Lord. Perhaps he will forgive your evil thoughts, for I can see that you are full of bitter jealousy and are held captive by sin.*

JOHN 6:35, ESV • ***Jesus said to them, "I am the bread of life; whoever comes to me shall not hunger, and whoever believes in me shall never thirst."***

PRAY GOD'S PROMISE

Lord God, I come to you right now in confession. You know my heart. You know the jealousy I harbor deep inside. It's consuming me, and it's not good. It's not right. ❧ Whatever I might try to call it, using other words and names, I know it is jealousy, and jealousy is a sin. Forgive me, Lord. Take this vice away. ⚜ I receive these words, both as a promise and as correction, that *you are the bread of life and a spring that will always satisfy my thirsty soul*. There is nothing else I need. There is nothing that others possess that I must have. Help me embrace this truth, Lord. Help me overcome the sin of jealousy in my life.

Tell God the specific things you are jealous about. Let him speak of his love for you. Ask for his help to stop comparing yourself to others.

———————— ◈ ————————

JEALOUSY · LETTING GO OF SELF

Come to God and talk with him about your desire to get ahead. Let him speak to you. Open your heart and mind to his truth . . .

GOD'S PROMISE

JAMES 3:14-16, ESV · *If you have bitter jealousy and selfish ambition in your hearts, do not boast and be false to the truth. This is not the wisdom that comes down from above, but is earthly, unspiritual, demonic.*

JAMES 3:16, ESV · *Where jealousy and selfish ambition exist, there will be disorder and every vile practice.*

JAMES 3:17-18, ESV · *But the wisdom from above is first pure, then peaceable, gentle, open to reason, full of mercy and good fruits, impartial and sincere. And a harvest of righteousness is sown in peace by those who make peace.*

PRAY GOD'S PROMISE

Lord God, I'm aware that my passion to get ahead has started to take over my life. I sometimes think that I'm just wired this way, that I'm a born overachiever. But I know that in my ambition, I am simply desiring more of what others have—more possessions, money, and status to promote my own prestige and self-importance. ⸭ Forgive me, Lord, for I know that this is not pleasing to you. ⸭ Lord, help me embrace your promise. *I want to manifest those characteristics of selflessness—mercy, gentleness, purity, open-mindedness, sincerity, impartiality, and peace.* I want to be freed from my relentless pursuit of getting ahead. I long for your blessing as I seek to obey.

Think about those people you may have hurt in your efforts to get ahead. Ask God how you might make amends with them.

———————— ⟡ ————————

JUDGING ANOTHER • FINDING GOD'S GRACE IN A NEGATIVE RELATIONSHIP

You've developed strong negative feelings toward someone. You fault them for certain things. Perhaps you were wronged by them, but this has grown beyond that into something deeper and darker. Prayerfully bring to God your feelings against this other person . . .

GOD'S PROMISE

1 JOHN 2:11, ESV • *Whoever hates his brother is in the darkness and walks in the darkness, and does not know where he is going.*

MATTHEW 7:1-3, ESV • *Judge not, that you be not judged. For with the judgment you pronounce you will be judged, and with the measure you use it will be measured to you. Why do you see the speck that is in your brother's eye, but do not notice the log that is in your own eye?*

1 JOHN 3:16, 18-20, NIV • *This is how we know what love is: Jesus Christ laid down his life for us. And we ought to lay down our lives for our brothers and sisters. . . . Dear children,* **let us not love with words or speech but with actions and in truth. This is how we know that we belong to the truth and how we set our hearts at rest in his presence:** *If our hearts condemn us, we know that God is greater than our hearts, and he knows everything.*

PRAY GOD'S PROMISE

Lord God, I have dark feelings toward someone I believe has wronged me and others. My heart has become filled with animosity toward this person. ❧ I don't know what to do, Lord. I hear what you have to say about judging others, and I also know what this can do to me on the inside. I don't want these feelings. And yet it's difficult to get beyond what I feel. ❧ But I know your will in this, Lord. *And I receive your instructions that my actions need to demonstrate sincere love for this person, and that by doing so I will set my heart at peace in your presence.* Thank you, Lord, for this truth.

Talk with God about your feelings toward this person, and listen to his counsel regarding tangible ways in which you can show love.

LACKING GENEROSITY · DISCOVERING
A LIFESTYLE OF GIVING

God's model for money management is based on generosity and helping those in need. Enter God's presence and listen to his words for you . . .

GOD'S PROMISE

LUKE 12:33-34 · *Sell your possessions and give to those in need. This will store up treasure for you in heaven! And the purses of heaven never get old or develop holes. Your treasure will be safe; no thief can steal it and no moth can destroy it. Wherever your treasure is, there the desires of your heart will also be.*

PROVERBS 11:24, ESV · *One gives freely, yet grows all the richer; another withholds what he should give, and only suffers want.*

PROVERBS 19:17, ESV · **Whoever is generous to the poor lends to the LORD, and he will repay him for his deed.**

PRAY GOD'S PROMISE

Lord God, I confess that I have been reluctant to give away much, perhaps because I am concerned about having enough for myself. I keep thinking that I will be more generous someday—when my earnings increase and I have sufficient margin for myself. And yet even as my income has gone up, I still don't seem to have much more margin. ‖ I know I need to rethink this, Lord. Help me to learn your wise financial principles and apply them to my life. ‖ Your promises assure me that you will provide for me when I reach out to help others. *I want to embrace that promise, Lord, and give more of what I have. And in doing this, I will trust you to provide for me.*

Besides giving away some of your own financial blessings, there are other ways of being generous. Think of those who live near you. What needs do they have? How can you offer provision for those needs?

LACKING MONEY TO GIVE

• DISCOVERING THE GREATNESS OF LITTLE

To God, who has everything, what matters most is not *how much* we give. Enter into God's space right now and listen to his words about what he truly values . . .

GOD'S PROMISE

2 CORINTHIANS 8:3-5, ESV • *They gave according to their means, as I can testify, and beyond their means, of their own accord, begging us earnestly for the favor of taking part in the relief of the saints—and this, not as we expected, but they gave themselves first to the Lord and then by the will of God to us.*

MARK 12:42-44, ESV • *A poor widow came and put in two small copper coins, which make a penny. And he called his disciples to him and said to them, "Truly, I say to you, this poor widow has put in more than all those who are contributing to the offering box. For they all contributed out of their abundance, but she out of her poverty has put in everything she had, all she had to live on."*

DEUTERONOMY 16:17, ESV • *Every man shall give as he is able, according to the blessing of the LORD your God that he has given you.*

PRAY GOD'S PROMISE

Father, I pray right now for wisdom about financial matters. I sometimes think that what little I have doesn't mean much in your economy. What I give can't compare to others' gifts. ❧ I ask for your help and guidance in this matter as I seek to budget for the future. ❧ *Father, I think I understand your promise that we are to give according to the blessing you have provided.* And you have blessed me greatly. I want to give what I can because I am grateful for the blessings you've already given me. Though it may not look like much to outsiders, it is a small reflection of how wonderfully you have provided.

As you plan your finances for the period ahead, listen for God's leading in the matter of giving.

———————— ❖ ————————

LACKING PROVISION • GOD'S PROMISES FOR CHALLENGING TIMES

At this point, your worry is not only about finding a job, but also about making ends meet after a period of unemployment. Come to God with your concerns and worries . . .

GOD'S PROMISE

PSALM 13:2-3, ESV • *How long, O LORD? Will you forget me forever? How long will you hide your face from me? How long must I take counsel in my soul and have sorrow in my heart all the day? How long shall my enemy be exalted over me? Consider and answer me, O LORD my God.*

PSALM 105:4-5, NIV • *Look to the LORD and his strength; seek his face always. Remember the wonders he has done, his miracles, and the judgments he pronounced.*

1 CORINTHIANS 10:13, MSG • *No test or temptation that comes your way is beyond the course of what others have had to face. All you need to remember is that* **God will never let you down; he'll never let you be pushed past your limit; he'll always be there to help you come through it.**

PRAY GOD'S PROMISE

Lord God, I am losing hope. It's been quite a while now that I've been without a job. It seems there are no new opportunities out there. I had hoped something would open up by now, but you haven't yet provided it. I'm worrying, Lord. ❧ Still, this verse about all that you have done encourages me. I don't doubt the miracles you've done and can do. I just want to know that somehow something good will happen in my life. ❧ *I embrace your promise that no test will be more than I can handle, with your help.* And, Lord, again I pray for a job opportunity. I trust that you will be here for me as I continue to go through this. Thank you, Lord.

Spend some time recounting for God the amazing things that he has done in your life. Do you believe he'll do so again?

LACKING USEFULNESS · DISCOVERING NEW

PURPOSE AND WORTH

There are times in life when circumstances conspire to make us feel useless. We question if we have anything of value to offer anyone. Discover what God has to say about how valuable you really are to him and others . . .

GOD'S PROMISE

PSALM 71:9 · *Don't set me aside. Don't abandon me when my strength is failing.*

ISAIAH 40:30-31, ESV · *Even youths shall faint and be weary, and young men shall fall exhausted; but they who wait for the LORD shall renew their strength; they shall mount up with wings like eagles; they shall run and not be weary; they shall walk and not faint.*

PSALM 92:12-14 · *The godly will flourish like palm trees and grow strong like the cedars of Lebanon. For they are transplanted to the LORD's own house. They flourish in the courts of our God. Even in old age* ***they will still produce fruit; they will remain vital and green.***

PRAY GOD'S PROMISE

Oh Lord, I come to you in these moments of feeling completely useless. Because of recent events, I feel set aside and put on the shelf. I struggle to know what I can do to be valuable again. I pray for you to come alongside me and comfort me, Lord. ⚘ I am encouraged by your words of possibility—that in waiting for your direction and leading, my strength can be renewed. And most of all, I thrill to think about how I will be transplanted to your own house. ❦ So, Lord, I do claim your promise here, right now, *that I will still produce fruit, and that I will remain vital in some new situation or opportunity.* I believe that this can be true again, and I look to you for your next purpose for me.

Continue in prayer and ask God to point out to you some ways you may currently be more valuable to others than you think you are. Who will you encounter today that you can bless?

———————— ❖ ————————

LONELINESS · GOD IS LISTENING TO YOU

Sometimes our loneliness is due to the distance we feel after drifting away from God. In spite of this, his arms are open to you. Come to him, talk to him. He will hear you . . .

GOD'S PROMISE

PROVERBS 18:24, NIV · *One who has unreliable friends soon comes to ruin, but there is a friend who sticks closer than a brother.*

PSALM 34:18 · *The LORD is close to the brokenhearted; he rescues those whose spirits are crushed.*

PSALM 5:3, NIV · *In the morning, LORD, you hear my voice; in the morning I lay my requests before you and wait expectantly.*

PRAY GOD'S PROMISE

Dear God, I acknowledge I've kept my distance from you for quite a while. I'm afraid I've been too busy to carve out time to spend together. Forgive me, I pray. ❧ I know you are my friend—a friend who is even more devoted to me than my closest relative. I regret that I haven't been a good friend back. ❧ God, I want for us to have a better relationship. I want your presence in my life every day. *I claim your promise that you will rescue me from this brokenhearted loneliness. Help me commit time to you in the morning, when I know you will hear my voice.*

God wants to nurture his relationship with you, but first you must provide him with the opportunity to do so. Think of him as a friend who cares deeply for you and looks forward to spending quality time together.

LONELINESS • GOD IS THERE WHEN OTHERS AREN'T

You are not alone . . . there are times in every person's life when it seems that very few friends or relatives live close by. Reach out to God during this lonely time. Let him come close to you . . .

GOD'S PROMISE

PSALM 25:16, ESV • *Turn to me and be gracious to me, for I am lonely and afflicted.*

DEUTERONOMY 31:6, ESV • *It is the LORD your God who goes with you. He will not leave you or forsake you.*

1 PETER 5:7, NIV • *Cast all your anxiety on him because **he cares for you**.*

PRAY GOD'S PROMISE

Lord, I am in a life stage where I have no friends or family who are nearby. I face some limitations and can't connect with others as easily as I used to. I feel very alone. I pray for your help. ⚜ The emptiness is deep, Lord—and harsh. Please draw near to me in my isolation. ⚜ *Lord, I eagerly claim your promises that you go with me, that you will not leave me, and that you care for me.* I will try to cast my anxiety and worries at your feet. I pray that you would soothe my empty ache.

In these next moments, pray for God to bring someone new into your life. Let his presence fill the lonely void you're feeling.

LONELINESS · THE NEARNESS OF GOD

Everyone feels alone at some point in life. But don't give in to despair. Invite God into your loneliness. His presence is not a false comfort—it's a real thing. Let him speak to you right now . . .

GOD'S PROMISE

PSALM 102:7, ESV · *I lie awake; I am like a lonely sparrow on the housetop.*

ISAIAH 41:10 · *Don't be afraid, for I am with you. Don't be discouraged, for I am your God. I will strengthen you and help you.*

JEREMIAH 29:11, NIV · *"I know the plans I have for you,"* declares the LORD, *"plans to prosper you and not to harm you, plans to give you hope and a future."*

PRAY GOD'S PROMISE

Lord God, I suddenly find myself feeling very alone in my everyday life. Maybe this is simply a transition period—the beginning of a new adventure—but in this moment I still feel empty and alone. I'm asking for the comfort of your abiding presence. ❦ These Scripture verses remind me that you are indeed with me. I confess that too often I run ahead, forgetting to make time for you. Help me come to you in prayer every day, Lord. ❦ *I embrace this promise that you have plans for me.* How amazing that is, Lord! And I pray that as these plans unfold, I will continue to look for you by my side. I cannot travel this journey alone.

Schedule specific times to meet with God each day this week. Continue to pray for his tangible presence in your life, day by day.

———————————— ⬦ ————————————

LOSS OF A JOB · GOD'S PROVISION IN TRYING CIRCUMSTANCES

After the sudden news that you've been let go from your job, bring your hurt and frustration to God in a time of prayer. Let God's words reassure you . . .

GOD'S PROMISE

GENESIS 50:20, NIV · *You intended to harm me, but God intended it for good to accomplish what is now being done.*

PSALM 128:1-2, NIV · *Blessed are all who fear the LORD, who walk in obedience to him. You will eat the fruit of your labor; blessings and prosperity will be yours.*

PSALM 50:15, NIV · *Call on me in the day of trouble; I will deliver you, and you will honor me.*

PRAY GOD'S PROMISE

Lord God, I didn't expect this. It's a shock. I'm reeling from the news of it. I'm in anguish from the hurt of it. Oh Lord, I need your help desperately. ❦ I don't know what I will do or where I will go. But I do trust that you have your purpose in this, Lord. You intend this for good in my life. I may not see that now, but I trust you and your plan. ❦ *I embrace your promise that as I call upon you in this day of personal trouble, you will deliver me.* Thank you. I trust you in this circumstance. I will honor you and stay close to you. Help me, Lord.

Think about the ways in which this development might have good out-comes. Express these possibilities to God, and listen as he speaks to you in response.

———————— ❖ ————————

LOSS OF SOMEONE CLOSE

• GOD'S COMFORT IN MOURNING

In this time of deep loss, come into God's presence and pour out your heart to him. First, listen to his words for you . . .

GOD'S PROMISE

ISAIAH 3:26, ESV • *Her gates shall lament and mourn; empty, she shall sit on the ground.*

REVELATION 1:18 • *I am the living one. I died, but look—I am alive forever and ever! And I hold the keys of death and the grave.*

PSALM 34:18, NIV • *The* LORD *is close to the brokenhearted and saves those who are crushed in spirit.*

PRAY GOD'S PROMISE

Lord God, I'm having a difficult time making sense of what's happened. Someone close to me is now gone. ❧ It has crushed me, Lord—partly because I cannot understand it. I don't know your purpose in it and ask for you to show me the meaning behind this tragic event. ❧ Lord, I pray for you to come close to me . . . soothe my soul and ease my aching heart. I ask for clarity of mind. *And Lord, help me embrace your promise that you will draw near and save me from a deeper depression.* Thank you that you've heard my prayer for wisdom and comfort. I trust that as you grant me understanding and perspective, I will have some measure of peace.

Let your tears flow as you open up the floodgates of your heart. Let God minister to your deep hurt.

———————————— <❖> ————————————

LUST • OVERCOMING THE LURES OF THE WORLD

Quiet your heart, mind, and body. Come to God for a time of confessing your sin and listening to his words . . .

GOD'S PROMISE

MATTHEW 5:28 • *But I say, anyone who even looks at a woman with lust has already committed adultery with her in his heart.*

1 JOHN 2:16, ESV • *All that is in the world—the desires of the flesh and the desires of the eyes and pride of life—is not from the Father but is from the world.*

PSALM 119:9-10, MSG • *How can a young person live a clean life? By carefully reading the map of your Word. I'm single-minded in pursuit of you; don't let me miss the road signs you've posted.*

PRAY GOD'S PROMISE

Lord God, I come to you asking that you would forgive the sin of lust in my life and grant me strength in overcoming temptation in the days to come. ❧ The lure of sexuality is everywhere, and I can hardly avoid it. But I confess that sometimes I don't *try* to avoid it. Have mercy on me, Lord. ❧ In moments of temptation, please let me be mindful of how temporal and superficial these lust lures are. *And Lord, thank you for this promise that gives me hope—by focusing on your Word, I can avoid the sins of my flesh.*

Develop a simple prayer of just a few words that you can memorize and repeat when you find yourself being tempted.

LUST · REFOCUSING ON THE HOLINESS OF GOD

Come into God's presence for a quiet time of conversation with him about the sexual struggles you've been facing . . .

GOD'S PROMISE

1 THESSALONIANS 4:3-5 • *God's will is for you to be holy, so stay away from all sexual sin. Then each of you will control his own body and live in holiness and honor—not in lustful passion like the pagans who do not know God and his ways.*

1 THESSALONIANS 4:7-8 • *God has called us to live holy lives, not impure lives. Therefore, anyone who refuses to live by these rules is not disobeying human teaching but is rejecting God, who gives his Holy Spirit to you.*

PHILIPPIANS 4:8-9, ESV • *Finally, brothers, whatever is true, whatever is honorable, whatever is just, whatever is pure, whatever is lovely, whatever is commendable, if there is any excellence, if there is anything worthy of praise, think about these things.* **What you have learned and received and heard and seen in me—practice these things, and the God of peace will be with you.**

PRAY GOD'S PROMISE

Lord God, I pray for deliverance from the sin of lust. Lately it seems to have taken over my life. I find it difficult to say no when I'm tempted. I need your help. ⸙ Lord, I understand that succumbing to lust is not only a sin against you but also against my own body. I want to be free of this, Lord. ⸙ I know the struggle to resist will continue, but I ask you to walk with me through it. *And I will cling to your promise that as I focus on you and all that is pure and true, your peace will be upon me.*

Talk with God about the specific temptations you face. Listen for his wisdom to help you overcome them.

—————— ‹◊› ——————

LYING · CHANGING A LIFESTYLE OF DECEPTION

Often, we are blind to the ways in which we convey deception to ourselves and others. Consider what you have said and done in recent weeks. Have you been fully and completely truthful? Prepare yourself to be brutally honest with God about yourself in these next moments. Open yourself to his words . . .

GOD'S PROMISE

PROVERBS 12:22-23 · *The LORD detests lying lips, but he delights in those who tell the truth. The wise don't make a show of their knowledge, but fools broadcast their foolishness.*

LUKE 8:17 · *For all that is secret will eventually be brought into the open, and everything that is concealed will be brought to light and made known to all.*

JOHN 8:32 · **You will know the truth, and the truth will set you free.**

PRAY GOD'S PROMISE

Father God, I confess to you in these moments that I have not been truthful in my life about things I have done. I have been deceiving others about some things and lying openly about other things. ✤ My secrets and lies plague me with anxiety as I fret about being discovered. And I know very well that eventually they will become known. I understand that you know all things—especially the deceit of my heart. Forgive me, Father. ✤ I come before you wanting to change my life. I want to eliminate lying and deceit from my lifestyle. *I want to claim your promise that the truth will set me free.*

In the next minutes think about the one untruth in your life that is the most significant in scope or degree. How will you come clean about that and start to rebuild your life in the freedom of God's truth?

--- ❖ ---

LYING · DISCLOSING THE SECRETS OF YOUR HEART

As you approach God today, prepare your heart to confess the lies that you've been harboring. Exchange them for his truth . . .

GOD'S PROMISE

PSALM 44:21, ESV · *Would not God discover this? For he knows the secrets of the heart.*

EPHESIANS 4:25-26 · *Stop telling lies. Let us tell our neighbors the truth, for we are all parts of the same body.*

EPHESIANS 4:15-16 · *We will speak the truth in love, growing in every way more and more like Christ,* who is the head of his body, the church. He makes the whole body fit together perfectly. As each part does its own special work, it helps the other parts grow, so that the whole body is healthy and growing and full of love.

PRAY GOD'S PROMISE

Lord God, I come to you in these moments to acknowledge that I have not been truthful in my life with others or with you. I know this is wrong, but often I just feel I can make things work out in a better way if I tell a lie or deceive someone. I think it's just a "little thing" in those situations, but I know it's really much bigger. And it's wrong. ✚ Lord, I also realize that there is nothing I can hide from you. You know the truth, and you know the secrets of my heart. ✚ *I receive the promise here that as I start to live truthfully, with love, I will become more and more like you.* I realize that if I submit myself to your control and direction, you will make my relationships and other aspects of my life work together in greater harmony.

In the next few minutes, think about those you have lied to and wronged. How is God telling you to remedy those wrongs?

———————————— ‹◇› ————————————

MARRIAGE CONFLICT · HELP FOR HUSBANDS AND WIVES

Conflict in marriage is natural, but sometimes it creates distance between a husband and wife. Come to God at this point when you feel alienated in your marriage. Allow him time and space in your heart to speak to you . . .

GOD'S PROMISE

GENESIS 2:23-24 • *This one is bone from my bone, and flesh from my flesh! She will be called "woman," because she was taken from "man." This explains why a man leaves his father and mother and is joined to his wife, and the two are united into one.*

1 CORINTHIANS 11:11 • *Among the Lord's people, women are not independent of men, and men are not independent of women.*

1 CORINTHIANS 13:4-7 • *Love is patient and kind. Love is not jealous or boastful or proud or rude. It does not demand its own way. It is not irritable, and it keeps no record of being wronged. It does not rejoice about injustice but rejoices whenever the truth wins out. Love never gives up, never loses faith, is always hopeful, and endures through every circumstance.*

PRAY GOD'S PROMISE

I come to you, Lord, twisting and turning inside because I feel more conflict than ever in my marriage. Little things have led to an emotional distance, a spiritual vacuum. I pray for your help. ❧ I read your words about your design for marriage, and they are reminders that whatever I am experiencing now, I need to see this bigger picture. I know you have a plan and a purpose for us both, together. ❧ Implicit in these words from you is the truth that love is not about receiving but about giving. *I claim your promise that in endeavoring to love one another sacrificially, we can endure through this rough time.* I pray that soon we will both experience the joy of a healed marriage.

Unburden your heart before God about all those little things that add up and cause strife. Let him share his wisdom with you about how to handle each one.

———————————— ‹◇› ————————————

MARRIAGE ROLES · LEARNING THE
PARTNERSHIP OF MARRIAGE

You're dealing with a power struggle in your marriage. Come before God during this time of stretching. Share with him your concerns. Listen to his words of comfort and counsel . . .

GOD'S PROMISE

1 CORINTHIANS 11:11, MSG · *Neither man nor woman can go it alone or claim priority.*

EPHESIANS 5:33 · *I say, each man must love his wife as he loves himself, and the wife must respect her husband.*

1 PETER 3:8-9, MSG · *Be agreeable, be sympathetic, be loving, be compassionate, be humble. That goes for all of you, no exceptions. No retaliation. No sharp-tongued sarcasm. Instead, bless—that's your job, to bless. You'll be a blessing and also get a blessing.*

PRAY GOD'S PROMISE

Lord, I come to you at a point of conflict in my marriage. Lately we've been at odds regarding so many things. I need your help. ❦ It seems we're each trying to take the lead, to exert authority, to make decisions on our own. I hear your words about how we need to work together. Help me become a more helpful partner. ❦ *And Lord, these verses point out to me how my attitudes and behaviors in my marriage need to change. Thank you for your promise that as I'm obedient, I will be a blessing to my spouse and to others.* Help me, Lord, to shape and live my life according to these commands.

Talk with God further about the blessings these verses speak of. Bring your spouse into this conversation with God.

MARRIAGE STRUGGLES · THE POWER OF GIVE-AND-TAKE

The relationship between a husband and wife is not automatic. It takes work and sacrifice. And at times, the process of making a marriage work is overwhelming. Listen to God's words at a time when you're struggling in your marriage . . .

GOD'S PROMISE

GENESIS 2:18, MSG · *GOD said, "It's not good for the Man to be alone; I'll make him a helper, a companion."*

HEBREWS 13:4 · *Give honor to marriage, and remain faithful to one another in marriage. God will surely judge people who are immoral and those who commit adultery.*

1 CORINTHIANS 13:4-7, MSG · *Love never gives up. Love cares more for others than for self. Love doesn't want what it doesn't have. Love doesn't strut, doesn't have a swelled head, doesn't force itself on others, isn't always "me first," doesn't fly off the handle, doesn't keep score of the sins of others, doesn't revel when others grovel, takes pleasure in the flowering of truth, puts up with anything, trusts God always, always looks for the best, never looks back, but keeps going to the end.*

PRAY GOD'S PROMISE

Father, I come to you at a time when my spouse and I

are struggling in our marriage. I know there are things I can do differently, and maybe better. But sometimes it seems like too much work. Forgive me, Father, but this is a struggle for me. ⚜ I embrace your design for my marriage, and I believe you have a plan and a purpose for us as a couple. Help us as we walk forward through life together. ⚜ *Father, I want to take to heart these words about love—that true love is focused on giving rather than taking.* I know I'm guilty of some of the selfish behaviors that love is *not*. I pray for help and strength to pursue a more giving love in my marriage. Thank you, Father.

Talk to God about each phrase from 1 Corinthians 13:4-7. Be open and honest with him about your struggles with giving love. Receive his forgiveness, mercy, and strength to grow in this area.

MENTAL ILLNESS · GOD'S PRESENCE IN TIMES OF CONFUSION

Perhaps someone you know, someone close to you, is facing mental troubles. Maybe you yourself are struggling. Whether a temporary confusion of muddled thoughts or a more serious mental condition, God's whisper can be heard through the noise in a way no other voice can . . .

GOD'S PROMISE

ISAIAH 43:1 • *Listen to the LORD who created you. O Israel, the one who formed you says, "Do not be afraid, for I have ransomed you. I have called you by name; you are mine."*

ROMANS 12:2, NIV • *Do not conform to the pattern of this world, but be transformed by the renewing of your mind. Then you will be able to test and approve what God's will is—his good, pleasing and perfect will.*

ISAIAH 43:2 • **When you go through deep waters, I will be with you.** *When you go through rivers of difficulty, you will not drown. When you walk through the fire of oppression, you will not be burned up; the flames will not consume you.*

PRAY GOD'S PROMISE

Father God, I hear your voice calling me by name. You formed me, created me, and love me as your child. You say you have ransomed me, and by your voice, I can be free. ❦ You know that I sometimes struggle with confusion. I feel overwhelmed by everyone around me. At times I feel as if I'm drowning. But you promise to deliver me. ❦ Right in this very moment, I look to you for deliverance, strength, and protection. *I claim your promise that as I go through deep waters, you will be with me.*

In these moments, let God's whisper be the only thing you hear. Allow him to speak directly into your thoughts. Let his words calm your troubled mind and reassure your heart.

———————————— ❖ ————————————

NATURAL DISASTERS • THE PROMISE OF
PEACE FROM THE GOD OF CREATION

Nature is often beautiful and majestic, but at other times frightening. As conditions threaten you now, come to God in a time of prayer for his assurance and protection . . .

GOD'S PROMISE

PROVERBS 30:5 • *Every word of God proves true. He is a shield to all who come to him for protection.*

PSALM 46:1-3, MSG • *God is a safe place to hide, ready to help when we need him. We stand fearless at the cliff-edge of doom, courageous in seastorm and earthquake, before the rush and roar of oceans, the tremors that shift mountains.*

JOHN 16:33, NIV • *I have told you these things, so that in me you may have peace. In this world you will have trouble. But take heart! I have overcome the world.*

PRAY GOD'S PROMISE

Lord God, we are facing something significant that poses possible physical dangers and even threatens our home. Please come close to us right now. We ask for your deliverance. 🍃 Help us to trust in you. Help us find refuge in you. We ask you to shield us from these impending natural forces. 🍃 *And we claim this promise of your peace. Help us to embrace your peace, Lord, and tuck it deep inside our hearts.* We know that your power is greater than anything. We ask for you to keep us safe, Lord.

Sing hymns of praise aloud to God. Pause between each one and listen for his voice speaking to you.

NEED FOR CLOTHING • GOD WILL PROVIDE

God will provide. Come and tell him what you and your family need. When we rely on God, we experience his presence and greatness in astonishing ways . . .

GOD'S PROMISE

PROVERBS 27:25-27, NIV • *When the hay is removed and new growth appears and the grass from the hills is gathered in, the lambs will provide you with clothing.*

MATTHEW 6:28-30 • *Why worry about your clothing? Look at the lilies of the field and how they grow. They don't work or make their clothing, yet Solomon in all his glory was not dressed as beautifully as they are. **And if God cares so wonderfully for wildflowers that are here today and thrown into the fire tomorrow, he will certainly care for you.***

PSALM 30:11-12 • *You have turned my mourning into joyful dancing. You have taken away my clothes of mourning and clothed me with joy, that I might sing praises to you and not be silent. O LORD my God, I will give you thanks forever!*

PRAY GOD'S PROMISE

Lord God, I pray to you because my family and I have been struggling. We've had to decide between meeting one basic need or another. And as a result, we are in need of clothing. ❧ I pray to you, Lord, for your help. Thank you that your Word declares a time of renewal—a new spring for us—and with it there will be hefty provision. I will look for that expectantly. ❧ *But for now, Lord, I want to claim your promise that you will certainly care for us and provide for our immediate clothing needs.* I trust you to be faithful, Lord. Thank you.

Allow God to help you through other people. Have you spoken to them about your need? Let God speak to you about this right now . . .

———————— ‹•› ————————

NEED FOR FOOD · LEANING ON THE GOD OF ABUNDANT PROVISION

If you're literally struggling to make ends meet, come to God and ask him to meet your need. He is the Bread of Life in more ways than one . . .

GOD'S PROMISE

PSALM 132:15, NIV · *I will bless her with abundant provisions; her poor I will satisfy with food.*

LUKE 9:16-17 · *Jesus took the five loaves and two fish, looked up toward heaven, and blessed them. Then, breaking the loaves into pieces, he kept giving the bread and fish to the disciples so they could distribute it to the people. They all ate as much as they wanted, and afterward, the disciples picked up twelve baskets of leftovers!*

MATTHEW 4:4 · *People do not live by bread alone, but by every word that comes from the mouth of God.*

PRAY GOD'S PROMISE

Lord Jesus, I am facing such tough times financially. I worry about having enough to feed my family. I ask you for provision, a miracle to provide what we need to eat and live. ⚜ Your words remind me that when you were on earth, you not only helped people spiritually but also physically. You took a little portion of food and, after giving thanks, transformed it into enough to feed thousands of people. ❦ Jesus, I believe that you can do the miraculous for my family as well. *I claim your promise that you will bless us with your abundance and you will satisfy us with food.* Thank you, Lord.

Even in this time of scarcity, look around to see how you might help someone else. God works through his people, blessing them through each other.

———————— ‹•› ————————

NEED FOR GOD · CONFESSING GOD AS LORD

Perhaps your attempt at doing life alone has failed. Maybe you've come to a sense of your need for God. In these next moments, enter into God's presence. Confess to him that he is the Almighty Lord over all of Creation, and now the Lord of your life . . .

GOD'S PROMISE

ACTS 17:30-31 · *God overlooked people's ignorance about these things in earlier times, but now he commands everyone everywhere to repent of their sins and turn to him. For he has set a day for judging the world with justice by the man he has appointed, and he proved to everyone who this is by raising him from the dead.*

ROMANS 10:9, ESV · *If you confess with your mouth that Jesus is Lord and believe in your heart that God raised him from the dead, you will be saved.*

ROMANS 10:10 · *It is by believing in your heart that you are made right with God, and it is by openly declaring your faith that you are saved.*

PRAY GOD'S PROMISE

God, I come before you with a deep sense of my unworthiness and my sin. Not only sins I commit, but also my whole sinful nature. I know you have sent your Son to pay for my sins. Now the ball is in my court. I need to claim your forgiveness. ⚜ God, I want to be made right with you. I want to live in obedience to you. I pray for that now. ⚜ *I claim your promise that if I confess with my mouth that your Son, Jesus, is Lord and believe that you raised him from the dead, I will be saved.* I do believe, and Jesus is now Lord of my life. Thank you, God. Thank you, Jesus.

As you go through your day and through this coming week, come to God in prayer frequently. Thank him for saving you. Start to read his Word on a regular basis.

NEED FOR HEALING · THE SAVING TOUCH OF JESUS

In the midst of illness, we are reminded of Jesus and the many he healed during his time on earth. Take a moment to focus your mind and heart on God. Ask him for his healing touch in these next minutes . . .

GOD'S PROMISE

LUKE 7:6-7 · *Just before they arrived at the house, the officer sent some friends to say, "Lord, don't trouble yourself by coming to my home, for I am not worthy of such an honor. I am not even worthy to come and meet you. Just say the word from where you are, and my servant will be healed."*

LUKE 7:9-10 • *When Jesus heard this, he was amazed. Turning to the crowd that was following him, he said, "I tell you, I haven't seen faith like this in all Israel!" And when the officer's friends returned to his house, they found the slave completely healed.*

JAMES 5:15, ESV • **The prayer of faith will save the one who is sick, and the Lord will raise him up.**

PRAY GOD'S PROMISE

Jesus—Son of God and my healer—thank you for this account of a man who had faith and believed you could heal people. Because of his faith, you healed his servant. Through this example from the Bible, I hear you saying to me that healing and faith go hand in hand. ⚜ And so I come to you today with my own need for healing. And Jesus, I believe. I believe you are God. I believe you can heal people of all kinds of sicknesses. I believe you can heal *me*. ⚜ In this moment, with this prayer of faith, *I claim your promise to save this one who is sick*. I pray for your healing touch, Jesus.

Quietly whisper to Jesus each of your aches, pains, hurts, and symptoms of sickness. Let his words of healing wash over you.

———————— ⟨⋄⟩ ————————

NEEDING HELP • GOD'S DELIVERANCE IN TIME OF NEED

Overwhelmed by needs on so many fronts, you can ease your mind by entering into God's presence with an expectant heart . . .

GOD'S PROMISE

PSALM 22:11, ESV • *Be not far from me, for trouble is near, and there is none to help.*

ISAIAH 41:10, ESV • *Fear not, for I am with you; be not dismayed, for I am your God; I will strengthen you, I will help you, I will uphold you with my righteous right hand.*

PSALM 72:12, NIV • **He will deliver the needy who cry out, the afflicted who have no one to help.**

PRAY GOD'S PROMISE

Lord, I feel so down because there are so many ways in which I need help. Work, money, health. I'm really facing it right now. ✻ I need your hand of strength. I need your helping presence in my life. I need you, Lord, to just walk alongside me. ✻ *You say that you will deliver those who cry out. Well, Lord, I am crying out. And I will hold your promise close to my heart.* I am the afflicted, Lord, and I look to you for my help and salvation.

Right now, just take some quiet time with God. Let him speak to your heart and soothe your soul.

—◇—

NEEDING HELP • GOD'S RESCUE WHEN LIFE IS TOO MUCH

Let go of your needs and worries, and open your heart as you prepare to spend this time with God. Listen for his voice . . .

GOD'S PROMISE

JOHN 14:1, NIV • *Do not let your hearts be troubled. You believe in God; believe also in me.*

PSALM 54:4, ESV • *God is my helper; the Lord is the upholder of my life.*

PSALM 34:17-18 • *The* LORD *hears his people when they call to him for help. He rescues them from all their troubles.* **The** LORD **is close to the brokenhearted; he rescues those whose spirits are crushed.**

PRAY GOD'S PROMISE

Lord, I have so many needs and so many worries. I come to you overwhelmed by my life. I am struggling to keep going, not knowing where help will come from. ❦ I ask you to provide those things that I need but do not yet have. I pray you will be with me through this, Lord. ❦ Thank you for your promise that you hear my prayers. *And for the promise that you will rescue me, as I am truly crushed by life.* I will trust you for provision. Thank you.

Tell God about your most immediate needs, one by one. Pray about each. Watch for God to work in your life in coming days.

———————————— ❖ ————————————

OBSESSION WITH A SIN • FINDING LIGHT AFTER DARKNESS

That's it—you're done with it. Ready to be finished with what's controlling you. Now quiet your mind and heart and body. Allow yourself to focus on Jesus. Seek his peace . . .

GOD'S PROMISE

1 JOHN 1:5-6, NIV • *This is the message we have heard from him and declare to you: God is light; in him there is no darkness at all. If we claim to have fellowship with him and yet walk in the darkness, we lie and do not live by the truth.*

1 PETER 4:1-2 • *If you have suffered physically for Christ, you have finished with sin. You won't spend the rest of your lives chasing your own desires, but you will be anxious to do the will of God.*

JOHN 16:33 • *I have told you all this so that you may have peace in me. Here on earth you will have many trials and sorrows. But take heart, because I have overcome the world.*

PRAY GOD'S PROMISE

Jesus, I hear your words about light and darkness, and I confess to you what you already know—so much of my life is lived in deep darkness. I cannot escape it. Please shine your light on my life. ❧ I encounter this verse about being finished with sin and no longer chasing my own desires—and I find myself wanting that, Lord. I really want that. Help me to be finished with sin. ❧ I long for the peace you speak of. *I claim your promise that even through my trials and sorrows, I can have that peace.* I know you have overcome the world. Help me to overcome mine. Jesus, I pray, give me that peace.

Talk to God specifically about your struggles; ask him to be the power you rely on to overcome them.

———————— ❖ ————————

OPPOSITION · GOD IS AT YOUR SIDE IN BATTLE

When others stand in your way, it can feel overwhelming. Call out to God, and let him come to your rescue . . .

GOD'S PROMISE

2 CHRONICLES 14:11, NIV · *LORD, there is no one like you to help the powerless against the mighty. Help us, LORD our God, for we rely on you.*

DEUTERONOMY 20:1 · *When you go out to fight your enemies and you face horses and chariots and an army greater than your own, do not be afraid. The LORD your God . . . is with you!*

EXODUS 14:13-14, ESV · *Fear not, stand firm, and see the salvation of the LORD, which he will work for you today. . . . **The LORD will fight for you, and you have only to be silent.***

PRAY GOD'S PROMISE

Father God, I come to you in prayer facing big opposition—people who want to undermine me and hurt me. They stand over me, are more powerful, and are quite capable of derailing my life in significant ways. ⁂ I pray to you for deliverance, strength, and support for this battle ahead. ⁂ *I claim your promise that you will fight for me.* Help me not to be afraid.

As the verse instructs, be silent right now. Allow God to equip your mind and heart for the conflict ahead.

OPPRESSION · STRENGTH IN THE MIDST OF PERSECUTION

As you feel surrounded by people who are persecuting you for your faith, sit for a few minutes in the presence of God and listen to his words . . .

GOD'S PROMISE

PSALM 88:17, NIV • *All day long they surround me like a flood; they have completely engulfed me.*

PSALM 23:5, ESV • *You prepare a table before me in the presence of my enemies; you anoint my head with oil; my cup overflows.*

MATTHEW 5:11-12, NIV • ***Blessed are you when people insult you, persecute you and falsely say all kinds of evil against you because of me. Rejoice and be glad, because great is your reward in heaven,*** *for in the same way they persecuted the prophets who were before you.*

PRAY GOD'S PROMISE

Jesus, I am being ridiculed for my faith. I'm made fun of and in various ways insulted. It is much to bear. It wears me down. I need your help and strength, Lord. ❦ I thank you for your reassurances and for this picture of dining with you in the midst of my enemies. I need that feeling of peace and calmness as I deal with this. ❦ And Lord Jesus, *I claim your blessing of a reward in heaven for standing strong against my persecutors*. I ask for your wisdom and power as I endure this for your glory. Amen.

Know that your persecutors are not the only ones watching what takes place. There may be others who are bolstered by seeing the courage that results from your faith.

———————— ◇ ————————

OPPRESSION · GOD'S POWER IN THE FACE OF OPPOSITION

You're in a terrible place of being opposed and oppressed by others. Come into God's presence to find healing and peace for your weary soul . . .

GOD'S PROMISE

PSALM 9:9, ESV · *The LORD is a stronghold for the oppressed, a stronghold in times of trouble.*

PSALM 10:17-18, ESV · *O LORD, you hear the desire of the afflicted; you will strengthen their heart; you will incline your ear to do justice to the fatherless and the oppressed, so that man who is of the earth may strike terror no more.*

ROMANS 8:31-34 · *If God is for us, who can ever be against us? Since he did not spare even his own Son but gave him up for us all, won't he also give us everything else? Who dares accuse us whom God has chosen for his own? No one—for God himself has given us right standing with himself. Who then will condemn us?*

PRAY GOD'S PROMISE

Father, you know I have been facing opposition and oppression at the hands of others. I come to you with deep wounds from what's been said and done to me. I need your help. ♪ I pray for your healing touch, Father. Strengthen my body and encourage my heart. ♪ In spite of this trial I'm facing, I know that you're on my side, Father. *I claim your promise that you will give me what I need throughout this difficult time. I embrace the fact that since you are for me, no one can stand against me!* Thank you for choosing me to be an overcomer through your Son, Jesus.

Talk with God specifically about the situation you face. Allow him to speak to you and provide wise counsel about what you can do to overcome this situation.

PAST HURTS · GOD'S HEALING OF PAST WOUNDS

Come to God prepared to pour out to him the pains you feel from your past. Listen to him whisper to you . . .

GOD'S PROMISE

ROMANS 9:2, NIV · *I have great sorrow and unceasing anguish in my heart.*

PSALM 119:82, MSG · *My eyes grow heavy watching for some sign of your promise; how long must I wait for your comfort?*

REVELATION 21:4, NIV · *He will wipe every tear from their eyes. There will be no more death or mourning or crying or pain.*

PRAY GOD'S PROMISE

Lord God, I continue hurting from things that happened a while ago, which have left me with deep personal anguish. And my inner turmoil keeps multiplying. I don't know how to deal with this, Lord. I need your help. ❧ The pain has lasted for a long time, Lord. I pray that you would give me some relief. Most of all, I need your soothing touch upon my life. ❧ *Lord, I claim your promise that you will wipe away every tear from my eyes. I pray for no more crying or pain.* Be with me, Lord, in some special way, and relieve these burdens on my heart.

Tell God specifically of your past hurts, where they come from, and how they affect you today.

PEOPLE CONFLICTS · TURNING FRUSTRATION INTO FORGIVENESS

Set aside your agitation and anger about recent things that have taken place. Put a hold on thoughts you're having about those who've hurt you. Declare a truce in your mind and heart as you come to God in these moments, open to receive what he has for you . . .

GOD'S PROMISE

PSALM 71:10-11 · *My enemies are whispering against me. They are plotting together to kill me. They say, "God has abandoned him."*

ROMANS 8:31-34 · *If God is for us, who can ever be against us? Since he did not spare even his own Son but gave him up for us all, won't he also give us everything else? Who dares accuse us whom God has chosen for his own? No one—for God himself has given us right standing with himself. Who then will condemn us? No one—for Christ Jesus died for us and was raised to life for us, and he is sitting in the place of honor at God's right hand, pleading for us.*

PSALM 23:5 • *You prepare a feast for me in the presence of my enemies. You honor me by anointing my head with oil. My cup overflows with blessings.*

PRAY GOD'S PROMISE

Father, I face some people who seem to get in the way of the work I have to do. My life these days is just filled with people conflicts. I don't claim that everything I do is wonderful—it's certainly not perfect—but it can be demoralizing to have this person, then that person, interfering. ⚘ I need to take in the words you've given me here: that if you are for me, who can be against me? Father, I know I need to trust that since I am yours, no one can condemn me. ⚘ My heart is comforted to hear that familiar verse as a promise. And *I embrace this promise right now as well: that you will prepare a feast for me in the presence of my enemies.* Yes, Father, thank you for your love, your presence, and your protection.

Take the extra step right now to pray for those people, one by one, who are against you.

PERFECTIONISM · BEAUTY IN DROPPING THE POSE

Come to God and confess the way perfectionism has grabbed hold of your life. Listen to him speaking to you . . .

GOD'S PROMISE

2 CORINTHIANS 12:9 · *He said, "My grace is all you need. My power works best in weakness." So now I am glad to boast about my weaknesses, so that the power of Christ can work through me.*

2 CORINTHIANS 11:30 · *If I must boast, I would rather boast about the things that show how weak I am.*

PHILIPPIANS 1:6 · *I am certain that God, who began the good work within you, will continue his work until it is finally finished on the day when Christ Jesus returns.*

PRAY GOD'S PROMISE

Lord God, I confess to you this problem I have with trying to appear perfect in front of others. I know I am far from perfect, and yet I try to make others think I am. In fact, Lord, a lot of things in my life are quite a mess. ✣ I think I'm afraid of what others would think if they knew the real me. Help me to let down my pose, Lord; help me to have the courage to allow others access to my heart and life. ✣ I pray that in my weakness and imperfection you will work through me. *I claim your promise that you will continue perfecting this imperfect soul until your work in me is finished.*

Select some problem or imperfection in your life and share it with another person. Pray right now that God will help you find the right time to confess your imperfection to this person.

————————— ⟨•⟩ —————————

PERFECTIONISM · FOCUSING ON WHAT REALLY MATTERS

The familiar story of Mary and Martha is a lesson about perfectionism. Come into God's presence and allow him to speak to your heart . . .

GOD'S PROMISE

LUKE 10:38-39 • *As Jesus and the disciples continued on their way to Jerusalem, they came to a certain village where a woman named Martha welcomed him into her home. Her sister, Mary, sat at the Lord's feet, listening to what he taught.*

LUKE 10:40 • *But Martha was distracted by the big dinner she was preparing. She came to Jesus and said, "Lord, doesn't it seem unfair to you that my sister just sits here while I do all the work? Tell her to come and help me."*

LUKE 10:41-42 • *But the Lord said to her, "My dear Martha, you are worried and upset over all these details!* **There is only one thing worth being concerned about. Mary has discovered it, and it will not be taken away from her."**

PRAY GOD'S PROMISE

Lord Jesus, I come to you with an understanding that I have a problem with perfectionism. I know that it causes others to feel alienated (so I've been told!), but I'm beginning to understand that it's a hindrance in my spiritual life as well. Help me, I pray. ⚜ I readily identify with this story about Martha trying to create the perfect dinner. How many times have I been in that same situation? And yet it was Mary who knelt at your feet. ⚜ Lord, I want to let go of my perfectionism. I want to refocus my life on you, as Mary did. *Thank you that I, too, am discovering that following you is the most important priority in life. And I claim your promise that the peace that comes from being in your presence will not be taken away from me.*

Talk with God about the major items on your agenda this next week. Ask him to help you let go of obsessing about the details and be content in what he has for you instead.

PERSECUTION · GOD'S COMFORT FOR YOUR SUFFERING

You're living in a difficult situation, and you're paying a price for your faith. You have survived yet more hardship, so let God's healing comfort attend to your wounds . . .

GOD'S PROMISE

2 CORINTHIANS 4:8-10 · *We are pressed on every side by troubles, but we are not crushed. We are perplexed, but not driven to despair. We are hunted down, but never abandoned by God. We get knocked down, but we are not destroyed. Through suffering, our bodies continue to share*

in the death of Jesus so that the life of Jesus may also be seen in our bodies.

1 PETER 4:16, ESV • *If anyone suffers as a Christian, let him not be ashamed, but let him glorify God in that name.*

PSALM 23:4, ESV • ***Even though I walk through the valley of the shadow of death, I will fear no evil, for you are with me; your rod and your staff, they comfort me.***

PRAY GOD'S PROMISE

Lord, I have gone through rounds of persecution for your name's sake, and I am facing more and more. I do not waver in the face of this, but it is rough and tough. I need your help. ✠ I continue to be proud to call myself a Christian, even if others attack me for that. I continue to overcome these assaults by the grace of your presence, Lord. ✠ I come to these familiar words of Scripture, and they soothe my soul. *I claim the promise of those words, that as I continue through this valley, I will not be afraid, for your presence is with me, and your rod and staff will comfort me.* Yes, they comfort me, Lord. Thank you for the love and life I have in you.

In the silence of these moments, let God speak to you, his good and faithful disciple.

———————— ❖ ————————

PERSECUTION · WE ARE MORE THAN CONQUERORS

You find yourself in the midst of people who challenge you, ridicule you, and maybe even threaten you because of your faith. In these difficult times, listen to God's words . . .

GOD'S PROMISE

2 TIMOTHY 3:12-13 • *Everyone who wants to live a godly life in Christ Jesus will suffer persecution. . . . Evil people and impostors will flourish. They will deceive others and will themselves be deceived.*

MATTHEW 5:10, MSG • *You're blessed when your commitment to God provokes persecution. The persecution drives you even deeper into God's kingdom.*

ROMANS 8:35, 37, NIV • *Who shall separate us from the love of Christ? Shall trouble or hardship or persecution or famine or nakedness or danger or sword? . . . No, in all these things we are more than conquerors through him who loved us.*

PRAY GOD'S PROMISE

Lord Jesus, I'm in a difficult place, surrounded by people who want to hurt me for being a follower of you. Without question, I am your defender, but right now I am weary and beaten down. ❧ I know the truth of your Word—that persecution drives me deeper into your Kingdom. That has been so true, and I am grateful. But Lord, I need your assurance and comfort. ❧ *Thank you for the promise that nothing can separate me from your love, Jesus, and that in all things, ultimately, I am a conqueror because of your love.* Help me to hold these thoughts in my heart, Lord. Thank you, Jesus.

Take a few moments to memorize these key verses from Romans. Keep them in your heart as God's promise to you in coming days.

PERSEVERANCE · HELP COMES FROM THE LORD

It's been such a long journey, and you feel yourself faltering along the road. Let God refresh and revive you . . .

GOD'S PROMISE

JOHN 14:1, NIV · *Do not let your hearts be troubled. You believe in God; believe also in me.*

HEBREWS 10:39, MSG · *We're not quitters who lose out. Oh, no! We'll stay with it and survive, trusting all the way.*

PSALM 121:2-3 · *My help comes from the LORD, who made heaven and earth! He will not let you stumble; the one who watches over you will not slumber.*

PRAY GOD'S PROMISE

Lord God, I have persevered for so long on so little, and I am tired and exhausted. I have great needs, financially and physically, and I've tried to make this all work. But it's been so difficult. And this has been a long haul. ⚜ I need your help, Lord. I need your strength and power. I ask for your help, right now in these moments, so that I don't just give up. ⚜ *I claim the promise that you won't let me stumble, that you will watch over me, and that you will be my help.* Lord, thank you. Through all of this, I know I have you.

Let God speak to your heart and soul about his coming provision for you. Expect him to come through. He'll be there. Trust him.

———————————— ❖ ————————————

PERSONAL TRAGEDY · COMFORT IN GOD'S JUSTICE

Allow God to speak to you during this difficult time of personal anguish. Prepare your heart and mind to receive his words . . .

GOD'S PROMISE

PSALM 126:6 · *They weep as they go to plant their seed, but they sing as they return with the harvest.*

ROMANS 12:19, ESV · *Beloved, never avenge yourselves, but leave it to the wrath of God, for it is written, "Vengeance is mine, I will repay, says the Lord."*

ISAIAH 61:1-2, NIV · *He has sent me to bind up the brokenhearted, to proclaim freedom for the captives and release from darkness for the prisoners, to proclaim the year of the LORD's favor and the day of vengeance of our God, to comfort all who mourn.*

PRAY GOD'S PROMISE

Lord, there's so much to say, and yet I have no words to say it. What has happened is very difficult and has hurt me deeply. I'm angry that I've been dealt such an unfair hand. ❧ I pray to you, Lord, for your comfort and peace. I need your presence to help me deal with this indignation that I fear could even become rage. ❧ *Lord, I need your help to claim this promise that my weeping will turn into singing. I ask for your comfort at this time.* I accept that we will continue to experience injustice, but let me trust in your vengeance and your justice, not my own.

Let yourself sit with God in these moments of silence. Allow him to speak into your life, assuage your deep hurt, and ease your anger.

———————————— ‹◇› ————————————

PHYSICAL DECLINE · HOPE DURING THE PROCESS OF AGING

It's difficult in a culture that values mobility and activity to accept the gradual process of physical decline our bodies go through as we age. But God tells us age can bring a deeper and more developed inner life with him, one of renewed wisdom. Quiet your heart. Listen to God in these next moments . . .

GOD'S PROMISE

PSALM 90:12 · *Teach us to realize the brevity of life, so that we may grow in wisdom.*

2 CORINTHIANS 4:16, ESV · *We do not lose heart.* **Though our outer self is wasting away, our inner self is being renewed day by day.**

JOB 12:12-13 · *Wisdom belongs to the aged, and understanding to the old. But true wisdom and power are found in God; counsel and understanding are his.*

PRAY GOD'S PROMISE

Lord God, I pray to you today because I am feeling distressed about the ways my body is declining. It seems that every day there is yet another thing I cannot do as easily as before—or without pain. There are even some things I'm no longer able to do at all. I confess it's getting me down. ❧ Lord, I think about your words, that true wisdom and power are found in you. I want to access your understanding and counsel. ⚜ And Lord, you encourage me not to lose heart by promising that *even though my outer self is wasting away, my inner self is being renewed every day. I receive that promise from you.* Thank you, Lord, for deepening my experience of you.

Spend some additional time with God in prayer right now. Talk with him about one thing you could do that would deepen your wisdom and renew your heart.

PHYSICAL PAIN · GOD'S STRENGTH FOR
THE HURTING

God knows the pain you've gone through and are experiencing now. Come to him in these next moments and share with him your hurts while listening to his soothing voice . . .

GOD'S PROMISE

PSALM 56:8, MSG • *You've kept track of my every toss and turn through the sleepless nights, Each tear entered in your ledger, each ache written in your book.*

1 PETER 4:19, ESV • *Let those who suffer according to God's will entrust their souls to a faithful Creator while doing good.*

PHILIPPIANS 4:11-13, ESV • *I have learned in whatever situation I am to be content. I know how to be brought low, and I know how to abound. In any and every circumstance, I have learned the secret of facing plenty and* *hunger, abundance and need. **I can do all things through him who strengthens me.***

PRAY GOD'S PROMISE

Lord God, I'm really going through a lot right now. The pain I'm experiencing is significant. Besides the harshness of it physically, it's also so distracting—I can hardly do anything else with my life. I ask for your help. ‡ I want to know more about entrusting myself to you while doing good. Teach me, God. How do I do that? Help me to be productive through this experience. ‡ ***Above all, dear God, I believe in the promise that I can do all things through you, and I embrace the words that you will indeed strengthen me.*** Thank you, God. Make use of me during this time of stress and pain.

Allow God to minister to you personally in these quiet, private moments. Listen for his voice.

PHYSICAL PAIN · THE HOPE OF FUTURE RELIEF

Sometimes our physical aches and pains are almost more than what we can endure. Come into God's presence and pray for relief from your pain, but also let him talk with you about the pain-free life to come . . .

GOD'S PROMISE

JOB 30:16-17, MSG · *My life drains out, as suffering seizes and grips me hard. Night gnaws at my bones; the pain never lets up.*

ROMANS 8:18, ESV • *I consider that the sufferings of this present time are not worth comparing with the glory that is to be revealed to us.*

REVELATION 21:4, NIV • *He will wipe every tear from their eyes. There will be no more death or mourning or crying or pain, for the old order of things has passed away.*

PRAY GOD'S PROMISE

Lord God, I come to you after another long bout with a lot of physical agony. I despair because I fear this pain will always be with me. ❧ I pray, Lord, for your deliverance from this trial. Please give me some relief. ❧ But I also look to you as the conqueror of pain and death. *I claim your promise that you will wipe away every tear from my eyes.* I believe that you are bringing in a new reality, physically and spiritually, and I look forward with great expectation to the day when the pain will be gone and your glory will be revealed.

Allow God to come alongside you right now. Listen to his whispers.

PREJUDICE • FINDING FORGIVENESS FOR JUDGING

Has your walk with God been hindered because you have been harboring judgmental feelings toward those of a different race or ethnicity? Talk with him now about this problem and listen to his words . . .

GOD'S PROMISE

GALATIANS 3:28, MSG • *In Christ's family there can be no division into Jew and non-Jew, slave and free, male and* *female. Among us you are all equal. That is, we are all in a common relationship with Jesus Christ.*

JAMES 2:9 • *If you favor some people over others, you are committing a sin. You are guilty of breaking the law.*

EPHESIANS 4:32 • **Be kind to each other, tenderhearted, forgiving one another, just as God through Christ has forgiven you.**

PRAY GOD'S PROMISE

God, I am realizing that I have been wrongly judging others; specifically, I am guilty of prejudice toward people of other ethnic groups and races. I know this attitude likely originated from certain experiences I've had and, to some degree, from how I was raised. But these words from Scripture make me painfully aware that my judgmental words and actions are sinful. ⚜ I ask for forgiveness, God. I really don't want to be like this. ⚜ I understand your teaching that in Christ we are one body, where each part is not greater or lesser than the other. *And I embrace your promise of forgiveness as I learn to be kind and forgiving toward others.*

As you continue to talk with God, think of those you may have offended. Do you need to go to them personally to ask for forgiveness?

A PRIDEFUL HEART · LETTING GO OF SELF

Whether you label it as pride or the more modern term of narcissism, you've become aware of its harmful effect on your behavior and character. Come to God about this, and listen to his words for you . . .

GOD'S PROMISE

PROVERBS 30:12, NIV • *[There are] those who are pure in their own eyes and yet are not cleansed of their filth.*

2 TIMOTHY 3:2, 5, NIV • *People will be lovers of themselves . . . having a form of godliness but denying its power.*

MATTHEW 5:5, MSG • *You're blessed when you're content with just who you are—no more, no less. That's the moment you find yourselves proud owners of everything that can't be bought.*

PRAY GOD'S PROMISE

Lord, I confess I have been guilty of prideful thoughts and behavior. For some reason, I've wanted to convince myself that I'm better than others around me, and I'm afraid I've even taken this stance in public settings. ❧ Forgive me, Lord, for I know this is displeasing to you. ❧ These words from the Bible help me understand that I need to be content with who you've made me to be. *And I will claim your promise that by letting go of my self-importance, I will discover my true place as your very own child, which is the most valuable identity I could ever ask for.* I'm amazed, Lord, by your goodness to me!

In further moments of stillness with God, confess some specific thoughts and actions that were prideful. Turn each one over to him. Let God reassure you of your true value in his Kingdom.

———————— ❖ ————————

A PRIDEFUL HEART · SUBMITTING TO GOD'S RENOVATION OF YOU

Perhaps because of what someone has said, you are coming to God at this time regarding the problem of pride in your life. Focus your heart and mind, and open yourself to what God has to say to you . . .

GOD'S PROMISE

PROVERBS 29:23 · *Pride ends in humiliation, while humility brings honor.*

ROMANS 12:3-6, NIV · *Do not think of yourself more highly than you ought, but rather think of yourself with sober judgment, in accordance with the faith God has distributed to each of you. For just as each of us has one body with many members, and these members do not all have the same function, so in Christ we, though many, form one body, and each member belongs to all the others. We have different gifts, according to the grace given to each of us.*

JAMES 4:6-8, ESV · *He gives more grace. Therefore it says, "God opposes the proud, but gives grace to the humble." Submit yourselves therefore to God. Resist the devil, and he will flee from you. Draw near to God, and he will draw near to you.*

PRAY GOD'S PROMISE

Lord, I know that the way I've been living my life hasn't been up to your standards. I'm aware especially of the problem of pride in my heart. I confess that I have often compared myself to others and convinced myself of my superiority over them. ❦ And Lord, this has played out in both my actions and speech. I know it has at times hurt others. Please forgive me, Lord. Help me to eliminate this problem of pride from my life. ❦ I ask for you to work in me. I ask for your grace. *I claim your promise that as I submit to this renovation of my heart, you will draw near to me.* I realize my value is nothing apart from you, Lord.

Talk with God about specific people you may have hurt by allowing pride and conceit to creep into your heart. What counsel is he giving you for how to make amends?

PRIORITIES · FIXING YOUR EYES UPON GOD

Enter God's presence and listen for his words of instruction about your focus and priorities . . .

GOD'S PROMISE

EXODUS 20:3 · *You must not have any other god but me.*

PROVERBS 21:21, MSG · *Whoever goes hunting for what is right and kind finds life itself—glorious life!*

ROMANS 12:2, MSG · *Don't become so well-adjusted to your culture that you fit into it without even thinking. **Instead, fix your attention on God. You'll be changed from the inside out.** Readily recognize what he wants from you, and quickly respond to it. Unlike the culture around you, always dragging you down to its level of immaturity, God brings the best out of you, develops well-formed maturity in you.*

PRAY GOD'S PROMISE

Father God, I am fully aware that I have gotten side-tracked from my pursuit of you. Instead of seeking you, I have become preoccupied with the surrounding culture. The world around me is so glittery and fast paced . . . I just get caught up in the thrill of it all. ⚜ I'm sorry, Father, that my selfishness has displaced your rightful place in my life. Your words here say that *you* should be the only God in my life. Forgive me for getting so distracted. ⚜ I pray for your help in readjusting my priorities. *I claim your promise that as I fix my attention on you, your Spirit will transform me from the inside out.* Bring out the best in me, Father.

What areas of your life need to change so that you can refocus your priorities? Talk with God about how you can make him first.

PRIORITIES · RETURNING TO THE PATH OF LIFE

As you examine your heart regarding your current life priorities, listen to God's words . . .

GOD'S PROMISE

LUKE 12:34, MSG · *It's obvious, isn't it? The place where your treasure is, is the place you will most want to be, and end up being.*

MARK 8:36-37 · *What do you benefit if you gain the whole world but lose your own soul? Is anything worth more than your soul?*

PSALM 16:8-11, ESV • *I have set the LORD always before me; because he is at my right hand, I shall not be shaken. Therefore my heart is glad, and my whole being rejoices; my flesh also dwells secure. For you will not abandon my soul to Sheol, or let your holy one see corruption.* **You make known to me the path of life; in your presence there is fullness of joy; at your right hand are pleasures forevermore.**

PRAY GOD'S PROMISE

Lord, I am troubled by my preoccupation with some things in my life that while not wrong, are also not focused on you. I'm asking for your insight into this problem because I want to live a life that honors you, praises you, and is all *about* you. ❧ And yet, Lord, so many other things rush in and seem to hijack my priorities. ❧ Help me find ways to make sure you are always at the center of what I do. Help me to follow you on this journey. *I embrace your promise that as I do so, you will guide me down a path that overflows with pleasures and the gladness that comes from being in your presence.* Thank you, Lord!

Tarry in God's presence as he helps you refocus your life toward him.

———————————— ❖ ————————————

PROBLEM PEOPLE • GRACE IN DEALING WITH
A DIFFICULT PERSON

Come, talk to God about this person who is getting the best of you. Share with him your frustration and listen to his words . . .

GOD'S PROMISE

GALATIANS 6:7-8, MSG • *What a person plants, he will harvest. The person who plants selfishness, ignoring the needs of others—ignoring God!—harvests a crop of weeds.*

1 CORINTHIANS 13:4-5, NIV • *Love is patient, love is kind. It does not envy, it does not boast, it is not proud. It does not dishonor others, it is not self-seeking, it is not easily angered, it keeps no record of wrongs.*

ROMANS 5:3-4, MSG • *We continue to shout our praise even when we're hemmed in with troubles, because we know how **troubles can develop passionate patience in us, and how that patience in turn forges the tempered steel of virtue,** keeping us alert for whatever God will do next.*

PRAY GOD'S PROMISE

Lord God, I find myself at odds with a person in my life who deeply frustrates me. I feel that this person is working and talking against me. It's difficult for me. I need your help, Lord. ⚜ I hear your words about love. And patience. Not being self-seeking. Keeping no record of wrongs. Do I need to address these things in my own heart? ⚜ Lord, your promise here is wrapped up in seeing this as an opportunity for growth. *I claim your words, Lord, that this situation can increase my patience and help me develop stronger character.* And I pray for your specific wisdom in dealing with this person.

Tell God about the specifics of your frustration. Consider how you might apply some aspects of 1 Corinthians 13 to this person and situation. Listen for God's voice during this time.

PROBLEMS WITH FRIENDS · MAKING
THINGS RIGHT AGAIN

As you wrestle with tensions and disappointments in a particular friendship, God has some thoughts for you . . .

GOD'S PROMISE

ROMANS 12:10, NIV · *Be devoted to one another in love.*
Honor one another above yourselves.

ROMANS 12:3, NIV · *Do not think of yourself more highly than you ought, but rather think of yourself with sober judgment, in accordance with the faith God has distributed to each of you.*

ROMANS 12:4-6, NIV · *As each of us has one body with many members, and these members do not all have the same function, so in Christ we, though many, form one body, and each member belongs to all the others.* ***We have different gifts, according to the grace given to each of us.***

PRAY GOD'S PROMISE

Lord God, I come to you right now with a heavy heart after a close friendship has soured. What was once such a good relationship has grown silent and cold. I am grieving this, Lord, and I ask for your help. ⸙ I hear your words. I know that a true friendship is a mutual, equal relationship. I'm sure we've both probably done some things that have been self-serving. ⸙ *I pray for an understanding of how each of us is valuable. Help me learn how to honor my friends above myself and to celebrate their unique gifts.* Thank you, Lord, for helping me to grow in this area.

Talk with God specifically about this friend. Review with him the things that happened. Let him speak to you about the best way to seek reconciliation.

———————— ‹◇› ————————

PROBLEMS WITH FRIENDS · MENDING
A BROKEN RELATIONSHIP

As you're dealing with a fraying friendship, talk with God about the problem that has come between the two of you. Listen to his words for you . . .

GOD'S PROMISE

1 JOHN 3:17, MSG • *If you see some brother or sister in need and have the means to do something about it but turn a cold shoulder and do nothing, what happens to God's love?*

PROVERBS 18:24, ESV • *A man of many companions may come to ruin, but there is a friend who sticks closer than a brother.*

EPHESIANS 4:29-32, NIV • **Do not let any unwholesome talk come out of your mouths, but only what is helpful for building others up according to their needs, that it may benefit those who listen. . . . Get rid of all bitterness, rage and anger, brawling and slander, along with every form of malice. Be kind and compassionate to one another, forgiving each other, just as in Christ God forgave you.**

PRAY GOD'S PROMISE

Father in heaven, I confess that there's much I need to learn about being a friend to someone else. This current friendship is falling apart, and I ache because of it. I come to you for wisdom and learning and help. ✦ Father, I think in some ways I've been "taking" a lot in this relationship and not "giving" enough. I've maybe even taken this friend for granted. Forgive me, Father. ✦ *Right now I claim this picture of friendship that is painted for me in your Word—I want this kind of friendship, one without bitterness and ill feelings, one that is compassionate and forgiving.* I realize I have to work at that, Father. Help me to build up my friend and mend this relationship.

Talk over with God some specific areas of this friendship you need to work on. Listen to his direction for you about mending fences.

RACISM · OVERCOMING PREJUDICE

Come before God prepared to confess to him how you have allowed the sin of racism to affect your actions toward others. Listen to God speaking to you . . .

GOD'S PROMISE

MATTHEW 7:1-2 · *Do not judge others, and you will not be judged. For you will be treated as you treat others. The standard you use in judging is the standard by which you will be judged.*

MATTHEW 7:3-5 · *Why worry about a speck in your friend's eye when you have a log in your own? How can you think of saying to your friend, 'Let me help you get rid of that speck in your eye,' when you can't see past the log in your own eye? Hypocrite! First get rid of the log in your own eye;*

then you will see well enough to deal with the speck in your friend's eye.

COLOSSIANS 3:12 • *Since God chose you to be the holy people he loves, you must clothe yourselves with tenderhearted mercy, kindness, humility, gentleness, and patience.*

PRAY GOD'S PROMISE

Lord God, I ask right now that you would forgive me for the sin of racism. It's become painfully clear that this offense lurks inside me. I ask not only for your forgiveness but also for your help in having a respectful attitude toward others with different ethnic origins than my own. ❧ And Lord, I am deeply affected by these words about judging others while being blind to my own shortcomings and sins. I am truly sorry, Lord. ❧ Help me to change. When I start to say something hurtful, even hateful, *remind me of your promise that I am also of a different race—a member of your very own chosen people. And as such, you expect me to show kindness to all.* Thank you, Lord, for such an honor and privilege.

As you continue to confess to God, listen to what he says to you. Ask to share his heart of love for people of all races.

A REBELLIOUS HEART · A RETURN TO
OBEDIENCE

When we have disobeyed God and later come face-to-face with
what we've done, we ache inside because we know that our actions
grieved God. Come into God's presence right now, and in these
next few moments, let him hear the distress of your heart. Confess
to him . . .

GOD'S PROMISE

LAMENTATIONS 1:20 · *LORD, see my anguish! My heart is
broken and my soul despairs, for I have rebelled against
you.*

PSALM 31:10 · *I am dying from grief; my years are shortened
by sadness. Sin has drained my strength; I am wasting away
from within.*

PSALM 32:1-2 · **Oh, what joy for those whose disobedience
is forgiven, whose sin is put out of sight! Yes, what joy
for those whose record the LORD has cleared of guilt, whose
lives are lived in complete honesty!**

PRAY GOD'S PROMISE

Lord God, I come before you with a heavy heart. I grieve
over what I have done. I know it was an act of disobedience
against you, and I know I did it willingly. And now I am
in despair. Oh, how I hurt inside over what I have done. ※
I don't want to continue living this way—in rebellion. I
don't want to keep feeling this soul ache. I am sorry for my
actions, for my disobedience. ※ **You promise to forgive, and
you say that you will put my sin out of sight. I claim that**

promise, Lord. I know you can and will turn my anguish into joy.

Continue in prayer time with God. Talk to him about your desire to obey him and come closer to him.

———————— ‹◆› ————————

A REBELLIOUS HEART · THE REWARDS
OF OBEYING GOD

God gives us a beautiful picture of what obedience to him can accomplish in our lives. Listen as Jesus tells a parable, and think about what it means for your life . . .

GOD'S PROMISE

LUKE 6:46, ESV · *Why do you call me "Lord, Lord," and not do what I tell you?*

LUKE 6:47-48, ESV · *Everyone who comes to me and hears my words and does them, I will show you what he is like: he is like a man building a house, who dug deep and laid the foundation on the rock. **And when a flood arose, the stream broke against that house and could not shake it, because it had been well built.***

LUKE 6:49, ESV · *But the one who hears and does not do them is like a man who built a house on the ground without a foundation. When the stream broke against it, immediately it fell, and the ruin of that house was great.*

PRAY GOD'S PROMISE

Lord Jesus, I come to you at a time when I've been feeling torn about some decisions I've made that steer my life in a particular direction opposite of what you would have me do. I pray for your guidance, Lord, even as I know what I should be doing. ❧ Lord, this picture of life based on doing your will versus a life that defies you shows me how my life could be better and stronger and more meaningful long-term. I want that, Lord. ❧ *And I claim the reward you promise to those who live a life of obedience—a house built on a deep foundation, upon you and your words . . . one that is solid and rooted and cannot be shaken.* Lord Jesus, I want that kind of life.

What does the house built upon a solid foundation look like for you? Talk with God about how you can build your life on his will.

REJECTION · CHOSEN BY GOD

Jesus himself experienced the pain of rejection that you are facing right now. Come to him and open your heart in his presence . . .

GOD'S PROMISE

HEBREWS 4:14-15 · *Since we have a great High Priest who has entered heaven, Jesus the Son of God, let us hold firmly to what we believe. This High Priest of ours understands our weaknesses, for he faced all of the same testings we do, yet he did not sin.*

1 THESSALONIANS 5:9, MSG · *God didn't set us up for an angry rejection but for salvation by our Master, Jesus Christ.*

1 PETER 2:9-10, MSG · *You are the ones chosen by God, chosen for the high calling of priestly work, chosen to*

be a holy people, God's instruments to do his work and speak out for him, to tell others of the night-and-day difference he made for you—from nothing to something, from rejected to accepted.

PRAY GOD'S PROMISE

Lord Jesus, I had such high hopes and wanted this so much, but instead I've been let go and rejected. Oh, this hurts so much, Lord. I am broken and crushed. ✦ Jesus, I know that you experienced the same thing—indeed so much more. I know you understand the hurt I feel. Thank you for standing with me. ✦ *I hold on to this promise that as one chosen by you, I am called to do your work and to tell others of what you've done for me.* That alone puts my heartache and so much else into perspective.

Continue opening up your heart to God. Let him speak to you as you release your tears to him.

—✦—

REJECTION · GOD'S PLEASURE IN YOU

As you wrestle with feeling cast aside, let God touch your heart . . .

GOD'S PROMISE

PSALM 27:10 · *Even if my father and mother abandon me, the LORD will hold me close.*

PSALM 147:3 · *He heals the brokenhearted and bandages their wounds.*

EPHESIANS 1:4-5 · *Even before he made the world, God loved us and chose us in Christ to be holy and without fault in his eyes. God decided in advance to adopt us into his own family by bringing us to himself through Jesus Christ. This is what he wanted to do, and it gave him great pleasure.*

PRAY GOD'S PROMISE

Lord God, I come to you brokenhearted and shattered. This rejection I just experienced severely undermines my sense of self. It hurts deeply. ᛬ Lord, comfort my heart. Please heal my wound. ᛬ *I want to embrace your words reminding me that you chose me, accepted me, and brought me into your family.* And I cherish the thought that choosing me brought you great pleasure. I pray that this reminder will help me overcome these difficult feelings and restore my sense of value. Thank you, Lord.

Just spend quiet time with God right now. Let your heart speak to him. Listen for his soothing words of acceptance.

———————————— ⟨⋄⟩ ————————————

RESENTMENT · FINDING RESOLUTION IN A DIFFICULT RELATIONSHIP

Come to God in these next private minutes and open up to him about the issues you have toward this other person. Listen for what God wants you to do . . .

GOD'S PROMISE

JOB 5:2 • *Surely resentment destroys the fool, and jealousy kills the simple.*

MARK 11:25 • *When you are praying, first forgive anyone you are holding a grudge against, so that your Father in heaven will forgive your sins, too.*

COLOSSIANS 3:13-15, NIV • *Bear with each other and forgive one another if any of you has a grievance against someone. Forgive as the Lord forgave you. And over all these virtues put on love, which binds them all together in perfect unity. Let the peace of Christ rule in your hearts, since as members of one body you were called to peace.*

PRAY GOD'S PROMISE

Lord God, I pray to you because I am well aware that this feeling of resentment is harmful to me and this other person. I want to be rid of it, and yet I can't help but feel wronged and bitter. Help me, Lord. ⚜ I hear your instruction to forgive this person, just as you forgave me. I will try to do that, but please give me your direction and counsel about how to go about it. ⚜ *And Lord, I claim your promise that by forgiving these grievances and putting on love, I will find the peace of Christ,* which right now is absent from my heart. I want that, Lord.

Ask God for his advice on how you should go about approaching this person and what you need to do to make things right.

———————————— ⟨⋄⟩ ————————————

RIDICULE • GOD IS ON YOUR SIDE

As a follower of Christ, you will likely come to a time when you are made fun of, threatened, and bullied for what you believe. Listen to God's words of encouragement . . .

GOD'S PROMISE

ZEPHANIAH 3:19 • *I will save the weak and helpless ones; I will bring together those who were chased away. I will give glory and fame to my former exiles, wherever they have been mocked and shamed.*

1 PETER 4:16 • *It is no shame to suffer for being a Christian. Praise God for the privilege of being called by his name.*

ISAIAH 50:7-9 • **Because the Sovereign LORD helps me, I will not be disgraced.** *Therefore, I have set my face like a stone, determined to do his will. And I know that I will not be put to shame. He who gives me justice is near. Who will dare to bring charges against me now? Where are my accusers? Let them appear!* **See, the Sovereign LORD is on my side!**

PRAY GOD'S PROMISE

Lord God, I am feeling hurt these days by what some people have said about me. It comes from their reactions to my faith in you. I know what I believe. Standing up for you is the right thing to do. And yet these words and actions leveled against me are sometimes deeply hurtful. ❦ I think part of my struggle is that I question if I have the fortitude to do this. I don't know if I have the inner strength to deal with ridicule, and I'm not sure how to handle being shamed day after day. ❦ I pray, Lord, for your strength. And I thank you for these encouraging words from the Bible. *I will embrace your promise that you, the Sovereign LORD, will help me . . . that I will not be disgraced . . . and that you, God, are on my side.*

Tell God about the specific incidents you have faced in recent days. Listen to his response and his affirming encouragement.

———————— ◆ ————————

SADNESS · FINDING GOD'S STRENGTH AND HOPE

Your heart is discouraged and your mind feels trapped in darkness. Trust that he hears you in this time of sorrow. Spend some time with God right now and offer to him the cares of your heart . . .

GOD'S PROMISE

PSALM 102:1-3, NIV • *Hear my prayer, LORD; let my cry for help come to you. Do not hide your face from me when I am in distress. Turn your ear to me; when I call, answer me quickly. For my days vanish like smoke; my bones burn like glowing embers.*

ISAIAH 41:10 • *Don't be afraid, for I am with you.* **Don't be discouraged, for I am your God. I will strengthen you and help you. I will hold you up with my victorious right hand.**

2 CORINTHIANS 1:6-7 • *Even when we are weighed down with troubles, it is for your comfort and salvation! For when we ourselves are comforted, we will certainly comfort you. Then you can patiently endure the same things we suffer. We are confident that as you share in our sufferings, you will also share in the comfort God gives us.*

PRAY GOD'S PROMISE

Dear God, I am in a dark place right now. I feel lost, sad, and deeply discouraged. ⸭ I ask that you would hear my prayer and lift me out of this abyss. I pray for your deliverance from this melancholy. ❧ God, I need your presence. Be close to me. *I hear your promise that you will strengthen me and help me.* I claim that promise. Please rescue me from this deep valley.

Let God speak into your heart in these next minutes. Let him be close to you. Receive his strength and encouragement.

———————————— ⟨⋄⟩ ————————————

SEEKING FORGIVENESS · RELIEF IN
CONFESSING TO GOD

Our sin not only grieves God and hurts others but also burdens our own hearts with guilt and worry. Whatever we have done, God is ready to receive us, listen to our confession, and forgive our sins. Come before him now and open your heart to him . . .

GOD'S PROMISE

JEREMIAH 36:7 · *Perhaps even yet they will turn from their evil ways and ask the LORD's forgiveness before it is too late. For the LORD has threatened them with his terrible anger.*

1 JOHN 1:8 · *If we claim we have no sin, we are only fooling ourselves and not living in the truth.*

1 JOHN 1:9-10 · *If we confess our sins to him, he is faithful and just to forgive us our sins and to cleanse us from all wickedness. If we claim we have not sinned, we are calling God a liar and showing that his word has no place in our hearts.*

PRAY GOD'S PROMISE

God, I'm coming to you now because I'm troubled by things I have done. ⚜ I know I have claimed before that I don't need to ask for forgiveness, but you are right—I have not been living in the truth. I have not lived as I should have. I have not treated others well. I have not listened to and obeyed you, God. ⚜ I pray that you would hear my prayer. Forgive me for my sins. Forgive me for the life I've been leading. Help me to turn things around and follow you. God, *I hold on to your promise that by confessing my sins to you here, you will forgive me.* Cleanse me from all my wickedness. Thank you, God.

Tell God specifically the sins you have committed. Allow him to speak to you about each one. Hear him whisper to you in these moments.

———————————— ◇ ————————————

SEEKING FORGIVENESS · THE POWER OF CONFESSING TO OTHERS

Let go of trying to be in control of your life. No longer conceal from others the wrongs you've committed against them. God wants you to be free. Open your mind to his words for you . . .

GOD'S PROMISE

PROVERBS 28:13 • *People who conceal their sins will not prosper, but if they confess and turn from them, they will receive mercy.*

EPHESIANS 4:2 • *Be patient with each other, making allowance for each other's faults because of your love.*

JAMES 5:16 • *Confess your sins to each other and pray for each other so that you may be healed. The earnest prayer of a righteous person has great power and produces wonderful results.*

PRAY GOD'S PROMISE

Lord God, I find it so difficult to apologize to others, and in this one particular situation, I find it nearly impossible. It's true that I have done this person wrong, but I've been wronged as well. It doesn't seem fair. ❧ Yet I know that failing to ask forgiveness is only hurting myself. Lord, I don't want to conceal my transgression from this person or from you. ❧ I know that harboring this thing is only eating away at me from within. Lord, help me to apologize. *Help me to confess my wrong. I receive your promise that in confessing my sins to another, I myself will be healed.*

In a deeper time with God, let him speak to you about what you should say to this other person, and how you should say it.

--- ❖ ---

SELFISHNESS · A LOVE THAT DOESN'T DEMAND ITS OWN WAY

Enter God's presence prepared to confess your self-centered behavior. Listen to his words to you about this . . .

GOD'S PROMISE

1 JOHN 3:17, MSG • *If you see some brother or sister in need and have the means to do something about it but turn a cold shoulder and do nothing, what happens to God's love?*

LUKE 14:11 • *Those who exalt themselves will be humbled, and those who humble themselves will be exalted.*

1 CORINTHIANS 13:4-7 • *Love is patient and kind. **Love is not jealous or boastful or proud or rude. It does not demand its own way.** It is not irritable, and it keeps no record of being wronged. It does not rejoice about injustice but rejoices whenever the truth wins out. Love never gives up, never loses faith, is always hopeful, and endures through every circumstance.*

PRAY GOD'S PROMISE

Lord God, I come to you with a problem and a confession. Lately I have become more and more self-absorbed and self-serving. I fail to think much about others or to even care about what's happening outside of my own world. I know this is sin, Lord, and I ask for your forgiveness. ⚜ Your words are reminders that I should be pursuing what I can do to encourage and provide for people around me. I want to change, Lord. ⚜ *Thank you for these Scriptures that cast vision for a life of true love. I embrace this picture of love that doesn't demand its own way.* Help me to make this vision a lifestyle.

In a deeper time with God, relate to him recent specific incidents when your behavior left someone feeling hurt or ignored. What is his response?

SELFISHNESS · DEVELOPING A SERVING HEART

You have recently become aware of some of your actions, how they serve you at the expense of others. Come into God's presence with a spirit of confession . . .

GOD'S PROMISE

GALATIANS 5:26, NIV • *Let us not become conceited, provoking and envying each other.*

2 TIMOTHY 3:2-5, ESV • *People will be lovers of self, lovers of money, proud, arrogant, abusive, disobedient to their parents, ungrateful, unholy, heartless, unappeasable, slanderous, without self-control, brutal, not loving good, treacherous, reckless, swollen with conceit, lovers of pleasure rather than lovers of God, having the appearance of godliness, but denying its power.*

PHILIPPIANS 2:1-4, NIV • ***If you have any encouragement from being united with Christ, if any comfort from his love, if any common sharing in the Spirit, if any tenderness and compassion,*** *then make my joy complete by being like-minded, having the same love, being one in spirit and of one mind. Do nothing out of selfish ambition or vain conceit. Rather, in humility value others above yourselves.*

PRAY GOD'S PROMISE

Lord, I'm feeling guilty about some of my recent behaviors. I have been seeking my own best interests, sometimes at the expense of others. Forgive me, Lord. ❦ This passage from the Bible describes how most people are filled with selfish ambition, and I don't want to be like them. ❦ ***Lord, I thank you for promising your love to me, along with the fellowship and fruit of the Holy Spirit.*** Since you have given me these gifts, I can and will overcome my selfish ambition. I want to put others first. Please help me develop a serving heart. Thank you, Lord.

Let God point out the needs around you. Talk with him right now about specific ways you can help. Start today.

———————————— ◈ ————————————

SERIOUS ILLNESS · CLAIMING THE HEALING POWER OF GOD

Quiet your heart. Set aside your fears. Bring yourself to God in this moment and let yourself fall into his arms of love and healing . . .

GOD'S PROMISE

PSALM 102:3-5, 11, MSG • *I'm wasting away to nothing, I'm burning up with fever. I'm a ghost of my former self, half-consumed already by terminal illness. . . . There's nothing left of me—a withered weed, swept clean from the path.*

PSALM 102:12, MSG • *Yet you, GOD, are sovereign still, always and ever sovereign.*

PSALM 102:15, 17, MSG • *The godless nations will sit up and take notice . . . when he attends to the prayer of the wretched. He won't dismiss their prayer.*

PRAY GOD'S PROMISE

Father in heaven, in this moment I hear these words that you are sovereign. ⚜ The entire universe bows before your supreme power; yet even in all of your greatness, you stoop to hear the prayer of those in deep need. ⚜ *Right now, Father, I claim your promise that you are attending to the prayer of this wretched one. Thank you that you won't dismiss my prayer.* I embrace your sovereignty over everything, including this terrible disease. I pray for healing, Father, but most of all, I thank you for being present with me in this difficult time.

As you talk with God, listen to him. Be silent for long enough to hear his voice. What is he saying to you?

---◇---

SEXUAL TEMPTATION · DEFEATING DEADLY DESIRES

Prepare your heart for meeting with God right now. Be honest with him about the temptations that plague you. Know that he loves you and wants what's best for you . . .

GOD'S PROMISE

GALATIANS 5:17, ESV · *The desires of the flesh are against the Spirit, and the desires of the Spirit are against the flesh, for these are opposed to each other, to keep you from doing the things you want to do.*

JAMES 1:14-15 · *Temptation comes from our own desires, which entice us and drag us away. These desires give birth to sinful actions. And when sin is allowed to grow, it gives birth to death.*

1 JOHN 2:16-17 · *The world offers only a craving for physical pleasure, a craving for everything we see, and pride in our achievements and possessions. These are not from the Father, but are from this world. And this world is fading away, along with everything that people crave. **But anyone who does what pleases God will live forever.***

PRAY GOD'S PROMISE

Lord Jesus, I confess to you today that I experience significant sexual temptations every day. I know that these things that tempt me are not pleasing to you—nor are they honoring to those they exploit, who are likewise your loved ones. I am trying to resist, but sometimes I am weak. ⚜ I understand your words about sexual temptation giving way to death—that it is hurtful to people's bodies and spirits. ⚜ In this moment, *I claim your promise that pleasing you is what matters most for gaining eternal life.* I ask for your strength as I live each day. I pray for a fresh focus on you as I live my life in this culture.

Spend some time telling God about the sexual temptations you encounter. Be specific. Let God's light shine over those temptations and reveal them for what they really are.

SHAME · DISCOVERING THE DEPTH OF GOD'S LOVE

Shame is a feeling of deep humiliation and unworthiness that can hinder your intimacy with God. Though these feelings are intense, don't give in to their lies. Come into God's presence right now and open your life to him. Let him embrace you and tell you that you are worthy . . .

GOD'S PROMISE

ISAIAH 1:18, ESV • *Though your sins are like scarlet, they shall be as white as snow.*

ISAIAH 61:7, ESV • *Instead of your shame there shall be a double portion; instead of dishonor they shall rejoice in their lot; therefore in their land they shall possess a double portion; they shall have everlasting joy.*

EPHESIANS 1:4-6, MSG • *Long before he laid down earth's foundations, he had us in mind, had settled on us as the focus of his love, to be made whole and holy by his love. Long, long ago he decided to adopt us into his family through Jesus Christ. (What pleasure he took in planning this!) He wanted us to enter into the celebration of his lavish gift-giving by the hand of his beloved Son.*

PRAY GOD'S PROMISE

Lord God, I am living under a great weight of shame. I am deeply aware of the extent of my sins. And even though I have confessed them, and I know you have forgiven me, I'm struggling with the humiliation of my past life. Please help me, Lord. ❧ I feel so unworthy of anything and anyone. I feel so far away from you, Lord. Please come close to me, even as undeserving as I am. ❧ You speak to me about my scarlet sins becoming as white as snow, about my shame being turned into a double portion of joy. I want that, Lord. *And I eagerly claim your promise that in spite of my sin and shame, your love for me exceeds anything I can imagine.* Oh Lord, thank you. With this hope I can forget what is behind and press on toward my high calling in you.

Understand that once God has forgiven your sins, you are restored to him. He doesn't see you as guilty any longer. Remaining in shame is simply allowing the enemy's lie to prevent you from experiencing God's lavish love.

A SICK CHILD · CHRIST'S LOVE FOR YOUR CHILD

In the next few minutes, unburden your heart before God, sharing with him how you ache for your child in this moment of sickness. Listen to the story about a young girl he healed . . .

GOD'S PROMISE

MARK 5:23 · *"My little daughter is dying," he said. "Please come and lay your hands on her; heal her so she can live."*

MARK 5:40-42 · *He took the girl's father and mother and his three disciples into the room where the girl was lying. Holding her hand, he said to her, "Talitha koum," which means "Little girl, get up!" And the girl, who was twelve years old, immediately stood up and walked around! They were overwhelmed and totally amazed.*

MARK 9:37 · *Whoever welcomes one of these little children in my name welcomes me; and whoever welcomes me does not welcome me but the one who sent me.*

PRAY GOD'S PROMISE

Lord Jesus, it is no accident that you have brought me to the account of this man and his daughter—how you not only brought her out of death but also completely healed her. My heart goes out to her father; I feel his desperation. ❧ Jesus, you know I hurt so deeply right now for my own child, but I believe that you can and will heal my child. ❧ *I claim your promise of healing right now, Jesus. Hold my child's hand. Relieve the pain and suffering, and please bring my child to recovery.* I pray these things in faith that you are indeed the God who heals.

As you pray for the healing of your own child, think of other children—of friends, loved ones, acquaintances—who may also need healing. Pray for Jesus to wrap his arms around them in a special way and for his healing touch to be at work in their lives as well.

---<◇>---

A SICK PARENT · GOD'S HEALING AND PRESENCE

In this difficult time of uncertainty, bring the concerns of your heart to God in prayer. Listen to his words of comfort . . .

GOD'S PROMISE

EPHESIANS 6:2-3, ESV · *"Honor your father and mother" (this is the first commandment with a promise), "that it may go well with you and that you may live long in the land."*

PSALM 41:3, ESV · *The LORD sustains him on his sickbed; in his illness you restore him to full health.*

JEREMIAH 30:17, MSG · *As for you, I'll come with healing, curing the incurable, because they all gave up on you and dismissed you as hopeless.*

PRAY GOD'S PROMISE

Lord God, I come to you with a heartfelt petition. I have been caring for my ailing parent for some time, and I need your encouragement. I know this disease is relentless, but I also know you are a great God. Please come to our side. ❦ I pray for myself as well, as this has been a trying time. The demands of bedside care have been substantial and difficult. I don't complain, for I would do nothing less than this, but I am weary, Lord. ❦ *I claim your promise that you will come with healing, even curing the incurable. I trust that your heart's desire is to bring us deliverance from this disease.* I also look to you for my own sustenance and strength in the days to come.

Let God see your tears of weariness and concern. Share your heart with him.

———————————— ⋅⟐⋅ ————————————

SICKNESS · HOW ILLNESS BRINGS US CLOSER TO GOD

Sometimes a time of illness can be a time-out from life. It provides a short season in which to focus on God. Despite your hurts and aches, right now quiet yourself. Enter into God's presence . . .

GOD'S PROMISE

PSALM 6:2-3 · *Have compassion on me, LORD, for I am weak. Heal me, LORD, for my bones are in agony. I am sick at heart. How long, O LORD, until you restore me?*

PSALM 41:10 · *LORD, have mercy on me. Make me well again.*

MATTHEW 13:15, NIV · *This people's heart has become calloused; they hardly hear with their ears, and they have closed their eyes. **Otherwise they might see with their eyes, hear with their ears, understand with their hearts and turn, and I would heal them.***

PRAY GOD'S PROMISE

Lord God, your words suggest sickness and illness are sometimes related to a person's mental or spiritual condition. Well, yes, I confess that I have drifted away from you lately, and I am sorry for my distance from you. ⚜ At times my eyes have been closed. Forgive me, Father, for not seeing you, not looking for you. ❦ I come to you today realizing that your promise is this: ***You will heal those who choose to see, hear, and understand your truth.*** And so I claim that promise, Lord, along with a renewed commitment to seek you more regularly in my daily life.

Examine your life and how your busyness has perhaps distracted you from God. Confess these things to him right now. What might you change to make sure you have time with him when you're well again?

SICKNESS · HOW ILLNESS GROWS COMPASSION FOR OTHERS

During this time of suffering, use your illness for good. Pray for others who are ailing. Right now, shut out other distractions, allow God's presence to envelop you, and listen to him speaking to you . . .

GOD'S PROMISE

MATTHEW 4:23 • *Jesus traveled throughout the region of Galilee, teaching in the synagogues and announcing the Good News about the Kingdom. And he healed every kind of disease and illness.*

MATTHEW 8:7 • *Jesus said, "I will come and heal him."*

PSALM 41:1, 3, NIV • *Blessed are those who have regard for the weak; the LORD delivers them in times of trouble. . . . The LORD sustains them on their sickbed and restores them from their bed of illness.*

PRAY GOD'S PROMISE

Father, I need your healing touch today in the midst of this nasty sickness. I hear these encouraging words— that you went about healing and doing good. ⚜ But you remind me that there are others who are likewise ill and weak and have their own needs. I think of them right now and want to pray for them too. ⚜ I thank you that this time of sickness gives me a chance to spend more time with you in the Word and in prayer. And yes, *I claim your promise to restore me.* I ask you for healing, greater strength, and deeper rest. I thank you for your care, your promises, and for your abiding love.

As you continue in prayer, bring to God each one of your symptoms and ask for his healing touch on these friends you are thinking of. Praise him for how he has healed you in the past and how he has restored others you know.

SIN · FREEDOM FROM THE MESS WE'VE MADE

Sometimes a particular sin takes hold of us and refuses to let go. Only God can free us. Come to him right now in confession and expect him to do a new work in your life . . .

GOD'S PROMISE

ROMANS 7:19 · *I want to do what is good, but I don't. I don't want to do what is wrong, but I do it anyway.*

ROMANS 3:23-24, MSG · *Since we've compiled this long and sorry record as sinners (both us and them) and proved that we are utterly incapable of living the glorious lives God wills for us, God did it for us. Out of sheer generosity he put us in right standing with himself. A pure gift. He got us out of the mess we're in and restored us to where he always wanted us to be. And he did it by means of Jesus Christ.*

2 CORINTHIANS 5:17 • *Anyone who belongs to Christ has become a new person. The old life is gone; a new life has begun!*

PRAY GOD'S PROMISE

Lord Jesus, I confess to you right now that I have sin in my life. You know very well what I am struggling with. You see how I wind up doing things I don't want to do. I'm sorry, Lord. ❧ I ask for your help in overcoming these harmful patterns. I know the solution lies in living in your presence on a regular basis. I have not done that. ❧ *Lord, since I belong to you, I claim this promise that I have become a new person.* Help me to come to you daily, to spend time with you, and to seek your help when I'm facing temptation.

Plan to spend time regularly with Jesus. Talk with him now about your intentions, and ask him to help you make time in your life for prayer and Bible reading.

———————————— ❖ ————————————

SIN • GOD WANTS YOU BACK

Come into God's presence. Open your heart to him . . .

GOD'S PROMISE

JAMES 4:17, ESV • *Whoever knows the right thing to do and fails to do it, for him it is sin.*

1 JOHN 1:10, NIV • *If we claim we have not sinned, we make him out to be a liar and his word is not in us.*

JOHN 3:16-17, MSG • *This is how much God loved the world: He gave his Son, his one and only Son. And this is why: so that no one need be destroyed; by believing in him, anyone can have a whole and lasting life. **God didn't go to all the trouble of sending his Son merely to point an accusing finger, telling the world how bad it was. He came to help, to put the world right again.***

PRAY GOD'S PROMISE

Lord God, I come before you right now asking you to forgive my sin. Sometimes I lead myself to believe that I don't sin much, yet deep down I realize there are many times when I know the right thing to do but just don't do it. ⚜ I can no longer claim I haven't sinned or even rationalize that "I'm not that bad." There is sin in my life, and it's clear that you don't approve. ⚜ Yet I find relief, Lord, knowing that you are eager to forgive me. *I embrace the promise that you aren't pointing at me with an accusing finger, but instead are reaching out to me with your arms open wide.* Thank you, Lord. Help me walk with you.

Quiet yourself before God. Listen for his voice. Can you sense his joy that you have returned to him?

———————————— ‹◇› ————————————

SIN · THE PROMISE OF GOD'S FORGIVENESS

Come to God with an open, truthful heart. Know that he receives you with open arms . . .

GOD'S PROMISE

GALATIANS 5:19-21, ESV • *The works of the flesh are evident: sexual immorality, impurity, sensuality, idolatry, sorcery, enmity, strife, jealousy, fits of anger, rivalries, dissensions, divisions, envy, drunkenness, orgies, and things like these. I warn you, as I warned you before, that those who do such things will not inherit the kingdom of God.*

1 JOHN 1:8-9, NIV • *If we claim to be without sin, we deceive ourselves and the truth is not in us. If we confess our sins, he is faithful and just and will forgive us our sins and purify us from all unrighteousness.*

PSALM 32:5 • *I confessed all my sins to you and stopped trying to hide my guilt. I said to myself, "I will confess my rebellion to the LORD." And you forgave me! All my guilt is gone.*

PRAY GOD'S PROMISE

God, I come to you at a time when I have become deeply aware of my sin. The guilt I feel is like none I've experienced before. I don't deserve your forgiveness, but I desperately need it. ❧ I know that I have been willful in my sins, and I have repeated some of them over and over. I ask for your help in changing my ways. ❧ *I claim your great promise that if I confess my sins, you will forgive them.* I have indeed confessed, Lord, and I trust you now to take away my guilt. Thank you for your amazing kindness!

Start a new era in your life by spending time with God every day. Discover the blessings of his intimate presence in your life.

———————— ◇ ————————

SIN OF INFIDELITY · GOD RESTORES BROKEN MARRIAGES

Come to God to confess your sin. Listen to his words to you . . .

GOD'S PROMISE

HEBREWS 13:4 · *Give honor to marriage, and remain faithful to one another in marriage. God will surely judge people who are immoral and those who commit adultery.*

MATTHEW 19:4-6, ESV · *Have you not read that he who created them from the beginning made them male and female, and said, "Therefore a man shall leave his father and his mother and hold fast to his wife, and the two shall become one flesh"? So they are no longer two but one flesh. What therefore God has joined together, let not man separate.*

JAMES 5:16, ESV · **Confess your sins to one another and pray for one another, that you may be healed.**

PRAY GOD'S PROMISE

God, I come to you with tremendous guilt and shame. I have committed adultery and violated my marriage vows. In deep anguish I ask for your forgiveness. ⚜ I never meant for this to happen, yet I confess that I consciously made the choice. I have sinned. ⚜ Lord God, I ask that you would point the way for making amends with my spouse. I pray for restoration of my marriage. I know I must stand up and be accountable for this terrible sin. *And I believe your promise that if I confess my sins, you will heal me.*

And not only me, but also my marriage. Thank you, Lord, for your tremendous mercy.

Talk with God in these moments about your next steps. Listen to his voice of wisdom and counsel. Talk to another person—a pastor or counselor—about how you should proceed.

———————————— ❖ ————————————

SLEEPLESSNESS · FINDING REST IN THE ARMS OF GOD

If you are experiencing a bout with persistent insomnia, consider bringing the problem to God in prayer. Listen to his words and his comfort . . .

GOD'S PROMISE

PSALM 77:4-6 • *I am too distressed even to pray! I think of the good old days, long since ended, when my nights were filled with joyful songs. I search my soul and ponder the difference now.*

PSALM 132:4-5, MSG • *I'm not going to sleep, not even take time to rest, until I find a home for GOD, a house for the Strong God of Jacob.*

PSALM 4:8 • **In peace I will lie down and sleep, for you alone, O LORD, will keep me safe.**

PRAY GOD'S PROMISE

Lord God, this matter seems like a trivial thing to bring to you, and yet it's a major concern for me. Lately I've had a hard time falling asleep at night, and the lack of rest I'm feeling is stretching me thin. I pray for relief from this insomnia, Lord. ⚜ I hear your words in this psalm about taking time to provide a home for you, Lord. Long ago, this was the Temple in Jerusalem. Now, we who believe have become your very own temple! Help me to build up your home—this temple—by reading your Word and coming to you in prayer. Then my soul shall truly rest. ⚜ *And I claim your promise that my body, too, will rest—in peace I will lie down and sleep.* I trust that you can make this happen for me, Lord. Thank you so much.

The next time you have a problem falling asleep, make it a time for communing with God. Sing a hymn of praise. Pray for the people in your life. Read the Bible. Listen to his soothing whisper.

SORROW · OVERCOMING THE LOSS OF SOMEONE CLOSE

The weight of losing a loved one is a heavy burden—one that may seem impossible to escape. This is a time for you and God. Bring to him the sorrows of your heart and listen to his words . . .

GOD'S PROMISE

ISAIAH 25:8 · *He will swallow up death forever! The Sovereign LORD will wipe away all tears.*

PSALM 23:4, ESV · *Even though I walk through the valley of the shadow of death, I will fear no evil, for you are with me.*

REVELATION 21:4 · **He will wipe every tear from their eyes, and there will be no more death or sorrow or crying or pain. All these things are gone forever.**

PRAY GOD'S PROMISE

Lord, I confess I am depressed these days because of the loss of someone close. My life is emptier, and I feel the vacancy deeply. I am down because the reality of death is, frankly, overwhelming. ¾ I come to you, Lord, for your comfort and your embrace. I surely do feel like I am walking through the shadow of death. Help me, Lord. ¾ I do know that you have conquered death, and I believe you have also overcome the effects that someone's death has on those who are left behind to grieve. *I claim your promise that one day you will wipe the tears from my eyes.* Be with me, Lord as I walk through this valley.

Pour your heart out to God right now. Tell him the things you miss about the one in your life who has passed on.

SPIRITUAL DROUGHT · REFRESHING

THE DUSTY LIFE

Like the seasons, sometimes our spiritual lives go through dry spells. Enter into God's presence to quench your thirst for him . . .

GOD'S PROMISE

PSALM 81:10, NIV · *I am the LORD your God. . . . Open wide your mouth and I will fill it.*

COLOSSIANS 2:9-10, MSG · *Everything of God gets expressed in him, so you can see and hear him clearly. You don't need a telescope, a microscope, or a horoscope to realize the fullness of Christ, and the emptiness of the universe without him.*

When you come to him, that fullness comes together for you, too.

EPHESIANS 3:17-19, NIV • *I pray that you, being rooted and established in love, may have power, together with all the Lord's holy people, **to grasp how wide and long and high and deep is the love of Christ, and to know this love that surpasses knowledge—that you may be filled to the measure of all the fullness of God.***

PRAY GOD'S PROMISE

Oh Lord, I come to you right now in a time of spiritual drought. I feel I've reached a long, dry valley in my journey, and there's only dust and dirt. I am thirsty and empty. ⚜ There's nothing in my world right now that fills me up or quenches my thirst. I need you, Lord. ⚜ *I claim your promise that in grasping how immense your love is for me, Jesus, I will be filled with your fullness.* Refresh my spiritual world, Lord.

Give God some time right now to speak into your life and fill you up with his presence.

———————————— ‹·› ————————————

SPIRITUAL WARFARE · GOD OVERCOMES THE WORLD

As you face resistance in your life and experience the work of the enemy, quiet your mind and heart. Come into God's space prepared for him to speak powerfully to you . . .

GOD'S PROMISE

EPHESIANS 6:18, MSG • *Prayer is essential in this ongoing warfare. Pray hard and long. Pray for your brothers and sisters. Keep your eyes open. Keep each other's spirits up so that no one falls behind or drops out.*

EPHESIANS 6:11, MSG • *Take everything the Master has set out for you, well-made weapons of the best materials. And put them to use so you will be able to stand up to everything the Devil throws your way.*

1 JOHN 5:4-5, NIV • *Everyone born of God overcomes the world. This is the victory that has overcome the world, even our faith. Who is it that overcomes the world? Only the one who believes that Jesus is the Son of God.*

PRAY GOD'S PROMISE

Lord God, I am facing opposition in my life on a number of fronts. I feel oppressed. I know it's the enemy, and I'm not sure I'm in a good place to fight against him. ❦ I pray for your strength, Lord, and for your help. I pray for others also, my brothers and sisters in you, who are likewise facing challenges. I pray that you would keep us alert and aware. ❦ *I claim your extraordinary promise, Lord, that we who are born of you—we who believe in Jesus—will overcome the world and the enemy's schemes.* I take that as a tremendous assurance in the face of this battle I'm in. Thank you, Lord. Thank you.

Tell God some of the specifics regarding the warfare you're in right now. Listen for his responses and look for his help in days to come.

SPIRITUAL WARFARE · STRENGTH FOR THE BATTLE

In the midst of spiritual assault, come to God for his strength, assurance, and marching orders . . .

GOD'S PROMISE

1 PETER 5:8-9, NIV · *Be alert and of sober mind. Your enemy the devil prowls around like a roaring lion looking for someone to devour. Resist him, standing firm in the faith.*

EPHESIANS 6:12, NKJV · *We do not wrestle against flesh and blood, but against principalities, against powers, against the rulers of the darkness of this age, against spiritual hosts of wickedness in the heavenly places.*

ISAIAH 40:31, NIV · *Those who hope in the LORD will renew their strength. They will soar on wings like eagles; they will run and not grow weary, they will walk and not be faint.*

PRAY GOD'S PROMISE

Lord God, in recent days I've been under attack. I know it's the enemy trying to undermine me, my testimony, and your authority. Help me face this assault and overcome. ❧ I am keenly aware of the significance and reality of spiritual warfare, and I ask for your protection, deliverance, and power in fighting back. ❧ *I claim your words of promise, that by hoping in you I will renew my strength for the fight, and that I will walk and run and soar, even in the midst of fighting this battle.* Thank you, God.

In these next moments, tell God about the specific ways in which you have been under attack. Allow him time to speak to you about each one.

———————— ◆ ————————

SPIRITUALLY DISTANT · FINDING YOUR
WAY BACK TO GOD

God is always with us, but sometimes when we lose our focus, we also lose our way in life. Take time to shut out the distractions and draw near to him . . .

GOD'S PROMISE

JEREMIAH 50:6 · *My people have been lost sheep. Their shepherds have led them astray and turned them loose in the mountains. They have lost their way and can't remember how to get back to the sheepfold.*

LUKE 19:10 · *The Son of Man came to seek and save those who are lost.*

REVELATION 3:20, ESV · *I stand at the door and knock. If anyone hears my voice and opens the door, I will come in to him and eat with him, and he with me.*

PRAY GOD'S PROMISE

God, I have felt that you've been far away from me lately—distant. I don't know how to explain it or what this feeling is exactly. It's like we got disconnected somehow. ❧ It's possible that I am the one who has strayed away, although I don't know exactly when that happened. I've been busy, I know. Distracted. This isn't fun, God. I hate feeling like I'm all alone on this path. ❧ Help me open the door to you so we can reconnect. *I claim your promise that you will come in so we can be together once again.* Forgive me for not making time for you. Forgive me for closing my life's door to you.

In these moments, reestablish with God a time when you'll seek to connect with him each day to enjoy his presence.

———————— ❖ ————————

SUFFERING · THE GLORY OF PARTNERING WITH CHRIST

Your situation is difficult and filled with much pain. But in these trying times, learn how physical suffering connects you to Christ in a special way . . .

GOD'S PROMISE

JOB 33:19, ESV • *Man is also rebuked with pain on his bed and with continual strife in his bones.*

JOB 33:26, ESV • *Then man prays to God, and he accepts him; he sees his face with a shout of joy, and he restores to man his righteousness.*

1 PETER 4:12-13 • *Don't be surprised at the fiery trials you are going through, as if something strange were happening to you. Instead, be very glad—for these trials make you partners with Christ in his suffering, so that you will have the wonderful joy of seeing his glory when it is revealed to all the world.*

PRAY GOD'S PROMISE

Lord Jesus, the pain I'm suffering is substantial at times. Only you can understand what it's really like. I look to you for some way of easing this pain and soothing my hurt. ❧ Lord, I want to stay positive and keep my eyes open to the good things in my life—even with this pain— and find joy in them. Help me do that, Jesus. ❧ *I claim the promise of having wonderful joy when your glory is revealed, and I pray you will help me understand and experience this partnership in your suffering.* If in just a small way I can more deeply know the extent of your sacrifice, then this is all worth it.

In these next moments, tell God about the pain you feel. Allow him then to speak to you. Listen to his words for you.

TEMPTATION · OVERCOMING THE SEDUCTIONS OF SATAN

You find yourself struggling to deal with temptations the enemy is throwing at you. Right now quietly come before God. Share these things with him . . .

GOD'S PROMISE

1 JOHN 4:4 · *You belong to God, my dear children. You have already won a victory over those people, because the Spirit who lives in you is greater than the spirit who lives in the world.*

JAMES 4:7 · *Humble yourselves before God. Resist the devil, and he will flee from you. Come close to God, and God will come close to you.*

1 PETER 1:7 • *These trials will show that your faith is genuine. It is being tested as fire tests and purifies gold— though your faith is far more precious than mere gold. So when your faith remains strong through many trials, it will bring you much praise and glory and honor on the day when Jesus Christ is revealed to the whole world.*

PRAY GOD'S PROMISE

Lord God, you know I am struggling. Many things in the world challenge what I believe throughout my day. I'm also aware that it is the enemy—Satan—who is behind this, lurking to draw me away from my faith. ❦ So God, I come to you humbly, asking for strength, steadfastness, and clarity of mind. ❦ I am encouraged by these words about my faith being more precious than gold. *And I claim your promise, Lord, that my faith will overcome these trials and ultimately bring me glory and honor.* I want my life to be a testimony of praise to you.

In these moments, experience God coming close to you. In silence feel his arms embracing you. Speak to God about the many things he has done for you. Praise him for who he is!

———————— ❖ ————————

TEMPTATION • RESISTING THE WILES OF THE WORLD

Enter into this time with God just as you are, without pretense or posturing. It's just you and God together. Give yourself a time of quiet before you start, and don't forget to listen for his voice . . .

GOD'S PROMISE

JAMES 1:3, ESV • *You know that the testing of your faith produces steadfastness.*

ROMANS 12:21, ESV • *Do not be overcome by evil, but overcome evil with good.*

1 CORINTHIANS 10:13, ESV • *No temptation has overtaken you that is not common to man.* **God is faithful,** *and he will not let you be tempted beyond your ability, but with the temptation* **he will also provide the way of escape, that you may be able to endure it.**

PRAY GOD'S PROMISE

Father, I come to you today, struggling with the temptations of the culture around me. I know there are things I shouldn't allow into my life, and I am trying not to, but I am deeply tempted sometimes. Many of my friends are partaking of activities that would not be pleasing to you. I need your help. ❦ I hear your words that you will not allow me to be tempted beyond my ability, but I sometimes doubt my strength to resist certain things. ❦ I know I need to trust you and place my life in your hands. So yes, *I will embrace your promise that you are faithful. I will embrace your promise that you will provide a way of escape from temptation. And I will embrace your promise that I will indeed be able to endure these temptations.* Help me be strong, Father.

Take some minutes now to tell God the specific temptations you are facing. After each one, repeat the words, "Yet you are faithful."

‹◇›

A THREATENING WORLD · COURAGE IN
THE FORTRESS OF GOD

Quiet your heart and mind. Let God speak to you about his presence with you in a world that threatens . . .

GOD'S PROMISE

PSALM 27:14 · *Wait patiently for the LORD. Be brave and courageous. Yes, wait patiently for the LORD.*

ISAIAH 12:2, MSG · *Yes, indeed—God is my salvation. I trust, I won't be afraid. **God—yes God!—is my strength and song**, best of all, my salvation!*

PSALM 27:1 · ***The Lord is my light and my salvation—** so why should I be afraid? **The LORD is my fortress,** protecting me from danger, so why should I tremble?*

PRAY GOD'S PROMISE

Lord God, sometimes the events of this world are overwhelming. I listen to the news and can hardly bear the evil and danger all around. And sometimes these things strike close to home. ⚜ I know I should not live in fear, Lord. I know I need to trust you. ⚜ *Lord, I want to embrace your promises here—I want to rediscover you as my strength and song; I want to reclaim you as my light and salvation; I want to rest my heart and mind in you as my fortress.* Help me trust you for all these things. Thank you, Lord.

Talk with God specifically about the event that most troubles you. Allow him to whisper to you about this fear.

———————— ◇ ————————

A THREATENING WORLD

- A WORRY-FREE HEART IN THE STORM

Certain dangers feel as if they might strike close. Come to God, quiet your heart, and listen to his reassuring words for you . . .

GOD'S PROMISE

PSALM 119:114 • *You are my refuge and my shield; your word is my source of hope.*

JOB 42:2, MSG • *You can do anything and everything. Nothing and no one can upset your plans.*

JOHN 14:27, ESV • *Peace I leave with you; my peace I give to you. Not as the world gives do I give to you. Let not your hearts be troubled, neither let them be afraid.*

PRAY GOD'S PROMISE

Lord Jesus, you know what I am facing, and how I am filled with uncertainty and fear right now. I ask for you to come close to me in these moments. ❧ I pray for your reassurance to overcome these fears, and I ask for your comforting presence in my life. ❧ *Lord Jesus, I embrace the promise of your peace. I pray for a worry-free heart.* Displace the anxieties I harbor deep down with the reality of your glorious presence. Help me to trust you fully for your protection in this situation. Thank you, Jesus.

In moments of quiet, allow God to whisper to you about his great power and love and sovereignty over all things. He is in control.

—————————— ❖ ——————————

TOUGH CHOICES · DISCOVERING GOD'S DIRECTION

As you struggle with some significant life decisions, come close to God in these next moments. Ask him to shine his light on your inner debate . . .

GOD'S PROMISE

PSALM 138:8 • *The LORD will work out his plans for my life—for your faithful love, O LORD, endures forever.*

PROVERBS 19:21 • *You can make many plans, but the LORD's purpose will prevail.*

JEREMIAH 29:11-14 • *"I know the plans I have for you," says the LORD. "They are plans for good and not for disaster, to give you a future and a hope. In those days when you pray, I will listen. If you look for me wholeheartedly, you will find me. I will be found by you," says the LORD.*

PRAY GOD'S PROMISE

Lord God, I am facing some significant life decisions, and I want to seek your will in them. Yet I know I have some selfish desires in the plans I've started to make. I ask that you would, right now, speak to me about this. ❧ God, I want my life to be spent seeking you, pursuing you. I long for this closeness to you, and I desire in my days and years ahead to be in this place of personal communion with you. ❧ *I claim your promise, God, that you have plans for me, and that they are for good, plans that give me a future and a hope.* I want your will to become the blueprint for my life—not the plans that I so selfishly make.

In the next few minutes, quiet your voice and your heart and listen for God's direction about what he has for you.

———————————— ❖ ————————————

TOUGH CHOICES · LOOKING FOR GOD IN THE DECISIONS OF LIFE

Come to God in these next moments and listen to his assurances of what it means to seek and follow his will for your life . . .

GOD'S PROMISE

PSALM 138:8 · *The LORD will work out his plans for my life—for your faithful love, O LORD, endures forever.*

JOHN 6:38-40 · *I have come down from heaven to do the will of God who sent me, not to do my own will. And this is the will of God, that I should not lose even one of all those he has given me, but that I should raise them up at the last day. For it is my Father's will that all who see his Son and believe in him should have eternal life. I will raise them up at the last day.*

1 JOHN 2:17, ESV · **The world is passing away along with its desires, but whoever does the will of God abides forever.**

PRAY GOD'S PROMISE

Lord God, I seek your wisdom for my life right now. I don't doubt that I need to live in your will, but sometimes, given my options, it's hard to discern which one you want me to choose. ❦ Lord, today and in the coming weeks and months, make known to me your wisdom and advice. I need to know what you wish me to do. I ask for your guidance. Whisper your plans for me. ⚜ I know I need to have in mind the big picture, which is *a promise from you—that while the world is temporal and passing away, those who do the will of God will abide forever.* Thank you, Jesus.

Lay out before God the options you are considering. Pray about each one, then listen for God's direction throughout the following hours and days.

TRAGEDY · GOD'S WORK IN US IN THE MIDST
OF SUFFERING

When tragedy happens, it feels so random. We search for a reason, for some purpose, but there is none that we can see. Come into God's presence and lean on him for comfort . . .

GOD'S PROMISE

COLOSSIANS 1:13-14 · *He has rescued us from the kingdom of darkness and transferred us into the Kingdom of his dear Son, who purchased our freedom and forgave our sins.*

PSALM 34:18, NIV · *The LORD is close to the brokenhearted and saves those who are crushed in spirit.*

JAMES 1:2-4, ESV · *Count it all joy, my brothers, when you meet trials of various kinds, for you know that the testing of your faith produces steadfastness. And let steadfastness have its full effect, that you may be perfect and complete, lacking in nothing.*

PRAY GOD'S PROMISE

The unthinkable has happened, Lord, and it fills me with sadness. As I look around my community and the world at large, I am overwhelmed by all the evil and senseless violence the enemy has perpetrated. And now this. ❧ I am brokenhearted. I pray for your presence, Lord. Please come close in this time of confusion and tragedy. ❧ I pray that you would help me see the larger picture of your purposes in this world, Lord. *I ask that you would help me embrace your promise that these trials will at some point lead me to perfection—Christlike character that is a jewel in my crown and brings you great glory and honor.* I look forward to becoming more steadfast and devoted to you in the face of these kinds of tragedies. I need that, Lord. Thank you for working all things together for good.

Speak to God specifically about what has happened. Listen for his words of comfort.

——————————— ❖ ———————————

TRAGEDY · PEACE WHILE SEARCHING FOR GOD'S PURPOSE

Draw near to God with your heart full of sorrow and questions about what has happened . . .

GOD'S PROMISE

PSALM 121:1-2 • *I look up to the mountains—does my help come from there? My help comes from the LORD, who made heaven and earth!*

PSALM 91:2 • *He alone is my refuge, my place of safety; he is my God, and I trust him.*

JOHN 16:33, NIV • *I have told you these things, so that in me you may have peace. In this world you will have trouble. But take heart! I have overcome the world.*

PRAY GOD'S PROMISE

Lord God, what has happened is unfathomable. It is such a tragic situation, and it's hard for me to make sense of it. I am crushed. I pray to you, God, even though I don't have words to pray. ✦ I lean on you in these minutes and hours as my only strength. Let me feel your presence and find in you a refuge from the questioning and agony, Lord. ✦ *I want to claim your promise of having this peace that comes from resting in you.* Help me trust that you have a purpose in what has happened. Remind me that you have indeed overcome the world and its pain, and that in time, with your help, I will do the same.

Allow yourself to simply be silent in God's presence. Feel his arms around you as you listen to his words.

TRAGEDY · HOW GOD TURNS LOSS INTO JOY

In this time of heartbreak and unthinkable loss, sink into God's presence and hear him whisper to you . . .

GOD'S PROMISE

PSALM 13:2 • *How long must I struggle with anguish in my soul, with sorrow in my heart every day?*

JOHN 16:22 • *You have sorrow now, but I will see you again; then you will rejoice, and no one can rob you of that joy.*

JOHN 16:20-21 • *You will grieve, but your grief will suddenly turn to wonderful joy. It will be like a woman suffering the pains of labor. When her child is born, her anguish gives way to joy because she has brought a new baby into the world.*

PRAY GOD'S PROMISE

God, my Father, this is your child coming to you in great mourning and anguish. This loss has brought me waves of doubt, anger, and deep agony. I struggle with sorrow in my heart every day. ❧ But as I read these words of Scripture, I discover that in the future our sorrows will actually produce joy for us instead. I believe that, God. But I still must deal with the here and now. I ask you right now, Father God, to provide some comfort for my heart and soul. ❧ *Your promise is that at some point my grief will turn into wonderful joy.* It's hard for me to imagine that right now. But I do believe that you are God—you are sovereign and will triumph over death and tragedy and all of my sorrow.

Use these moments with God to pour out to him all that has happened. Tell him how it has affected you. Share with him your deepest hurt.

————————— ❖ —————————

TRAGIC CURRENT EVENTS

• GOD'S PRESENCE IN TIMES OF TROUBLE

You feel threatened by unsettling events that have occurred nearby, or perhaps they just feel "too close to home," and it worries you. Bring your anxieties to God in a time of prayer. Listen to him speak to you . . .

GOD'S PROMISE

PSALM 62:8, ESV • *Trust in him at all times, O people; pour out your heart before him; God is a refuge for us.*

PSALM 46:4-6, MSG • *River fountains splash joy, cooling God's city. . . . God lives here, the streets are safe, God at your service from crack of dawn. Godless nations rant and rave, kings and kingdoms threaten, but Earth does anything he says.*

PSALM 86:7 • *I will call to you whenever I'm in trouble, and you will answer me.*

PRAY GOD'S PROMISE

Lord, recent tragic events have felt closer to home than I am comfortable with. I know there are people around the world who live in the midst of violence and danger every day—and by comparison my worries are simple ones. But I am fearful, Lord, and I ask for your comfort. ♩ I hear your words that in "God's city" you keep the streets safe, and you are constantly present and powerful. Thank you for this reminder that no matter what is going on around me, your presence is my ultimate refuge. Help me to believe that you are indeed in control. ♩ *I claim your promise that as I call to you out of fear or need, you will answer me.* Soothe my worried heart and mind, Lord. Help me to trust in you.

As you converse with God, talk with him about events that have felt threatening in the past and how he has provided for your safety and well-being during those times.

TROUBLE · GOD IS IN CONTROL

You are facing troubles on many fronts. Come into God's presence and hear his words . . .

GOD'S PROMISE

DEUTERONOMY 31:6, ESV · *Be strong and courageous. Do not fear or be in dread of [the nations], for it is the LORD your God who goes with you. He will not leave you or forsake you.*

MATTHEW 6:33 · *Seek the Kingdom of God above all else, and live righteously, and he will give you everything you need.*

PROVERBS 19:21, MSG · *We humans keep brainstorming options and plans, but GOD's purpose prevails.*

PRAY GOD'S PROMISE

Lord God, I am concerned about a number of different matters in my life. I need your assurance that everything will be all right. ❧ I pray that you will indeed go with me, that you will walk this journey alongside me. *And help me believe this promise—that you are in control not only of my life but also of this world around me.* ❧ Thank you, Lord. Keep these troubles from distracting me; help me to focus on building your Kingdom instead.

Open your heart to God. Share with him the specific things that are troubling your heart.

TROUBLE · GOD'S CARE IN THE CHAOS

Bring to God the turmoil you are experiencing right now. Listen to his words for you . . .

GOD'S PROMISE

PSALM 27:5 · *He will conceal me there when troubles come; he will hide me in his sanctuary. He will place me out of reach on a high rock.*

ISAIAH 61:1-2 · *He has sent me to comfort the brokenhearted and to proclaim that captives will be released and prisoners will be freed. He has sent me to tell those who mourn that the time of the LORD's favor has come . . .*

JOHN 14:27, NIV · *Peace I leave with you; my peace I give you. I do not give to you as the world gives. Do not let your hearts be troubled and do not be afraid.*

PRAY GOD'S PROMISE

Lord God, I pray for your loving care and protection. Things in my life are all in a whirl. I'm feeling troubled, and even a little scared. Please come by my side. ⚜ Lord, I claim your promise of peace and a trouble-free heart. *And I cherish your promise to hide me in your sanctuary as troubles come. Thank you that you will place me far out of harm's way.* ⚜ Lord, I'm grateful for your comfort.

I eagerly look forward to experiencing more calm in the days ahead. I praise you for your favor in my life.

Talk with God about the things in your life that are especially unsettling. Let him soothe your heart about each one.

— ❖ —

TROUBLED BY THE FUTURE
• GOD'S PROVISION FOR WHAT'S TO COME

In this time of uncertainty, come to God with what's troubling you . . .

GOD'S PROMISE

DEUTERONOMY 31:8, ESV • *It is the LORD who goes before you. He will be with you; he will not leave you or forsake you. Do not fear or be dismayed.*

MATTHEW 18:20, MSG • *When two or three of you are together because of me, you can be sure that I'll be there.*

PHILIPPIANS 4:19 • **This same God who takes care of me will supply all your needs from his glorious riches, which have been given to us in Christ Jesus.**

PRAY GOD'S PROMISE

Lord God, I need your help. I am experiencing a time in my life when so many things are tentative and lack a definite commitment. I feel lost and uncertain about what's ahead for me. ❧ I pray for your presence and direction in my life these days, Lord. ❧ *And help me to embrace this promise—that you will take care of me and supply everything I need to fulfill my calling.* Encourage me to hold this hope close in my heart as I keep forging ahead in uncertain times. Thank you, Lord.

Talk with God in the next few minutes about the specific issues in your life that are troubling you.

———————— ⟨•⟩ ————————

TROUBLED SPIRITUALLY

• FINDING PEACE IN STRONG FAITH

Enter God's presence and express to him what you feel is lacking right now in your life and what you need spiritually. Listen to his voice speaking to you . . .

GOD'S PROMISE

JOHN 20:29 • *Jesus told him, "You believe because you have seen me. Blessed are those who believe without seeing me."*

PHILIPPIANS 1:6, ESV • *I am sure of this, that he who began a good work in you will bring it to completion at the day of Jesus Christ.*

JOHN 14:1, NIV • **Do not let your hearts be troubled. You believe in God; believe also in me.**

PRAY GOD'S PROMISE

God, I'm aware that right now I feel spiritually lost, and it troubles my heart. ⚜ I want a better relationship with you, but so many things seem to block me from that. I am reaching out to you right now for help. ⚜ I long for a deeper spiritual life—for a stronger faith and a genuine walk with you, Lord. Help me to not only believe but to also *live* a life of faith. **God, even though I feel far from you** *right now, I do know this—that I believe in you, through faith in your Son, Jesus Christ. Thank you for reassuring me that my heart need not be troubled if I have faith.* Help me to move forward now by living out my faith in you. Bring people into my life who can help me do that, Lord. Thank you that you will finish the good work of faith you started in me.

Have a conversation with God right now and talk with him as you would talk with a close friend. Share with him the things that have blocked your faith in the past. Listen to God's advice about that.

UNBELIEF · EXCHANGING DOUBT FOR FAITH

Many people in the Bible struggled to have faith in Jesus. Listen to the words of Scripture . . .

GOD'S PROMISE

MATTHEW 14:28-32, ESV · *Peter answered him, "Lord, if it is you, command me to come to you on the water." He said, "Come." So Peter got out of the boat and walked on the water and came to Jesus. But when he saw the wind, he was afraid, and beginning to sink he cried out, "Lord, save me." Jesus immediately reached out his hand and took hold of him, saying to him, "O you of little faith, why did you doubt?"*

JUDE 1:22, ESV · *Have mercy on those who doubt.*

1 CORINTHIANS 2:4-5, ESV · *My speech and my message were not in plausible words of wisdom, but in demonstration of the Spirit and of power, so that your faith might not rest in the wisdom of men but in the power of God.*

PRAY GOD'S PROMISE

God, I ask for mercy. I am a doubter. ⚡ At times, like Peter, I feel like I'm walking on water in faith, but then I falter and sink when I think about all the rational arguments against belief. Help me, God. ⚡ It's true that often I depend on common worldly wisdom for routine decisions. But deep inside I know there's a larger and higher truth I need to access. *I pray for your promise of a demonstration of the Spirit and power in my life.* Thank you, Lord. I will look for your presence in my life in the days to come.

Talk further with our supernatural God about the supernatural things you would like to see him do in your life.

UNBELIEF · FINDING THE ASSURANCE OF THINGS
HOPED FOR

We have faith in many things we cannot see, yet we want so much to see God with our own eyes before we commit ourselves to a life of faith. Listen to these words . . .

GOD'S PROMISE

JOHN 20:27-29, ESV · *"Put your finger here, and see my hands; and put out your hand, and place it in my side. Do not disbelieve, but believe." Thomas answered him, "My Lord and my God!" Jesus said to him, "Have you believed because you have seen me? Blessed are those who have not seen and yet have believed."*

HEBREWS 11:1, ESV • *Faith is the assurance of things hoped for, the conviction of things not seen.*

EPHESIANS 2:8, ESV • **By grace you have been saved through faith. And this is not your own doing; it is the gift of God.**

PRAY GOD'S PROMISE

God, I'm having trouble believing in things I can't verify. I'm like Thomas—I need to see first. Yet I *want* to believe there is more to this life than what I can physically experience. ❧ Your words here tell me there is evidence of you, God—evidence in the person of Jesus. I, too, want to touch the spear wound in his side and the crucifixion wounds in his hands. Since I can't do so in real time and space, I want to do it by faith. ❧ **And I claim your promise that I can be saved through this very same faith, because of grace, which is your gift to me, God. Thank you that I don't need to muster up faith on my own.** Help me to continue believing even though I have not seen you.

Can you imagine making time throughout this week for more conversations with God like this one? Is there anything more important to do?

———————————— ❖ ————————————

UNBELIEF • GOD'S PRESENCE IN TIMES OF DOUBT

Do you find yourself going through a period of doubt in your life of faith? Let these words speak to you . . .

GOD'S PROMISE

MARK 9:23 • *Anything is possible if a person believes.*

MARK 9:24 • *The father instantly cried out, "I do believe, but help me overcome my unbelief!"*

MATTHEW 21:21-22, ESV • *Truly, I say to you, if you have faith and do not doubt, you will not only do what has been done to the fig tree, but even if you say to this mountain, "Be taken up and thrown into the sea," it will happen. **And whatever you ask in prayer, you will receive, if you have faith.***

PRAY GOD'S PROMISE

God, I pray to you in the midst of doubt and uncertainty. I am like that father portrayed in the Scripture verse above—I believe, yet I also have unbelief mixed in, and I want to get past that. ‡ I pray for clarity in what I think and know about you, God. I pray for some pathway to faith. ‡ And in spite of my unbelief right now, I somehow know that your Word here is true—that anything is possible if I find the power to believe. Please help me to find it. *And I know it sounds funny, God, but since I have sincere faith in asking for faith, I claim your promise that I will receive what I've asked for.* Thank you that you'll take me to new levels of faith, God. I wait expectantly.

For now, just be quiet. Listen for God's voice whispering to you.

—<◊>—

UNCERTAINTY · OVERCOMING WORRY ABOUT
THE FUTURE

Perhaps you wake up in the morning feeling uncertain and insecure about having enough to eat today or next week or in six months. Where will the money come from? Let God speak to you his assurances about taking care of you . . .

GOD'S PROMISE

PSALM 139:23, NIV · *Search me, God, and know my heart; test me and know my anxious thoughts.*

MATTHEW 6:31-33, ESV · *Do not be anxious, saying, "What shall we eat?" or "What shall we drink?" or "What shall we wear?" For the Gentiles seek after all these things, and your heavenly Father knows that you need them all.* **But seek first the kingdom of God and his righteousness, and all these things will be added to you.**

PHILIPPIANS 4:19, MSG · *You can be sure that God will take care of everything you need, his generosity exceeding even yours in the glory that pours from Jesus.*

PRAY GOD'S PROMISE

Lord, I come to you now in the midst of my battle with feelings of insecurity. I don't know where my provision will come from in the future. Only you can help me, Lord. ⚜ Your words suggest that maybe my worries are distracting me from focusing on you, Lord. I accept that, but I must have your strength if I am to seek your Kingdom first. ⚜ I embrace your promise that *by laying aside these insecurities, and by seeking you and your Kingdom, all these things that I need will be added to my life*. Help me to trust you, Lord, for your provision.

Speak with God about the specific provisions you're concerned about. Tell him what you need; then let those things go. Spend time in his presence. Focus on God himself. Let him speak to you. Let him take care of you.

———————— ❖ ————————

UNCERTAINTY · SEARCHING FOR A FAITH IN GOD

For many, believing in God and Jesus is difficult, and life is filled with doubts. Know that God is patient and waits for that day when you will come to him . . .

GOD'S PROMISE

JUDE 1:22, ESV · *Have mercy on those who doubt.*

JOB 23:8-10, ESV · **Behold, I go forward, but he is not there, and backward, but I do not perceive him; on the left hand when he is working, I do not behold him; he turns to the right hand, but I do not see him. But he knows the way that I take; when he has tried me, I shall come out as gold.**

JOHN 14:1, ESV · *Let not your hearts be troubled. Believe in God; believe also in me.*

PRAY GOD'S PROMISE

God, as I come to you, I feel strange even just praying to you. I suppose I believe just enough to come to you right now in prayer. But not enough to believe everything that the Bible says. ❧ I think I'm simply asking for you to show me something. Help me believe in you. ❧ The words from the book of Job reveal a promise for me, *that even though I cannot see you, you are there. And in my journey of searching, you say that you know the way I go.* So I simply ask that you be patient with me. Show me your presence. Help me believe, God.

Sometimes we just need to look for God in our lives. And listen to him speak to us.

———————— ⟨◆⟩ ————————

UNEMPLOYMENT · THE PROMISE OF GOD'S PURPOSE

This time of "in between" is difficult and challenging, but it can also become a time of deep enrichment in the presence of God . . .

GOD'S PROMISE

MATTHEW 6:19-21, NIV · *Do not store up for yourselves treasures on earth, where moths and vermin destroy, and where thieves break in and steal. But store up for yourselves treasures in heaven, where moths and vermin do not destroy, and where thieves do not break in and steal. For where your treasure is, there your heart will be also.*

HABAKKUK 3:17-18, NIV · *Though the fig tree does not bud and there are no grapes on the vines, though the olive crop fails and the fields produce no food, though there are no sheep in the pen and no cattle in the stalls, yet I will rejoice in the LORD, I will be joyful in God my Savior.*

PHILIPPIANS 2:13, NIV • *It is God who works in you to will and to act in order to fulfill his good purpose.*

PRAY GOD'S PROMISE

Lord God, I have been without work for a little while, and I fear I may be unemployed for a while longer. I pray that some opportunities will open up for me. ❧ I also pray that this might become a deeper time for me with you. I hear your words about treasures in heaven versus treasures on earth. I know what really matters. Perhaps this is a time to refocus myself on those things that last forever. ❧ *I claim your promise, Lord, that you will work in me to fulfill your good purpose.* I pray for that and for you to clearly point me in the direction you have for me, Jesus.

Talk with God about what he has already provided for you. Praise him for each one.

———————— ❖ ————————

WILDERNESS JOURNEY

• GOD'S PROVISION IN DESERT PLACES

At times in our spiritual journeys we find ourselves in a desolate place. We feel we've lost our way. But God has a promise for those of us in the wilderness . . .

GOD'S PROMISE

NEHEMIAH 9:19 • *In your great mercy you did not abandon them to die in the wilderness.*

ISAIAH 35:8 • *A great road will go through that once deserted land. It will be named the Highway of Holiness.*

Evil-minded people will never travel on it. It will be only for those who walk in God's ways.

PSALM 65:12-13 • *The grasslands of the wilderness become a lush pasture, and the hillsides blossom with joy. The meadows are clothed with flocks of sheep, and the valleys are carpeted with grain. They shout and sing for joy!*

PRAY GOD'S PROMISE

Lord, I've been walking this path for a long time, but lately I feel as if I'm just trudging in dust. I've been so dry emotionally and spiritually. At times I can't even see the road I'm on. I need your help and your presence in a special way. ❧ I long for clarity, Lord. Help me see the road ahead. And I pray for a season of rich rain and warm sunshine. ❧ *Lord, I love this imagery of the wilderness becoming a lush pasture and hillsides blossoming with joy. Oh, I long for that. I pray it will become a reality in my life.* I want to shout and sing once again.

In these next moments, just be still in God's presence. Let his words rain upon you.

———————————— ❖ ————————————

WILL OF GOD • BECOMING THE NEW PERSON GOD WANTS

As you are asking questions about God's will for your life, enter into this time with God prepared to listen to his wisdom about you and the world around you . . .

GOD'S PROMISE

ROMANS 12:2 • *Don't copy the behavior and customs of this world, but* **let God transform you into a new person by changing the way you think. Then you will learn to know God's will for you, which is good and pleasing and perfect.**

EPHESIANS 5:10-14 • *Try to discern what is pleasing to the Lord. Take no part in the unfruitful works of darkness, but instead expose them. For it is shameful even to speak of the things that they do in secret. But when anything is exposed by the light, it becomes visible, for anything that becomes visible is light.*

EPHESIANS 5:15-19 • *Be careful how you live. Don't live like fools, but like those who are wise. Make the most of every opportunity in these evil days. Don't act thoughtlessly, but understand what the Lord wants you to do. Don't be drunk with wine, because that will ruin your life. Instead, be filled with the Holy Spirit, singing psalms and hymns and spiritual songs among yourselves, and making music to the Lord in your hearts.*

PRAY GOD'S PROMISE

Lord God, I receive these words from you as personal advice to me. Thank you for them. I need to be more aware of how my mind and my life are influenced by the world around me. ❦ I truly desire to live wisely, Lord, because I really do believe that is the path toward deep satisfaction. And yet I know at times I'm tempted to follow the ways of the world; sometimes it seems so immediately gratifying. Help me to resist these beckoning lures. ❦ ***Lord,***

I really do want to be transformed by you. I accept your promise here to do so. I desire a renewed mind, one that is in tune with you and your will for me. Thank you, Lord.

Spend these next moments with God by prayerfully committing to this next phase of your life.

———————————— ‹•› ————————————

WILL OF GOD · LETTING GO OF SELF

The will of God always starts with the right kind of life and the right kind of spirit. Settle yourself in these next moments and listen as God speaks into your life . . .

GOD'S PROMISE

1 THESSALONIANS 4:3-5 • *God's will is for you to be holy, so stay away from all sexual sin. Then each of you will control his own body and live in holiness and honor—not in lustful passion like the pagans who do not know God and his ways.*

1 PETER 4:1-2, MSG • *Since Jesus went through everything you're going through and more, learn to think like him. Think of your sufferings as a weaning from that old sinful habit of always expecting to get your own way. Then you'll be able to live out your days free to pursue what God wants instead of being tyrannized by what you want.*

1 PETER 4:19 • *Keep on doing what is right, and trust your lives to the God who created you, for he will never fail you.*

PRAY GOD'S PROMISE

Lord God, I confess that my life isn't always what it should be, and I have not lived as you would wish me to. I do want to pursue your will for my life, but I don't think I've realized how much my lifestyle steers me in a different direction and how much I simply live for "me." ⚜ I hear these words about a life of expecting to get my own way, and I know I've been chasing my own desires, seeking my own interests. Well, I want to be rid of that, Lord. ⚜ *I embrace your promise that, in doing what is right and trusting my life to you, you will never fail me.* Please help me, Lord, to follow your will in my daily life, to trust my life to you while letting go of my selfish interests.

Take some more time to be with God. Tell him your concerns for the day. Then, in silence, listen for his voice.

———————— ⟨◇⟩ ————————

WILL OF GOD · AVOIDING THE TRAP OF SEXUAL SIN

Many times when God talks about doing his will, he speaks about sexual behavior. As you seek God's will for your life, listen to his advice to you about the problem of sexual sin . . .

GOD'S PROMISE

1 THESSALONIANS 4:3-5 · *God's will is for you to be holy, so stay away from all sexual sin. Then each of you will control his own body and live in holiness and honor—not in lustful passion like the pagans who do not know God and his ways.*

1 JOHN 2:16-17 • *The world offers only a craving for physical pleasure, a craving for everything we see, and pride in our achievements and possessions. These are not from the Father, but are from this world. And this world is fading away, along with everything that people crave. But anyone who does what pleases God will live forever.*

1 PETER 4:2 • *You won't spend the rest of your lives chasing your own desires, but you will be anxious to do the will of God.*

PRAY GOD'S PROMISE

Dear God, I come to you today truly seeking your will. I confess that I struggle sometimes with my sexual behavior and doing what's right. ❧ I understand your words about the world offering only sexual craving and pride, for I see evidence of others—as well as myself—giving in to these temptations. ❧ God, I really do desire to be yours, to live in your will, and to discover and follow your plan for my life. *I embrace your vision for me here—that I won't spend the rest of my life chasing my desires, but will be eager to do your will.* I want to honor you, God. Help me lead a life that is pleasing to you.

In an extended time of prayer, tell God about the challenges you face in the world and the temptations you struggle with.

———————————— ❖ ————————————

WORLDLINESS · FINDING THE TRUE PLEASURES IN LIFE

You are troubled by your deepening involvement with worldly things. Come to God in prayer and listen to his words . . .

GOD'S PROMISE

1 JOHN 2:15, ESV · *Do not love the world or the things in the world. If anyone loves the world, the love of the Father is not in him.*

1 JOHN 2:16, ESV · *All that is in the world—the desires of the flesh and the desires of the eyes and pride of life—is not from the Father but is from the world.*

1 JOHN 2:17, ESV · **The world is passing away along with its desires, but whoever does the will of God abides forever.**

PRAY GOD'S PROMISE

Lord God, I've become aware that I'm no longer living for you. Instead I've become distracted by the world around me. I'm guilty of focusing my attention on pursuits that gratify me in the moment. Forgive me, Lord. ⚜ I know all this is fleeting, and I come to you now because I have sensed the emptiness of immersing myself in a culture that ignores your truths. I want a life that is filled with your presence, Lord. ⚜ *I believe your words here that the world is passing away, but those who are devoted to you will enjoy a deep, rich life that will never end.* This is what I want, Lord. I pray for a brand-new start. Help me to ignore the distractions of this world and follow you with all of my heart.

In these next moments, confess some of the specific things that have preoccupied you. Turn them over to God.

————————— <‹•›> —————————

WORLDLINESS · TRANSFORMED BY GOD INSTEAD OF CULTURE

Come to God in quiet prayer about how you've become enamored by the culture around you. Open your heart to his words for you . . .

GOD'S PROMISE

COLOSSIANS 3:2, ESV · *Set your minds on things that are above, not on things that are on earth.*

1 PETER 4:4-5, MSG · *Of course, your old friends don't understand why you don't join in with the old gang anymore. But you don't have to give an account to them. They're the ones who will be called on the carpet—and before God himself.*

ROMANS 12:2, MSG · *Don't become so well-adjusted to your culture that you fit into it without even thinking.* **Instead, fix your attention on God. You'll be changed from the inside out.** *Readily recognize what he wants from you, and quickly respond to it. Unlike the culture around you, always dragging you down to its level of immaturity, God brings the best out of you, develops well-formed maturity in you.*

PRAY GOD'S PROMISE

Lord God, I pray for a change of heart and mind. I have fallen back into some of my old ways—things I did before I knew you. I know I haven't been living for you, but rather for the people and culture around me. ⚡ I pray for your strength to stand up against the behaviors and customs of the world around me. ⚡ *I believe this promise—that I will be changed from the inside out so I can recognize your will for me.* I want a life, Lord, that is good and pleasing to you.

In a further time of prayer, talk with God about some specific things you can do right away to refocus your mind and heart on him.

———————— ❖ ————————

WORRY · TURNING ANXIETIES OVER TO GOD

Take a deep breath. Enter into God's presence. During this time, allow your anxieties to fade into the background and listen to the words God has for you . . .

GOD'S PROMISE

PSALM 139:23 · *Search me, O God, and know my heart; test me and know my anxious thoughts.*

PHILIPPIANS 4:6, MSG · *Don't fret or worry. Instead of worrying, pray.*

PHILIPPIANS 4:6-7, MSG · *Let petitions and praises shape your worries into prayers, letting God know your concerns. Before you know it, **a sense of God's wholeness, everything coming together for good, will come and settle you down**. It's wonderful what happens when Christ displaces worry at the center of your life.*

PRAY GOD'S PROMISE

God, you know that I've been living for some time with many anxious thoughts. These worries are controlling my days and even my nights. I desperately need your reassurance that things will work out well. I need a sense of your calm presence. ❧ I will try right now to replace my worries with prayers. Hear my prayers, God. ❧ And so in this moment *I claim your promise to replace my anxious thoughts with your wholeness. Settle me down.* Help me to trust you with each and every one of my anxieties.

For the next few minutes, use your own words to speak to God about the specific anxieties that are on your heart. Name them one by one, and tell God why each one troubles you. Then turn each one into a prayer: "God, I give this worry to you . . ."

WRONG CHOICES · RETURNING TO THE WILL OF GOD

Sometimes we know what God wants us to do, but we don't do it and instead take another path. Spend time with God in these minutes and restart your life. Get back on the right path . . .

GOD'S PROMISE

LUKE 6:46-49 • *Why do you keep calling me "Lord, Lord!" when you don't do what I say? I will show you what it's like when someone comes to me, listens to my teaching, and then follows it. It is like a person building a house who digs deep and lays the foundation on solid rock. When the floodwaters rise and break against that house, it stands firm because it is well built. But anyone who hears and doesn't obey is like a person who builds a house without a foundation. When the floods sweep down against that house, it will collapse into a heap of ruins.*

JOHN 5:30 • *I can do nothing on my own. I judge as God tells me. Therefore, my judgment is just, because I carry out the will of the one who sent me, not my own will.*

EPHESIANS 6:6-8 • *As slaves of Christ, do the will of God with all your heart. Work with enthusiasm, as though you were working for the Lord rather than for people. Remember that the Lord will reward each one of us for the good we do, whether we are slaves or free.*

PRAY GOD'S PROMISE

Father, I confess that I have followed my own way of late and haven't been seeking or following your will. I have made a mess of this, and I come to you right now in need. ⚜ I pray, first of all, that you will help me see the importance and wisdom of pursuing your will. I pray as well for your help in setting straight the things I've done that have gone so badly. ⚜ Father, I do accept your words here about not being able to do anything on my own. I see all too well where that's gotten me. *And I claim your promise that in following your will, in being a slave to Christ, you will reward me.* Help me, Father, to continue in my pursuit of your will in the coming months.

As you pray, commit to spending regular, daily time in prayer with God where you ask him to help you know his will for your life.

———————— ⟨⟩ ————————

GUIDE

→≫→

TO PRAYER TOPICS

EMOTIONAL

PHYSICAL

RELATIONAL

SPIRITUAL

SCRIPTURE INDEX

EMOTIONAL

309

PHYSICAL

SPIRITUAL